INDIA, PAKISTAN, CEYLON

India, Pakistan, Ceylon

EDITED BY
W. Norman Brown
UNIVERSITY OF PENNSYLVANIA

CORNELL UNIVERSITY PRESS
Ithaca, New York

CORNELL UNIVERSITY PRESS

April 1951

PRINTED IN THE UNITED STATES OF AMERICA BY THE
VAIL-BALLOU PRESS, INC., BINGHAMTON, NEW YORK

Foreword

AMONG the important political developments in Asia since the Second World War has been the emergence of India, Pakistan, and Ceylon from a dependent colonial position into full self-rule. Of these the first two were constituted from the old British "Indian Empire," which on August 15, 1947, was partitioned and each part granted dominion status in the British Commonwealth of Nations. Thus ended the epoch of British domination in the land which had had the unflattering distinction of being the world's greatest colonial possession. India formally proclaimed itself a sovereign republic on January 26, 1950, though it continues to be a member of the Commonwealth. Pakistan has remained a dominion. Similarly, on February 4, 1948, Ceylon passed from crown colony to dominion and retains that status today.

British control of the region now occupied by India, Pakistan, and Ceylon has been only a very recent matter, being a phenomenon of no more than two centuries in a known history of civilization extending over five millenniums. That region early evolved one of the world's great cultural complexes, the Indic, distinct from any other in many major features of religion, philosophy, art, social organization. This went abroad to central, eastern, and southeastern Asia, to contribute elements to civilizations there. Conversely, throughout recorded history and a long period of prehistory as well, this region has been recurringly subject to invasions from the northwest by peoples bringing in their own cultures. Characterized in its largest terms, the history of civilization there has been one of repeated cultural invasion, clash, amalgamation. In the case of the latest and greatest of these invasions, that of the Islamic way of life, the cycle has not been complete; amalgamation has not yet been accomplished. The irreconcilability of Indic and Islamic, more than any other cause, led to the partition of the old India in 1947 and the creation of the new nation Pakistan. At that time was once again effected the repeated and portentous division between the Northwest and the rest of India, which had been temporarily and superficially covered by a century of political union under Britain.

The purpose of this book is, partly, to give the background of these political changes. It is, still more, to describe the wider context of civilization in the area where these three newly liberated nations now exist. The book deals with geography and material resources, and the use that man has made of them in developing the arts of civilization. It restates, in brief form, what we know of prehistory and of recorded history. It describes achievements in thought, literature, the arts. It characterizes social structure, economic life, and law. The separate chapters were written as a series of articles for the *Encyclopedia Americana* and promote no ideology. Within the limitations of available space they aim to present the pertinent facts.

Something must be said about terminology. Until the political division of August, 1947, the region of the two present nations India and Pakistan was known by the single term India. This was in accordance with long practice. The ancient Greeks called it "India" (Ἰνδία), meaning the land of "the Indoi" (οἱ Ἰνδοί), that is, the people living near the river "Indos" (ὁ Ἰνδός) or, in the Latin form, "Indus." The adjective to indicate something pertaining to the region was "Indic" (Ἰνδικός), equivalent to our commoner adjective "Indian." From these sources come our familiar words "India, Indus, Indic." [1] The partition of 1947 has brought the use of these received terms into question. Since "Pakistan" and "India" now refer to two political units, the old term "India" has acquired a double usage. It is applied in a wide sense to the whole geographic area and in a narrow sense to the recently demarcated nation. Many people, especially those living in Pakistan, object to the wider usage. A similar problem exists with the phrases "subcontinent of India" and "Indian subcontinent," which for some time have been current among scholars writing on the area. Because India, in the wider geographic sense, is closely contained within the boundaries of the Hindu Kush and the Himalayas on the north, the mountains and desert of Afghanistan and Persia on the west, the mountains and marshes of Burma on the east, and the Bay of Bengal and the Arabian Sea embracing the peninsula in the south, it has had a degree of geographic and cultural isolation that seems to warrant calling it a subcontinent. But since partition in 1947 the use of "Indian" or "India" to characterize it has had some opposition. A certain vogue has attached to the designation "Indo-Pakistan subcontinent." Some writers have tried to use in place of the new and awkward compound the appellation "South Asia," which has an inclusive application to India, Pakistan, and Ceylon (with Nepal and Bhutan, and possibly also Afghanistan). What scholars will finally do with these various terms is unpredictable. At present most writers on almost all aspects of the subcontinent's life who are concerned with the period up to 1947 tend to retain the old and

[1] The basic Greek form "Indos" was an adaptation of an Old Persian and Avestan word *hindu* applied to the province of the Achaemenian empire adjacent to the river Indus and meaning "land of the [great] river." The Old Persian in its turn was cognate with the Sanskrit word *sindhu* "river," especially "the river Indus."

established forms "India" and "Indian," while commentators on current political affairs since 1947 sometimes use the newly coined "Indo-Pakistan." In this book the authors of the respective chapters follow the usual practice pertaining to the subjects which they treat.

Already India, Pakistan, and Ceylon as self-ruling nations have aspired to a place in world councils. India has assumed a prominent position in the United Nations, where she has stood somewhere between the Communist nations and the Western democracies and has tried to reconcile the disputes between the two sides. Pakistan, as the world's most populous Islamic state, seems a possible leader in the Moslem world. Ceylon occupies a peculiarly strategic point at the top of the Indian Ocean, midway on the lanes of communication between western Europe on one side and on the other the Far East with Indonesia and Australia. In the modern world these nations are acquiring an ever-growing political importance which increasingly calls our attention to them. More fundamentally important in the long-range view is their complex of civilizations, so different from that of the West, but full of meaning for the world. If this modest book can at all illuminate these nations and their cultural background for Western readers, it will satisfy its authors' aims.

W. Norman Brown

University of Pennsylvania
Philadelphia, December 30, 1950

Transliteration and Pronunciation

IN transliterating words from Oriental languages, the practice in this volume is that of the *Encyclopedia Americana,* which treats any term appearing in *Webster's New International Dictionary* as established in the English language and follows its style of spelling. Other words are transliterated according to the system used in many scientific Oriental journals and other publications, and are printed in italics.

In pronouncing the Sanskrit and other words from the languages of India, Pakistan, and Ceylon appearing in this volume, speakers of English should accent the next to the last syllable when it is long, and otherwise put the accent on the nearest long syllable before it. A long syllable is one which contains:

a vowel marked long: *ā, ī, ū;* or

a diphthong: *e, o, ai, au* (in Sanskrit *e* and *o* are always diphthongs and long; in most words from other languages appearing in this book they are also long); or

a vowel followed by more than one consonant, but note that *h* following a consonant usually represents an aspiration of the consonant, not a second consonant, and therefore does not serve to make the syllable long.

TRANSLITERATION

The pronunciation of vowels is approximately as follows:

a like *u* in English but
ā like *a* in English far
i like *i* in English pin
ī like *i* in English machine
u like *u* in English pull
ū like *u* in English rule
e like *ai* in English chair
ai like *ai* in English aisle
o like *o* in English go
au like *ow* in English how
ṛ like *ri* in English river

The following remarks apply to consonants:

c like *ch* in English church
g like g in English go
ś and *ṣ* like *sh* in English rush

The sounds represented by *t, d, n,* are made with the tongue farther forward than in the pronunciation of English *t, d, n,* while *ṭ, ḍ,* and *ṇ* are made with the tongue turned farther back, but casual users of words may in both cases employ the English sounds.

The aspirates *th, ph, kh* may be pronounced like the *t, p,* and *k* in tin, pin, kin; the nonaspirates *t, p, k* may be pronounced like the *t, p, k* of English stun, spin, skin. The aspirates *dh, bh,* and *gh* may be approximated by imitating the combinations of *d, b,* and g with *h* in English roundhouse, clubhouse, doghouse.

Otherwise the consonants are to be pronounced like the English consonants.

Contents

INDIA, PAKISTAN, CEYLON

CHAPTER I BY WILLIAM F. CHRISTIANS

The Land

INDIA, as the term is here used, refers to that vast subcontinent which occupies more than 1,500,000 square miles of southern Asia. Triangular in shape, it extends from Iran, Afghanistan, and the Arabian Sea on the west to China, Burma, and the Bay of Bengal on the east. From its southern tip at Cape Comorin (latitude 8° N.) to the northern frontier of Kashmir (latitude 37° N.) the distance is approximately 2,000 miles; from Iran eastward to China the maximum distance is some 2,200 miles. Included within the territory are several political units. The two largest and most important, which together occupy approximately 95 per cent of the total area, are the states of India and Pakistan, newly formed in 1947.

Partly due to its size, but chiefly because of its isolation from the rest of Asia, India is generally referred to as a subcontinent. On all land frontiers it is surrounded by high barrier mountains. Not a single railroad crosses its borders. Roads and tracks are few in number and difficult to negotiate. Malaria-infested jungles and waterless deserts further impede contact between India and its neighbors.

To the north is the world's highest mountain system, the towering Himalaya. Composed of a series of ranges separated by profound valleys, the Himalaya stretch for 1,500 miles, from the gorge of the Indus on the west to the gorge of the Brahmaputra on the east. The chain has an average crestline elevation of 20,000 feet and contains many of the world's highest peaks —Mount Everest (29,141 feet), Kanchanjanga (Kinchinjunga, 28,146 feet), and Mount Godwin Austin (28,251 feet). Access across this barrier to the north is possible only during the short summer season via high passes. Where transverse valleys exist they are too deep and narrow to provide feasible routes to the interior.

Flanking the Himalaya on both west and east are north-south ranges which separate India from Iran and Burma. Though not as high as the Himalaya, the western mountains (the Sulaiman and Kirthar) are complex and generally difficult of access. Two important passes do afford passage through or around these ranges. Near the northern end of the Sulaiman is the celebrated Khyber which leads from India to Kabul, the capital of Afghanistan, and at the southern end of the Sulaiman, between this range and the Kirthar, is the Bolan gate, a broad opening which is the principal gateway to Quetta and other areas of Baluchistan. But beyond to the west, re-enforcing the barrier character of the region, is the Dasht-i-Kavir, or Great Salt Desert, of Iran. The Burmese ranges, on India's eastern frontier, are generally higher than the mountains of the west. Composed of a series of individual parallel folds oriented north and south, these Burmese ranges rise from deep, malaria-infested valleys to elevations in excess 10,000 feet above sea level. Not a single east-west river breaks through the barrier and no easy crossing is available. Until World War II, when the Ledo and Burma roads were constructed, trails provided the only land routes between India and its eastern neighbors.

Although political frontiers penetrate the mountainous regions just described, the populous heart of India lies within the territory enclosed by the great arc of the mountain wall and by the seas and bays associated with the Indian Ocean. Within this area live about one fifth of the world's population. The census of 1941 showed a population of 389 millions. Estimates place the increase at 1.2 per cent, or nearly 5 million, per year. In 1950 the population of the subcontinent was probably between 400 and 425 millions, making India one of the most densely peopled areas of the world.

Within the populous heart, however, the population is not evenly distributed. Densities vary from the almost empty Thar, or Indian, Desert region to upwards of 1,000 per square mile (of nonurban population) in eastern Bengal. Since India is predominantly dependent upon agriculture for its economic existence, land forms, climate, soil conditions, and other features of the natural environment are all-important in understanding the wide variations in population distribution.

PHYSIOGRAPHY AND GEOLOGY . . . South of the mountain wall, India is composed of two great physiographic divisions: the Hindustan or Indo-Gangetic plain, and peninsular India.

The Hindustan plain is one of the greatest stretches of flat alluvium in the world. Scarcely any variation in relief is present. Between the Jumna River at Delhi and the Bay of Bengal, 1,000 miles away, into which it eventually flows by way of the Ganges River, the drop in elevation is only 700 feet.

In ancient times, the present area of the Himalaya was covered by a great arm of the sea which extended westward to Europe. During Eocene, Miocene, and Pliocene times, the sea gradually disappeared and was replaced by the high Himalaya of today. Between the hills and mountains of the north and the resistant plateau of the south, a great oceanic deep was created. Here, since late Pliocene times, exceedingly fine-grained alluvial and aeolian materials of enormous depth have been accumulating. Borings have been made to 1,000 feet without encountering any variation in the size of the particles. Some authorities estimate that the same type of material extends downward to depths of 30,000 or 40,000 feet.

Although similar physiographically, the plain, in terms of population densities, historical pattern of settlement, economic activity, and climate, is really made up of two major parts. The dividing zone lies in the vicinity of Delhi, the historical gateway between east and west. It is here that the highlands of southern India and the hills and mountains of the north most nearly approach each other and the plain reaches its narrowest dimensions. West of Delhi population densities are only about one fifth what they are to the east; wheat takes predominance over rice as the principal cereal crop; and rainfall decreases markedly. West of Delhi the plain averages 300 to 400 miles in width; along the Ganges to the east it is generally less than 200 miles wide.

South of the plain is a complex region for which it is difficult to find an all-inclusive, descriptive term. For convenience the term "peninsular India" will be used for all of the territory south of the Hindustan plain. The region, however, is not all peninsular, since a sizable portion lies north of the embayed arms of the Indian Ocean and is definitely a part of the major land mass of Asia. In order to comprehend the broad outlines of the structure and geology of this vast area, it will be necessary to subdivide it into two major divisions: the coastal plains and the plateau.

The coastal plains of India occupy narrow belts between the arms of the Indian Ocean and the western and eastern edges of the plateau, known respectively as the Western and Eastern Ghats. South of Goa the western coastal area is known as the Malabar Coast. It is a densely populated alluvial plain hundreds of miles long. Lagoons and dune-covered bars separate the plain proper from the Arabian Sea on its seaward margin. The shallow character of the water, combined with the even nature of the coastline, precludes the formation of any good natural harbors.

Cochin, the largest port and a center for trade in rubber, spices, coconuts, and rice, has an entirely artificial harbor. The eastern or Coromandel Coast is composed of alternating coastal plains, delta plains, and small remnant hills. Like the Malabar Coast, the Coromandel is densely populated and handicapped by the absence of good natural harbors. The chief port, Madras, like Cochin on the Malabar, has an artificial harbor.

The main portion of peninsular India is considered by geologists to be a remnant of the hypothetical continent Gondwana land, supposed to have extended through southern Africa to India. It is an area of long-continued geological stability and geologists cannot yet fully explain its origins and developments. In broad outlines, it is a region of granite foundations over which there have been sedimentary deposits and lava flows. In several places basins and trenches have been formed by folding, faulting, and erosion of the surface. In general the plateau lies at elevations between 1,000 and 3,000 feet above sea level and slopes gently eastward from the Western Ghats to the Eastern Ghats. The Western Ghats have an average elevation of about 3,000 feet, while the Eastern Ghats average about one half that elevation. In the extreme south are the Nilgiri and Cardamon Hills. It is here that peninsular India attains its highest elevation in Mount Dodabetta (8,760 feet).

The nature of the plateau proper is best understood if it is divided into two major parts. By drawing a line from Banaras (Benares) to Goa, the plateau is divided into two areas which are strikingly different in character. East of this line is a region of hard crystalline rock covered with a thin layer of poor reddish soil. This region is further broken up into three massifs separated from each other by down-warped river valleys. These valleys (the Mahanadi and the Godavari) are, in general, fertile agricultural sections with dense population, whereas the massifs are areas of low productivity and sparse population. In fact, the northernmost of these massifs, the Chota Nagpur Plateau, is a wild, primitive, little-known country occupied largely by tribal groups. The Chota Nagpur Plateau does, however, contain India's chief coal deposit as well as other minerals and is the site of the works of the Tata Iron and Steel Company (Jamshedpur), one of the largest self-contained iron and steel plants in the world.

West of the Banaras-Goa line the plateau has been covered in many places with lava deposits. The southern half of this district is a rolling plains country interrupted by many small flat-topped hills. The soil is dark and fertile and cultivation is extensive. Unfortunately, much of this area is semiarid, but rainfall is generally sufficient for the growth of cotton, millet and other drought-resistant crops. The northern portion of this part of peninsular India is composed of a series of hills, river trenches, and small plateaus which eventually terminate in the north-sloping Aravalli Hills. Perhaps the most important subregion of this portion of India is the Narbada River valley. This deeply eroded trench, some 600 miles long, forms the principal natural route between the west coast and the Ganges plain. It is a densely populated agricultural land with deep, fertile alluvial soil.

CLIMATE . . . Only the barest outlines of the unusual meteorological conditions which produce India's unique climatic conditions can be presented here, but a few generalizations will help in an understanding of India's climate.

Except for a small section of northwestern India, practically all of the subcontinent's rainfall results from a gigantic land-sea breeze, operating on a seasonal basis, known as the monsoon. In the period of low sun (winter in the middle latitudes or the cool season in India) winds are prevailingly from the northeast. In the period of high sun (summer in middle latitudes) winds are mainly from the southwest. The chief reason for reversal of wind direction is the difference in pressures which result from the differential heating of land and water at the various seasons of the year. In the period of high sun the land is rapidly heated, a low pressure is created, and air flows north and northeastward from the surrounding cooler seas to the land mass of India. This is the period of the southwest monsoon. During the period of low sun (the northeast monsoon) the land cools more quickly than the surrounding seas and air flows outward from India in a general southerly or southwesterly direction.

During and just preceding the period of the southwest monsoon the northward-moving air becomes saturated over the vast expanses of the Indian Ocean. When it strikes the elevated portions of the subcontinent it is suddenly lifted and cooled, and heavy precipitation results. Probably 85 per cent of all of India's rain comes at this period. The areas of heaviest precipitation are those sections where cooling is greatest and most sudden: along the Malabar Coast on the seaward slopes of the Western Ghats, and in Bengal where the air is lifted by the outliers of the Himalaya and the hills associated with the Burmese borderlands. On the slopes of the Western Ghats, rainfall of over 200 inches is not uncommon; on the hills of Cherrapunji, just north of the Ganges-Brahmaputra Delta, the average precipitation is 457 inches per year. Rainfall in the Ganges Valley decreases rapidly from eastern Bengal westward. In the delta country precipitation averages 60 to 80 inches per year; at Allahabad it is 40 inches; at Delhi, 25 inches; at Lahore, 21 inches. Above Delhi generally arid and semiarid conditions prevail in the lowlands. Most of the Punjab and all of the Thar Desert and Sind do not receive enough rainfall to support crop agriculture without irrigation, except along the Himalayan fringe and in portions of the northern Punjab. This last region has enough winter rainfall for a limited production of winter (ragi or raggee) crops, especially winter wheat.

The plateau of India is relatively dry. The air as it passes over the high edges of the plateau loses the major portion of its moisture. Moreover, in descending from the higher slopes to the lower level of the plateau, the air is warmed and its moisture-holding capacity is increased. Fairly heavy precipitation (generally over 40 inches) occurs in the northeast, where the winds sweep in from the Bay of Bengal toward the heart of India. Throughout the balance of the plateau, rainfall averages between 20 and 40 inches. During the southwest monsoon period, the southeast coast of India gets little rain. Because of the configuration of the country, the winds moving up the Bay of Bengal bypass this area. Winds from the west have lost most of their moisture on the windward side of the Western Ghats and on the Nilgiri and Cardamon Hills.

CLIMATIC REGIONS . . . The character of its wind system governs in large measure the seasonal distribution of India's precipitation. Topography controls to a marked degree the amount of rain occurring in any particular place. As a result, five major climatic regions can be recognized:

(1) The Malabar Coast and eastern Bengal areas have what is known as a tropical rainforest climate. Rainfall is heavy (generally over 100 inches) and is concentrated in the period of the southwest monsoon. But there is either some rainfall in other seasons of the year, or the soil is sufficiently moisture-retentive to support vegetation which requires constantly moist conditions. The rubber tree (*Hevea brasiliensis*), for example, which cannot withstand any extended period of drought, thrives in Malabar. Temperatures are constantly high, averaging well over 75° F. every month of the year.

(2) Most of the plateau and all of the middle and upper Ganges Valley have a tropical savanna climate. Rainfall is generally less here than in the tropical rainforest, averaging between 40 and 60 inches annually, but occasionally exceeding 100 inches. The principal difference between this climate and the tropical rainforest lies in the marked seasonal pattern of the rainfall. Except in the Madras district, practically all the rain falls during

the southwest monsoon period. While seasonal temperature differences are somewhat more extreme than in the tropical rainforest, this difference is of far less importance than the contrast in the distribution of precipitation.

(3) Bordering the tropical savanna on the northwest and also forming a small pocket on the plateau, east of the central Malabar, are areas of tropical steppe. Temperature conditions are similar to those of the tropical savanna, but the rainfall is less (usually under 30 inches) and the rainy season is much shorter.

(4) Except for extreme northwest India, the balance of the country (the Thar Desert, Sind, portions of the Punjab, and Baluchistan) has essentially a low-latitude desert type of climate. Here rainfall is everywhere less than 10 inches per year. Temperatures express a somewhat greater seasonal and diurnal range than in the three preceding climates.

(5) In the extreme northwest is a region of middle-latitude steppe climate. Rainfall is scanty (generally under 20 inches per year), and there is a tendency toward a winter maximum. January temperature averages fall to 55° F. or lower and occasionally freezing temperatures may occur during the winter months. Aside from the mountain country, this is the only section of India not under a tropical regime.

FLORA AND FAUNA . . . In many parts of India, under the impact of long-continued intensive cultivation, the original vegetation cover has largely disappeared.

In the wetter eastern portion of the Himalaya, vegetation occurs in clearly defined altitudinal zones. From 5,000 to 9,000 feet evergreen oak forest prevails; from 9,000 to 12,000 feet temperate coniferous forests predominate; alpine vegetation is characteristic in the zone from 12,000 to 16,000 feet; and the permanent snow line comes in around 16,000 feet. In the western (drier) Himalaya, various types of temperate forest occupy the zone between 5,000 and 10,000 feet. In the drier areas, short grass and bushes are characteristic. The forested areas contain mixtures of broad-leaved oaks, needle-leaved pines, and deodars.

Along the southern edge of the eastern Himalaya (the sub-Himalayan zone) and in the Assam Valley along both sides of the Brahmaputra River, the characteristic vegetation is a tall, coarse, swamp grass. Toward the west this gives way to shorter grass and to patches of thorn forest.

So much of the Hindustan plain is under intensive cultivation that only remnants of the original vegetal cover remain. Tidal swamp covers the seaward margins of the Ganges-Brahmaputra Delta. A brushwood jungle occupies portions of central Bengal, while west of Calcutta is a region of scrub jungle. In the middle and upper Ganges Valley there are patches of tropical deciduous and sal forest. Largely because of the low ground-water table, waste scrub is characteristic in the Punjab plains. Short grass and scrub forest are typical in most of the remaining areas of the western Hindustan plain.

Peninsular India has a wide variety of natural vegetation. Along the west coast and on the seaward flanks of the Western Ghats are many forested areas. Here dense evergreen tropical forests cover much of the highland country. Coconut palms are typical on the coastal dunes of Malabar. Along the Coromandel Coast, mangrove swamps occur on the seaward edges of the large deltas. The slopes of the Eastern Ghats are covered with sal forest. On the plateau proper, tropical deciduous forest and grassland form the most typical vegetation. The forest cover predominates in the wetter areas, while grass and scrub occupy the drier portions.

The natural fauna of India, save for various types which might be classed as pests (wild hogs, rodents, snakes, insects, and the like) is confined largely to the less populous and more remote sections of the country. Here a considerable variety abounds. Among the large mammals, leopard, cheetah, tiger, wolf, bear, antelope, rhinoceros, and elephant are perhaps the most common. Of the cat family, the leopard is the most common and widespread, being found in all parts of India. The cheetah is found only in the Deccan, where it is trained to hunt antelope. The tiger, like the leopard, is found in all parts of India, but today it is seldom seen except in such remote and inaccessible places as the ill-drained, malaria-infested, eastern sub-Himalayan zone, among the swamps of the Ganges-Brahmaputra Delta, and in the jungles of the plateau.

Wolves frequent the drier areas of the Hindustan plain and the plateau, where they are a constant menace to sheep raisers. The common black bear is found in many parts of India, but especially in the hilly and forested districts of the northern mountains. Another species, the Himalayan sun bear, also frequents the mountain country. This species is migratory in its habits, going into the high mountains during the summer rains and descending to lower elevations during the cool season.

Antelope are widely distributed but occur in greatest numbers in Gujarat and Orissa. Various species of deer are found in the forested areas of India, in the swamp country of lower Bengal and Assam, and in adjacent Tibet.

The most common type of rhinoceros found in India is the single-horn variety, found primarily in the Brahmaputra River valley. In the Sundarbans (Ganges-Brahmaputra Delta), a smaller species of the single-horn type is also common. Some two-horned rhinoceroses frequent the area in and around Chittagong. Elephants today are found only in remote hill sections. The area of greatest numbers is along the Assam-Burma border. They are also obtained from the jungle country of the plateau, especially in the hill country of the extreme south, notably in Mysore.

Among the pests, the wild hog and various rodents deserve special mention. These animals cause widespread damage in cultivated areas. One species of rat, the bandicoot, sometimes attains a size of two feet in length and a weight in excess of three pounds. It is responsible for great damage in the rice fields and gardens of India. Mosquitoes are an omnipresent health hazard in moist, ill-drained areas, as are flies in all sections of the country.

MINERAL RESOURCES . . . Mineral production in India is very small, employing only about .1 per cent of the population, and yielding an annual per capita return of only about 25 cents. Undeveloped known resources, moreover, seem to give little promise of a prosperous future, especially when viewed in terms of the area and enormous population of the country. Additional supplies of minerals may yet be discovered, but the probability is low, to judge from the extensive geological surveys which were conducted under British direction. In many parts of India, too, the exploitation of low-grade mineral deposits is made possible only because of the availability of a very cheap labor supply.

India's principal mineral deposits are concentrated in three major areas: (1) in and on the edge of the Chota Nagpur Plateau (Bengal, Bihar, and Orissa); (2) in the Godavari Valley; and (3) in southern peninsular India (Madras, Mysore, and adjacent districts). In addition, there are small, widely scattered deposits.

Coal is one of India's chief mineral resources. Estimates of reserves range between 50 and 80 billion tons, much of it high-grade bituminous. Production averages between 25 and 30 million long tons per year, with the Chota Nagpur fields furnishing upwards of 90 per cent of the total. Other producing areas are in the Godavari and Mahanadi valleys. Iron ore is widely scattered in India and ranges in quality from low-grade lateritic ores of the plateau (30 per cent iron) to the rich hematite (60 per cent iron) in Chota Nagpur (Singhbhum district), where the Indians estimate reserves at 3,600,000,000 tons. A rich magnetite deposit is located in the Salem district of southern India, but no coal is available in the area and there are technological difficulties to be overcome before this ore can be profitably used. Iron ore production approximates 3,000,000 tons per year. India has important reserves of manganese, the largest deposits occurring in Madhya Pradesh (until 1950 known as Central Provinces and Berar), Bihar, and Orissa, and in Madras. Petroleum resources are very limited, though exploratory work indicates the possibility that extensive deposits may be located in Sind. There is a very limited production in the Punjab and Assam. Gold, valued at around $10,000,000 annually, is produced in the Kolar district of Mysore. Indian mica, most of which is muscovite, finds wide use in the electrical industry, where, because of its great purity, it is used for insulation. Annual production, valued around $5,000,000, accounts for three fourths of the world's high-grade sheet mica supply. India possesses only limited quantities of nonferrous metals. Small deposits of bauxite are widely scattered and limited supplies of copper and chromite are present, but there is a marked deficiency in tin, lead, and zinc.

BIBLIOGRAPHY

India, Meteorological Department, *Memoirs* (Delhi, 1876–1939).

The Imperial Gazetteer of India, 2d ed., vols. 1–4 (Oxford, 1907–1909).

Kenoyer, L. A., "Plant Life of British India," *Scientific Monthly,* January, 1924.

Kendrew, W. G., *The Climates of the Continents* (Oxford, 1927).

Sion, Jules, *Asie des Moussons,* vol. 2 (Paris, 1929).

Mukherjee, B. B., *An Economic and Commercial Geography of India* (Calcutta, 1931).

Brown, J. C., *India's Mineral Wealth* (London, 1936).

Champion, H. G., "A Preliminary Survey of the Forest Types of India and Burma," *Indian Forest Records,* vol. 1, no. 1 (Delhi, 1936).

Wadia, D. N., *Geology of India,* 2d ed. (London, 1939).

Behre, C. H., Jr., "India's Mineral Wealth and Political Future," *Foreign Affairs,* October, 1943.

Lobeck, A. K., *Physiographic Diagram of Asia* (New York, 1945).

INDIA, PAKISTAN, CEYLON

The Indian and Pakistan Year Book and Who's Who (Bombay, annually).

U.S. Department of Commerce, *Foreign Commerce Yearbook* (Washington, annually).

U.S. Department of the Interior, *Minerals Yearbook* (Washington, annually).

CHAPTER II BY DANIEL THORNER

Economic Development

THE development of the rural economy of India may be divided into four major periods: that of the pre-British society (to 1793); the period in which new land systems were introduced (1793–1850); that of the spread of commercial agriculture (1850–1914); and the contemporary period (from 1914).

PRE-BRITISH STRUCTURE OF INDIAN SOCIETY (TO 1793) . . . The outstanding feature of the economy of India before the advent of British power was the self-subsisting and self-perpetuating character of its typical unit, the village. Most Indian villages came close to being little worlds unto themselves. The only outside authority which they acknowledged was that of some local princeling who in turn might be subordinate to a distant overlord, whether Hindu raja or Moslem nawab. The chief sign of submission to that authority was the payment each year of a share of the village crops, in some periods amounting to one sixth or less, and in others to as much as one third or even one half. As a general rule, the responsibility for making this payment, whether in produce or in money, was joint or collective, resting upon the whole village considered as a single unit.

Within the little world of the village, social and economic relationships were governed by customary patterns and conventions of immemorial antiquity. The cattle were tended and the soil was tilled by peasants whose fathers had been cultivators and whose sons would take their places when they came of age. In some parts of India a kind of rough equality was maintained by a periodic throwing together of all the lands of the village, followed by a fresh redistribution of the land among the cultivating peasants. Cloth for the garments of the peasants was generally spun and woven by families whose ancestors had been weavers long beyond the living memory of man. The other crafts were carried on by families who in effect were servants of the village. Their occupations passed on traditionally from father to son: the blacksmith, potter, and carpenter, who made and repaired the implements and utensils of the village; the silversmith, who made the village jewelry; and the oilseed presser. For their services these craftsmen received a regular stipend from the crops of the villagers. In some areas hereditary servants and slaves attached to peasant households performed both domestic and agricultural duties and received from their masters food, lodging, and clothing.

The village itself consumed most of the foodstuffs and other raw materials it produced. Its needs for handicrafts were satisfied by the families of craftsmen associated with the village. It was this tight union of agriculture and hand industry which made the village economically independent of the outside world except for a few necessities like salt and iron. The share of the village crops which went to the local magnate and moved on from him in a diminishing stream upward to the highest political overlord sustained the structure of government and provided subsistence for the urban population. As the local chiefs often constituted a rallying point against the center, some emperors and kings tried to weaken their power by collecting the land revenue without their participation. In their stead they created tax farmers or operated through subordinate revenue officials controlled by the imperial courts.

With the exception of the pilgrimage centers, India's towns and cities generally were little more than headquarters for the top political overlords or imperial courts. The industries which were carried on in these cities were of two classes: those which met the minimum wants of the urban population (clothing and shelter), and those which provided mainly luxury goods for the upper classes or implements of war for the army. Economically the cities had a one-way relation with the countryside, taking foodstuffs as tribute but supplying virtually no goods in return.

This was the structure of Indian society which, with regional variations, the British found between 1750 and 1850 as they conquered one part of India after another. The basic land relationships were rooted in century-old custom and usage rather than in any formal, elaborate set of statutes, legal cases, and court procedures about property. So long as the peasants turned over to the local potentate his customary tribute and rendered him the usual services, their right to till the soil and reap its fruits was taken for granted. Local rulers who repeatedly abused this right were considered oppressive; if they persisted, the peasantry fled to areas where the customs of the land were better respected. As land was still available for settlement and labor was not too cheap, local chiefs had to be careful lest they alienate the villagers.

There was nothing in India comparable to the highly developed forms of private property in land which were the rule in late eighteenth-century England. There were no landlords and no tenants in the Western sense. The right to levy the land revenues was recognized to be the essence of political power. In effect, the supreme political authority was the supreme landlord.

The British conquest of India through the agency of the East India Company (see Chapter XIII) led to the most drastic changes in the Indian way of life of which we have record. The most fundamental of these changes was the disintegration of the older structure of the village community, partly as a result of new land systems introduced by the British, and partly as a result of the spread in the nineteenth century of commercial agriculture.

THE INTRODUCTION OF NEW LAND SYSTEMS (1793–1850) . . . In making arrangements for collecting land revenue from the peasants in the areas of India which they conquered, the British were primarily concerned with securing the largest possible revenue. For it was basically from these sums that British conquest and consolidation in India were financed. Two major types of land revenue systems were devised, each of which shook the older structure of village life in India. In Bengal and adjacent areas, beginning in 1793, the British converted the tax farmers and revenue collectors into private landlords, granting them rights of private property in the land. This was done on condition that the new landlords would raise greatly enhanced revenues from the cultivating peasants and pass the bulk of these revenues on to the state. This land revenue system is known as the zamindari system (Hindustani *zamīndārī,* from *zamīndār,* or landholder, a word which more and more has taken on the connotation of landlord). In effect, the zamindari system in Bengal turned the village lands into the private property of the new landlords. The hereditary rights of the cultivators to the soil they tilled were virtually ignored; the British land arrangements left the village communities of Bengal in the power of the newly created landlords.

An entirely different land system was devised for large parts of Bombay and Madras, and later applied to areas in northeastern and northwestern India. Here the British, instead of creating private landlords, dealt directly with the individual peasants on the land, for thereby they hoped to be able to obtain more revenue than under the zamindari system. Each peasant was recognized as holding the particular plot or plots he occupied, but his right to the land depended upon annual payment in full of a heavy money rent to the state. Because it dealt directly with the peasant or ryot (*ra'īyat*), the new system was called the ryotwari (*ra'īyatwārī*) settlement. Whereas the zamindari system made the landlords masters of the village communities, the ryotwari system cut through the heart of the village communities by making separate arrangements between each peasant cultivator and the state.

These two systems, with a number of variants introduced in the course of the nineteenth century, were the dominant land systems of British India from 1793 to 1947. Under both of them, the old body of custom was submerged by the formidable apparatus of law courts, fees, lawyers, and formal procedures. For with the introduction of private property in land the purchase and sale of zamindars' holdings were explicitly sanctioned by law. All of this was too much not only for the humble peasants but also for the new landlords. Most of the latter could not raise the heavy revenues required by the government and soon defaulted or sold out to merchants, speculators, and other sophisticated persons from the cities. These new landlords by purchase were interested only in the rents they could squeeze from the land; often they delegated the collection to middlemen who contracted to pay high sums annually. The latter in turn sublet to still other classes of middlemen, so that before long the unfortunate peasants of Bengal were supporting an impressive string of middlemen, speculators, and absentee landlords.

The ryotwari system also introduced some features of private property in land. The individual holders were registered and empowered to sell, lease, mortgage, or transfer their right to the use of the land. In contrast to the previous indigenous regimes, which had made more or less elastic demands upon the peasants, the British insisted rigorously upon prompt and complete payment of the stipulated sums. In cases of default livestock, household property, and personal effects might be attached, and the peasant might be evicted. The new land system thus made mobile both the land and the peasant, and left the way open for the growth in power of the moneylender and the absentee landlord.

SPREAD OF COMMERCIAL AGRICULTURE (*1850–1914*) . . . The older rural framework of India, weakened by the new land systems introduced between 1793 and 1850, was shattered by the spread of commercial agriculture between 1850 and 1914. Commercial agriculture—the production of cash crops for sale in distant towns or overseas markets, rather than for consumption within the village—grew rapidly because of a variety of conditions. One basic reason was the constantly recurring need of the peasants under the new land systems to find ways of getting money to meet the mounting demands upon them by the state and the landlords. Another basic reason for the rapid growth in the cultivation of cash crops was the fact that such a development was welcome to the British authorities in India, who did everything in their power to foster it. By the middle of the nineteenth century Britain itself had passed through the Industrial Revolution. British industries were then the greatest in the world, and they kept on expanding. British manufacturers clamored for raw materials and sought anxiously for good markets in which to dispose of their finished products. Under pressure from British merchants and manufacturers, India's coastal towns were linked with Britain in the 1840's by steamships and the interior of India was covered after the 1850's by the most elaborate railway network in Asia.

Once the railways were opened it became possible for the inland areas of India to produce for the world market. Wheat poured out of the Punjab, cotton out of Bombay, and jute out of Bengal. As commercial agriculture and money economy spread, the older practices associated with a subsistence economy declined. In some districts the peasants shifted over completely to industrial crops and had to buy their foodstuffs from dealers. Villagers sent to market the cereal reserves traditionally kept for poor years. They became less prepared to meet poor harvests. Years of successive drought in the 1870's and 1890's led to great famines and agrarian unrest.

To produce crops for distant markets the peasants required credit to tide them through the long period of turnover. They turned to the moneylender, who came to occupy a place of unprecedented importance. Although in pre-British times the local moneylender extended casual credit to meet occasional needs of the villagers, he occupied a subordinate place in the subsistence economy of the countryside. The new forms of landholding, land revenue systems, legal procedures, and commercial agriculture of the nineteenth century, however, opened up a golden age for the moneylender. The demand for his services became an inescapable part of the peasant's life; to the state the moneylender was of invaluable aid in converting the peasant's crops into cash and passing on the land revenue due to the government. The moneylender was encouraged to expand his activities by the fact that under the new order of things he could make a good and secure profit. If the peasants defaulted he could use the new legal procedures to attach their lands, livestock, and personal possessions. Furthermore, from the middle of the nineteenth century the price of land rose rapidly in value, thereby encouraging the moneylender to broaden his operations. He began to take over the peasants' land and rent it out. The moneylenders grew in number and in wealth.

The same railroads which carried away the commercial crops brought back machine-made industrial products to the villages. The village weavers and traditional handicraft servants had to compete in the second half of the nineteenth century with products like Lancashire cloth, which was then overrunning world markets. The village artisans no longer were sheltered by the friendly backwardness of the older village commune. Furthermore, the union of agriculture and hand industry which had been the basis of village life was disrupted. Under the impact of new forces the village could no longer remain the compact social and economic unit that it had been. The growing tendency was for each family to make ends meet as best it could. Deep in the interior of central India and in other areas difficult of access the handicrafts held on for a long time, and some still show strength. In the coastal zones and in the regions lying along the new railroads, however, the ancient village handicrafts declined. The village potter, tanner, dyer, oilman, and jeweler all faced strong competition from machine products, whether made in Britain or, after the close of the nineteenth century, in the new industrial centers that grew up in India. Since 1850 a dwindling proportion of the village artisans of the subcontinent have been able to subsist on what they have received for their services from the village. Millions of them have had to find other ways to gain a livelihood or to supplement their scanty earnings from the village. In most cases the only avenue open to them has been agriculture, and they have added steadily to the great pressure on the land which is one of the chief characteristics of contemporary Indian and Pakistani life.

CONTEMPORARY RURAL ECONOMY . . . The outstanding characteristic of the Indian rural economy on the eve of the partition of the subcontinent in 1947 was the striking concentration of landed property. One or two million great magnates, large landlords, and moneylenders owned or controlled about one half of all the cultivated land. With few exceptions the members of these groups had no productive function. They did not farm their land with modern machinery nor did they apply fertilizers or concern themselves with the latest techniques of scientific cultivation. Instead, they stayed in the cities and leased out their property in tiny patches to peasants at high rentals. The income of the landlord and moneylender thus was drawn almost exclusively from rent and usury, and practically never from profits gained by growing crops on their own land. On a much smaller scale the same was true of some 3,000,000 petty landlords and rent receivers, chiefly city dwellers, who obtained some income from their minor properties.

Less than one quarter of the land was in the hands of some two or three million substantial peasant proprietors who actually tilled the soil. Except for this relatively small number of well-off peasants, India's working population in the land consisted of poor proprietors, poor tenants, and propertyless agricultural laborers. These three groups, totaling more than 100,000,000 working men and women, existed below what by nineteenth-century standards would have been the barest minimum considered satisfactory. The level of debt was such that it exceeded in amount the total annual income of the small proprietor and tenant. A government handbook put out in 1938 by retired British officials noted tersely that "indebtedness, often amounting to insolvency, is the normal condition of a majority of Indian farmers."

Poor peasant proprietors and tenants are so dependent upon, and tributary to, the landlord-moneylender that their condition approaches that of servile or unfree labor. The clearest evidence for this is the character and extent of sharecropping. By the 1940's this accounted for one fifth of the sown area of Bengal and Bihar, one fourth of the United Provinces, one half of the Punjab, and large parts of southern India, Sind, and North-West Frontier Province. Half or more of the gross produce went to the landlord, who often as not provided neither seeds, implements, nor work animals.

At the bottom of the economic scale were 30,000,000 to 50,000,000 landless laborers. Since the 1870's they have increased more rapidly than any other significant part of India's population. The recruits to this class stemmed from peasants who had lost all their livestock and all their land to the landlord or moneylender. A striking number of them have come to serve in one or another form of unfree labor. Some were serfs who might be transferred from one master to another as the land changed hands. Others were bond servants who performed customary menial tasks for their masters.

Crop production methods have remained the time-honored ones dating back to pre-British times and passed on from generation to generation. There has been little or no impetus to technical progress because the benefits of improvements generally have been siphoned off by landlords, moneylenders, and middlemen. In most cases peasant holdings consisted of a number of fragments scattered among the various grades and types of land in the village. The basic unit of field production on large and small holdings alike has been a plot so tiny as to make modern methods irrelevant. In the Punjab two out of five peasants tilled units less than 2½ acres in size. In other provinces subdivision of holdings through inheritance proceeded so far that units of cultivation as small as $1/100$ of an acre have been found. The only important examples of production on single great holdings have been the tea, coffee, and rubber plantations, originally founded and managed by British capital. But even here cultivation has been by old-fashioned hand methods and the working force has consisted of indentured or semifree labor.

URBAN ECONOMY . . . One out of every seven Indians lives in a town with a population of 5,000 or more. The large cities which have sprung up or expanded since 1850 have functioned economically in a role supplementary to the needs of the British metropolitan economy. They have served as centers for handling the outward movement of raw materials and the inbound movement of manufactured goods from abroad. The factories which have come into existence in these cities either are devoted to consumers' goods and other light industries or are workshops for maintaining transport services, particularly the railroads.

Indigenous enterprise made slow headway in nineteenth-century India, partly because it came up against the power of the British mercantile houses. These houses had evolved a form of business enterprise peculiar to India: the managing agency. Under the managing agency system a single business organization runs the affairs of a dozen or more concerns operating in a number of different fields. The system arose when British merchant houses, like those which had pressed in the 1840's for the opening up of India, themselves later founded banks, opened coal mines, built jute factories, or started tea plantations. After 1850 the great British concerns played a predominant, almost quasi-monopolistic, role in the economic life of India. Indians desiring to enter fields in which British managing agencies already operated came to find it sound or advisable to place themselves under the protection of one or another of these houses. Throughout the nineteenth century would-be Indian captains of industry received little if any of the government help for infant industries which was so common in Europe and the United States. The first tariffs of even a moderately protective nature did not come into operation until the 1920's and up to 1947 the great British shipping lines were able to operate freely in the Indian coastwise trade.

The birth of modern industry in India has therefore been a prolonged and painful process. The total number of factory workers has never reached 1 per cent of the population, and since 1900 the urban craftsmen and other handicraft workers have declined not only in proportion to the rest of the population but even in absolute numbers. It is the exceptionally slow rate of industrialization combined with the decline of handicrafts which explains the otherwise astounding fact that since 1900 India has become more and more of an agricultural country. In 1891 three persons out of five gained a living from the soil; by the 1930's the proportion was about three out of four.

There are two chief centers of modern industry in India: Calcutta with its environs, and Bombay and Ahmadabad (Ahmedabad) in western India. Heavy industry is concentrated in the Calcutta area. At Jamshedpur, 155 miles west of Calcutta, is the well-known works of the Tata Iron and Steel Company, which produces annually about 1,000,000 tons of finished steel. The coal mines which supply Tata's needs and most areas of India as well are concentrated around Asansol, about 120 miles northwest of Calcutta. They employ some 250,000 miners who turn out each year about 25,000,000 tons of coal. Near Asansol is the only other sizable steel works in India, that of the Steel Corporation of Bengal (SCOB), with a capacity roughly one third that of Tata.

The heart of Indian industry in and around Calcutta itself is the spinning of jute and its weaving into burlap. More than 100 jute and burlap mills employing close to 300,000 workmen stretch along both banks of the Hooghly River, which connects Calcutta with the Bay of Bengal. Calcutta's services as India's greatest rail hub and one of its two chief ports require a wide assortment of transport and engineering workshops and small metalworking plants, which together form the city's second largest industry. The mills and mines of the Calcutta-Asansol-Jamshedpur industrial complex employ altogether about 1,000,000 workmen.

The great industry of Bombay and of Ahmadabad 300 miles to the north of it is the spinning and weaving of cotton. Bombay has about 100 cotton mills employing more than 150,000 workmen, while Ahmadabad also has 100 mills but only about 100,000 workers. Whereas, however, Ahmadabad economically is only a cotton town, Bombay matches Calcutta as a great port and even exceeds it as a center of diversified light industries. In addition to the two great clusters of mills and shops in Calcutta and Bombay there are about a dozen smaller industrial centers of lesser rank, such as Madras, Kanpur (formerly Cawnpore), and Bangalore. India's industrial position on the eve of war in 1939 may be summed up in three figures (at 1938–1939 prices), as follows: the value of capital invested in industrial plants was 6,750,000,000 rupees ($2,000,000,000); net annual output was worth 3,300,000,000 rupees ($1,000,000,000); and total factory employment was roughly 2,000,000 workers.

For India as a whole, the great bulk of the town dwellers are not factory workers but either hand artisans, unskilled laborers, or domestic servants. Estimates of the size of these three groups vary, but the total number of persons employed in them is at least 30,000,000. All three of these groups are employed by, or otherwise subordinate to and dependent upon, the urban middle classes. Large numbers of unskilled laborers are employed in construction and road building, and on docks and railways.

The bulk of the middle classes in the cities consists of petty traders, shopkeepers, middlemen, sweatshop owners, and small absentee landlords. From their families come lawyers, schoolteachers, and the lower ranks of government employees, such as clerks. For the middle classes generally, the struggle to make ends meet is a hard one, and only a small percentage of them achieve a moderate degree of comfort. In this more fortunate group fall the larger merchants and the successful lawyers, whose main practice is taken up with corporation law and suits about land.

Economic power and influence in the cities is tightly concentrated in the hands of a few thousand Indians who have successfully established themselves as industrialists and financiers. Perhaps even more striking than the concentration of control is the fact that most of the leading Indian businessmen have come from three tiny social groups: the Parsis (Parsees) of Bombay, the Marwaris of Rajputana, and the Jains of Gujarat.

Of the Parsis (see Chapter IX) the most famous family is the Tatas. Despite the doubts of his countrymen and the scoffs of British engineers and government officials, Jamsetji Tata (1839–

1904), relying almost solely on his own resources, succeeded in founding the great Tata Iron and Steel Company. Besides textiles, iron, and steel, his descendants have large holdings in such basic industries as electric utilities, chemicals, machine tools, and airlines. The Tata interests comprise probably the most solid single Indian business group.

The chief Indian rivals of the Parsis have been the Marwaris, who originally were a group of moneylenders and merchants from Indian states in the interior of Rajputana. Quick to take advantage of the new economic opportunities presented in the second half of the nineteenth century, the Marwaris moved south to Ahmadabad and Bombay, and east to Kanpur and Calcutta. Along with the Parsis they were among the first to set up cotton textile mills. From these they expanded into every conceivable type of business in India. The wealthiest of the Marwari houses, that of the Birla brothers, has interests in cotton textiles, sugar mills, paper companies, cement plants, jute mills, insurance companies, newspapers, and weekly magazines.

Like the Marwaris, the Jains (see Chapter IX) began their rise to prominence in the second half of the nineteenth century. In the cotton textile industry their holdings are second only to those of the Marwaris. The best known Jain concern is the house of Dalmia, which controls cement plants, airlines, sugar refineries, vegetable oil mills, daily papers, and periodicals.

Wealthy Moslems, whose income was derived chiefly from the land, did not attempt until quite late in the day to enter the fields of industry and banking. Up to 1947 not a single Moslem concern had holdings of dimensions comparable with those of the Parsis, Marwaris, or Jains. Of the substantial Moslem merchants and grain dealers, the best known was the Calcutta house of Ispahani, founded by immigrants from Persia.

The few great Indian houses have risen to their present position by dint of great effort in the face of many difficulties. Clashes among themselves and with their British competitors in India were frequent and severe in the opening decades of the twentieth century. Since World War II, by which time the Indian houses may be considered to have arrived, all the established firms have tended to work together to prevent outsiders from intruding into their domain. In organization and structure the dominant Indian firms resemble the old British managing agency houses.

The war years from 1939 to 1945 brought unprecedented profits to the large mercantile and industrial firms. Prolonged and intense shortages of food and cloth prevailed for half a dozen years after 1942. Many textile manufacturers and food merchants took advantage of this to extract large prices from the consumers.

A fifteen-year program for national economic development jointly sponsored by representatives of the leading Indian business houses was put forward early in 1944. The Bombay Plan, as it was called, proposed a great expansion of industry. It provided for a considerable degree of governmental planning and regulation of economic enterprise, so as to make the most rapid and efficient use of India's limited capital resources. At the time the Bombay proposals evoked much official and unofficial interest in planning, but developments since the end of the war were little influenced by blueprints of this sort. The postwar years were marked rather by a series of understandings between the great Indian houses and some of the largest manufacturing interests in Britain. Birla's, for example, reached agreement with the leading British firm of Nuffield's for the assembly, and for the manufacture later on, of automobiles in India. Tata's concluded an arrangement with the British cartel, Imperial Chemical Industries, Ltd., for the manufacture of dyes for the Indian textile industry. There were also negotiations in the direction of similar links with other important British and American concerns.

While carrying through these individual agreements, the Indian houses withdrew their earlier support of broad economic planning under governmental auspices. In the midst of the turmoil of the postwar years, culminating in the partition of India in 1947, the Indian houses campaigned for prompt abolition of wartime economic controls of prices and distribution. They also opposed measures to implement the plans which they themselves had previously drafted. With the establishment of the new Dominion of India in August 1947, Indian business attained both of its immediate objectives.

First, under its pressure, rationing and price control at the consumers' level were quickly ended. By the spring of 1948 prices had risen 50 per cent and more on many basic commodities, to the profit of Indian business and industry. This same price rise, however, was disastrous for the government of India, for India since World War II has been a food-importing area. The hasty ending of rationing and price control threw out of gear the country's delicately balanced food supply arrangements. To restore the balance, the government of India, in the winter of 1948–1949, had reluctantly to reimpose much of the rationing and price control it had previously terminated; and it had greatly to increase India's food imports. While these food costs were weighing heavily on the government of India, two other great costs were sapping the government's financial resources: the relief and rehabilitation of refugees from the great riots and migrations in the Punjab, consequent upon partition; and the financing of the clash with Pakistan over Kashmir, a heavy and steady drain after October 1947.

Second, in this setting, Indian business could persuade the government that broad economic planning would be beyond its strength. By 1949–1950, the bulk of the older plans had been abandoned, except for a number of multipurpose river control projects and a few other schemes.

ECONOMIC DEVELOPMENT

BIBLIOGRAPHY

Buchanan, Daniel H., *Development of Capitalist Enterprise in India* (New York, 1934).

Anstey, Vera, *Economic Development of India* (London and New York, 1936).

Mitchell, Kate, *India Without Fable* (New York, 1942).

Gadgil, D. R., *Industrial Evolution of India* (Bombay, 1944).

Jathar, G. B., and Beri, S. G., *Indian Economics* (Bombay, 1945–1947).

Wadia, P. A., and Merchant, K. T., *Our Economic Problem* (Bombay, 1945).

Davis, Kingsley, *Population of India and Pakistan* (Princeton, 1951).

Statistical Abstracts, annual publication of Government of India.

Ghose, B. C., *Planning for India* (New York, 1946).

Ghosh, Dwarkanath, *Pressure of Population and Economic Efficiency in India* (New York, 1946).

Venkatasubbiah, Hiryanappa, *The Foreign Trade of India, 1900–1940* (New York, 1946).

Darling, M. L., *Punjab Peasant in Prosperity and Debt,* 4th ed. (London, 1947).

Pillai, P. P., ed., *Labour in South East Asia* (New York, 1947).

Linton, Ralph, ed., "India and Pakistan," in *Most of the World* (New York, 1949).

CHAPTER III BY MARIAN W. SMITH

Anthropology and Sociology

THIS chapter offers an outline of Indic anthropology and sociology, within which a wealth of detail, impossible to cover here, may be incorporated. For this purpose, we will deal with five major topics: (1) the anthropological background of Indic history and existence; (2) the family in India and Pakistan; (3) the wealth and prestige system; (4) caste; and (5) the general nature of Indic society.

ANTHROPOLOGICAL BACKGROUND . . . The anthropological background of India and Pakistan may most conveniently be described under the four classical branches of anthropology: (1) archaeology; (2) physical anthropology; (3) linguistics; and (4) ethnology. In the last of these sections, we will touch briefly upon both the tribal areas and certain characteristics of the modern nations.

Archaeology.—Archaeological finds of southern and eastern Asia may be roughly dated relative to each other by the climatic rhythm of four pluvial, or wet and rainy, periods. These extend through the Pleistocene, and the earliest finds date from the second pluvial period in the Middle Pleistocene. The earliest Paleolithic artifacts of northwestern India are large, crude flakes called pre-Sohan (pre-Soan) from their stratigraphic position. There is, however, no apparent cultural continuity between these early finds and the Sohan core culture which begins later in the same period. They therefore stand alone without proven connections either in their homeland or in other areas.

The Punjab offers the clearest stratigraphy to date of any part of the subcontinent, and here two complexes, the Sohan and the Abbevilleo-Acheulean, developed independently through the second interpluvial and third pluvial periods. On the basis of existing data, these divergent cultures did not mix until the third interpluvial period, and after that Sohan continued alone through the remainder of the Pleistocene until the emergence of the highly developed Neolithic cultures of the Indus Valley sites under climatic conditions similar to those of the present day.

Sohan culture has affinities with the Far East. It is based upon choppers and chopping tools, and it now seems clear that it is to be regarded as a manifestation of a great complex of chopper-chopping-tool cultures found in southern and eastern Asia, including the Choukoutienian of China, the Anyathian of Burma, the Patjitanian of Java, and possibly the Tampanian of northern Malaya.

The Abbevilleo-Acheulean belongs to a hand-ax culture found also in the Middle East, Europe, and Africa. The region around Madras furnishes the closest approximation to stratigraphic sequence in southern India and the Madrasian belongs to this same Western hand-ax complex which, according to typology, has an extensive distribution in the peninsula. This culture has thus far not been found east of the Ganges. Since the classic western European sequence is absent from the Far East, it is clear that as early as the dawn of the Lower Paleolithic period, we have to deal with independent groups of core-tool cultures which have developed separately. They cover a span of perhaps 500,000 years. It is equally clear that both of these are represented in peninsular India.

In tracing the paths by which these divergent cultures reached the subcontinent, it is important to note that, although in the Late Cenozoic era Burma and northern India formed a continuous area with Villafranchian fauna, including *Equus, Elephas,* and *Bos,* as essentially an eastern extension of the upper Siwalik, direct connections between the two regions apparently ceased at the end of the Lower Pleistocene. Either the carriers of the Sohan complex came in before this break, a hypothesis for which there appears to be no evidence, or they had a choice of two routes: across the northern mountains or south of Burma. Both these routes from the east remain possibilities at the present time.

The path of direct contact with the west remained open, and it is small wonder that the great Indus Valley civilizations bear many elements in common with the high cultures of Mesopotamia and Egypt. Indeed, from the point of view of the Middle East, Mohenjo-daro and its related sites may be regarded as the farthest eastern extension of the Mesopotamian center. It would be unwise, however, to underestimate the local quality of many Indus traits. (See also Chapter XI.)

Physical Anthropology.—No human skeletal remains have as yet been found in Pleistocene deposits in the subcontinent. Sinanthropus at Choukoutien, near Peking, and the Pithecanthropus finds of Java establish early forms of man for the Far East, but their relations to western evolutionary sequences remain unclear. The American anthropologist, Earnest A. Hooton, has posited the existence of an even distribution of physical types at the Pithecanthropus-Sinanthropus stage extending down the eastern half of Asia from Peking to Java and westward to northern India. Such a distribution is so far uncorroborated in its western extension and the most we can do at present is to leave the subcontinent in doubt between various eastern and western sequences of fossil man.

Homo sapiens, or modern man, belongs to the Upper Paleolithic, and there is a hiatus between fossil forms and modern variants of *Homo sapiens* which is often difficult to bridge. Three major modern races of man are commonly recognized: the Negroid, the white or Caucasoid, and the Mongoloid. In their larger distributions the descriptive distinctions among these three are fairly clear, but unfortunately numbers of living men can only with difficulty be forced into such a classificatory system. Two of these recalcitrant small groups have representatives in the southeastern parts of the subcontinent. The first includes the Negritos, who are clearly a pygmy Negroid type and are to be found with identical characteristics in central Africa, the Andaman Islands, and the Philippines; the second covers the Veddoid peoples of Ceylon. The latter have sometimes been associated with the aborigines of Australia to form an Australoid group, but any such association is highly hypothetical at best and leaves other groups like the Ainu of Japan unaccounted for. Although features of these two types occur, they are relatively infrequent and are seldom combined in any one individual. A true pygmy or Veddoid type is difficult to find at the present time either in peninsular India or Ceylon.

Pure Mongoloid physical types appear in the subcontinent mainly along the borders of Nepal and, whenever found, they can be identified as relatively recent immigrants from the northeast. In addition, a few Chinese have taken up residence in Indian cities. Numerous Caucasoid types, also mainly in the cities, can be traced directly to the recent historical conquests of the subcontinent by European nationals. The bulk of the population bears odd resemblances to both Caucasoid and Negroid peoples: they are often dark skinned, with heavy, wavy black hair and black eyes; lips may or may not be full; noses are broad, or thin and high bridged; and the limbs are long in proportion to the trunk.

Migrations of Caucasoid peoples are known to have entered northern India via land routes from the west for at least 3,000 years. Armenoid characteristics are common, and a type similar to that of the strikingly tall and large-featured men of Afghanistan occurs throughout the northern regions. Blue eyes are not uncommon in the Punjab, and other physical features usually associated with Caucasoid types also occur. Aryan literature also makes it clear that early immigrants of light-skinned peoples found, and placed themselves as rulers over, an indigenous dark-skinned population. Following such data, some authorities place the peoples of the northern and western portions of the subcontinent with the Caucasoid racial group and describe the southern and eastern sections, including Bengal, as a mixture of Caucasoid and Negroid elements.

Numerous objections stand in the way of such a classification. It is certainly true that a band of dark-skinned peoples extends from Fiji across Melanesia, sweeps up to include India and reaches on to the African continent. The relations between the peoples of this great expanse, however, remain unclear and until more is known about the inheritance and origin of physical traits, and the prehistoric movements of people, they are not apt to be clarified. The population of the subcontinent is distinct enough to be named Hindu or Indic by some authors, forming a racial subclassification. More modern opinion tends to classify the dark-skinned Pacific Islands people as Mongoloid despite their color, and the most recent authorities, such as Alfred L. Kroeber, show no hesitation in placing all sections of the Indian subcontinent squarely within the Caucasoid or white race. Despite these classifications, the various evidences of relationship in physical type between the Indian subcontinent and the islands of the Pacific must not be lost sight of.

Linguistics.—Linguistic distributions in the subcontinent are dealt with in Chapter IV, and it remains in this section to note only that they suggest contacts to the east through the Munda (Kolarian) languages, ties through Indo-European tongues with the west, and an important Dravidian core, affiliations for which cannot be discovered outside peninsular India and Ceylon.

Ethnology.—We can pass directly, then, to ethnological evidence deriving from contemporary cultures. There is a rich anthropological literature on the so-called tribal areas of the peninsula. For a number of years certain peoples of these areas, such as the Toda of the Nilgiri Hills, were considered representative of some of the world's most ancient cultural heritages. It was usual to think of them retaining, because of their isolation, a mode of life truly primitive, superseded in more advanced areas by more highly civilized customs. They were regarded as handy living fossils through whom could be studied man's early cultural life. Such a view bears the unmistakable mark of nineteenth-century thought, and it has not been validated by twentieth-century investigations. Although it is true that many ancient practices have been retained in India, especially among tribal groups, their isolation from the main currents of Indic life seems to have been greatly exaggerated. Simple as their ways may appear, they bear the general stamp of Indic society. In the simplest terms, the tribes are distinct because they are in various stages of being absorbed into Hinduism, and they are backward due to economic as well as to historic circumstances. A central belt of such tribes crosses the great plateau of Chota Nagpur with an extension north across the Santal Parganas to the Ganges River at Rajmahal. After a gap, this belt then includes the Nilgiris separating Travancore from the east coast. A western belt of tribes lives in the western hills of Aravalli and Malwa, and various land frontiers from Baluchistan to the eastern coasts of Bengal, isolated because of the nature of their terrain, are likewise occupied by tribal groups. On the whole, these peoples may be distinguished according to whether they are sedentary or semisedentary agriculturists or pastoralists, or depend for their livelihood upon food gathering in the remote forest tracts.

Wandering tribes are also to be found in most sections of the subcontinent. They live, literally, on the fringes of sedentary society, garnering their living from the great peninsular population. They owe their continued existence not only to their own ingenuity, but also to the great tolerance of the peninsular social system, which can find a place for any people either within its own structure or just outside of it. Such groups exist beyond the social pale, but they continue to exist.

A third group of tribes should also be mentioned. They are today predominantly followers of Islam and live through the fastnesses of the western mountains from Quetta to Afghanistan, the most widely known occurring along the northwest frontier. These people are neither backward nor primitive in any accepted sense. They owe their designation as tribes to their warlike independence, which has guaranteed them a measure of political separateness for unknown centuries.

Ethnological materials for the nontribal areas of India and Pakistan and for the great bulk of the village and city dwellers are mainly conspicuous by their absence. In this respect, the situation in the subcontinent differs not at all from other so-called civilized portions of the globe. Some generalizations may, however, be useful for our present purposes.

The history of civilization is to a large extent the history of human inventions and of their cultural utilization. Many of the inventions upon which modern world society is based were apparently developed during the late Neolithic period. Some of these can be fairly accurately placed within the general area of the Middle East; others are more difficult to locate geographically. They include the domestication and utilization of certain animals, such as cattle, sheep, goats, and horses; the invention of the wheel, upon which both wheeled vehicles and engineering aids such as the pulley depend; stone architecture, with the centralization of population in cities; and the art of writing. To these was added at a later date the use of metals for tools. India's contribution to world culture, especially in the area of intellectual pursuits, should never be underestimated. Quite apart from such fields, however, the simple fact that she shared in all the tangible traits we have listed demonstrates her close ties with the areas west of her peninsular boundaries during the Neolithic period.

The distributions of elements within another great human invention—agriculture—lend modern peninsular India a more complicated background. The evidence of agricultural crops and diet indicates that the subcontinent faced east as well as west. Whereas the northern sections are primarily grain-consuming areas like the Middle East and Europe, with the same staples of millet, wheat, and barley, the southern and eastern portions depend upon rice, and must be placed with southern China and the Pacific in the rice basket of the world. The pig, which also has an eastern distribution, is apparently old in the subcontinent; and yams, which are staple in many islands of the Pacific, play an important dietary role in southern parts of the peninsula.

Without our entering into greater detail, it becomes evident that ethnological materials support our earlier conclusions. From the beginning of man's cultural life to the present, peninsular India has served as a kind of hub for influences from both east and west. Ties with the Pacific Islands appear on many factual levels. And it should be further noted that, although we have not dealt equally with such factors, many elements of Indic life have been reworked into a unique pattern of their own.

FAMILY . . . In turning to a description of the family in peninsular India, we are faced again with the fact that its basic pattern has a wide distribution. The architectural unit, or compound, within which are separately housed several generations of persons, including members of the extended family such as brothers and nephews, extends from Africa through the Middle East to China. One supposes that, like other great human inventions, it dates from the Neolithic period. Our main concern here, however, is with the contemporary expressions of this familial complex as they occur in the subcontinent.

The Indic joint family system was legally recognized in Hinduism at least as early as the eleventh century A.D., and may well have been developed in its present form long before that. It exists with only minor variations in most parts of the subcontinent today, and even the matrilineal systems of the Malabar Coast are incorporated within Hindu orthodoxy. The family is usually patrilineal, constituted of a number of related men—brothers, sons, grandsons, and cousins through the male line—and their wives. A female child remains within the joint family until marriage, when she enters the joint family of her husband. The affairs of the family, economic as well as social, are administered by the oldest able man, and the family regards itself as a single unit in both the production and consumption of economic goods. Distribution of privileges and property are theoretically divided evenly between the members of the family, but there is often considerable favoring of those persons who contribute most to family support or prestige. For its psychological significance, not less than its economic, it is important to note that a man may never be permanently alienated from his family by any act or series of acts. His position as a member of a family remains absolute. The same is true with only minor exceptions of a woman in her husband's family. After the birth of her children her security is as great as his.

Such a system immediately suggests monogamy, and the subcontinent is, indeed, essentially monogamous. In the north, plural wives are allowed only if the first wife is barren or becomes physically incapacitated and even in such circumstances are infrequent. Moslem law recognizes the legality of plural wives, but, except for certain overzealous—and well-to-do—individuals, the opportunities offered by the legal code are seldom realized. In any case, the earlier wife is not discarded. In the same way, divorce is legally recognized in both India and

Pakistan today, but the incidence of divorce is phenomenally low. Marriage ordinarily occurs early, and it is for life.

The tribal areas differ most from recognized Indic society in their wide acceptance of brittle monogamy and of recognized premarital intercourse. Such customs seem clearly residuary and are suggestive of practices widespread in the more distant islands of the Pacific. They are largely limited to the southern and eastern portions of the subcontinent.

Marriage is certainly the most important event in the social existence of peninsular India. Mates are chosen early, and marriage arrangements are in the hands of the parents. Everywhere regulations regarding possible mates are strictly adhered to. The variety of these rules, however, is bewildering. Marriage seldom occurs across caste lines, but between some castes hypergamy, or reciprocal intermarriage, is usual. Degrees of relationship are also specified. The prohibited, or sapinda (Sanskrit *sapiṇḍa*), relationships in the north ordinarily include six or four degrees' removal through the paternal and maternal lines, respectively. South of the Narbada River, however, sapinda relations are just opposite to this, and the preferred marriage for a man is with the daughter of a maternal uncle, and the next best marriage is with the daughter of a paternal aunt. Cross-cousin marriage is also common in Bengal and has therefore a southern and eastern distribution. Certain groups, such as the Parsis, marry closely within the family. Villages in the Punjab are exogamous, irrespective of relationship, whereas many southern and eastern villages are practically endogamous. Castes, which are regularly endogamous, nevertheless contain subcastes, often called gotra, which are exogamous. So it goes. But the range of one's possible mates is always circumscribed by the family and social facts of one's birth. In the West, incest rules include only the close members of one's immediate family. In peninsular India, they are extended to include a large number of distantly related, or even unrelated, individuals, and there is a remarkable solidarity of family ties within these widely extended family groups. (See also Chapter X.)

WEALTH AND PRESTIGE SYSTEM . . . Peninsular India has known the greatest personal concentrations of wealth in the modern world. Family groups make constant efforts to accumulate reserves of land and jewelry, or both. Because of the general poverty few of these attempts may succeed, but it is still true that a few families, especially of ruling princes, have accumulated rights to extensive land revenues and vast quantities of nonproductive wealth such as gold and precious gems. The total range of per capita or, more accurately, of family wealth thus extends from dire need to fabulous luxury. Modern economic planning in India and Pakistan aims to correct this situation. In the meantime, the struggle for survival is often difficult enough. Nevertheless, it is constantly coupled with a struggle for relative wealth and position. Indeed, survival is often accomplished only by successful jockeying for positions which seem on the surface to be quite valueless. Once obtained, wealth and position are often perpetuated by various devices commonly present in class societies throughout the world.

It is important to note, however, that the value systems of the subcontinent, with few exceptions, emphasize nonmaterial successes such as wisdom, learning, orthodoxy, and prowess in fields ranging from athletics to the arts. In the traditional Hindu four stages of human life, ashrama (Sanskrit *āśrama*), the second is devoted to gaining a livelihood, the third to retirement in the forest from this struggle and to cultivation of the purer virtues, and the fourth to wandering asceticism. Without further elaborating the point, we may say that a wealthy man, or one of worldly position, is liable to be suspected automatically of dishonesty and blind self-interest. Such a judgment does not serve greatly to reduce the struggle for relative position, but it has tremendous effects upon recognized leadership and the prestige system. Men who devote themselves solely to wealth, the typical banyas (banias), are at the same time fawned upon and despised. Humble villagers, who are thought of as being outside the range of the most virulent struggles for material gain, often command considerable respect in the subcontinent, and in this they are to be sharply contrasted to the European peasant. Persons who receive a hearing in family, social, economic, or government affairs are most often those with other qualifications than wealth. But the truly great leader is the one who has the power of wealth, yet refuses to use it solely for his own ends, and who clearly demonstrates his right to recognition on some quite different count.

CASTE . . . The word caste has been used by a number of modern social theorists to refer to particular situations in various class societies. Wherever the position of individuals within a class is determined more or less rigidly by circumstances of birth, the class is often likened to a caste. Thus, it has become usual to speak of the position of Negro groups in the southern portions of the United States in terms of caste and class, stressing the fact that features of the Negro physical type set certain persons apart, from birth, from the more usual American class mobility. Caste thus becomes synonymous with a kind of frozen class system. Although such theorists make no reference to the Hindu caste system, the reader makes an easy transition from caste in their terms to the caste system. As a matter of fact, the association between certain caste practices and the evils of Western society is by no means new, and has had important repercussions upon Indian-Western relations from an early period. The abuses which occur within the system have long been obvious, and reform movements have been directed against them by Indian leaders from the sixteenth century to the present. But our immediate concern is for a fuller understanding of the caste system itself.

Though explicit in Hindu doctrine, caste is by no means a solely religious phenomenon. The caste system is at the core of life in Ceylon, India, and Pakistan whatever the religions of their citizens, and despite the fact that Ceylon, as primarily Buddhist, and Pakistan, as nationally Moslem, both hold religious doctrines antagonistic to much of caste practice. Other Buddhist and Moslem countries do not have caste. As the English anthropologist, J. H. Hutton, has said, caste is an exclusively Indic phenomenon.

According to Hindu tradition the castes originated in the four varna (Sanskrit *varṇa*), and knowledge of this tradition is widely circulated. It was explicitly formulated in the Vedic period. Furthermore, Vedic documentation has been accepted by scholars in support of the common belief that caste took its present form during the Aryan invasions of the Vedic period. Various social origins of caste have been suggested: that it was the device of a conquering people invented to keep a subjugated people under control and was further extended to maintain the power of the priesthood; that some form of caste arises when different racial stocks come together and is an expression of social inferiority and superiority; that the system develops naturally when differentiation of occupation becomes traditional; and that it arises from emphasis upon ritual purity. Some authors combine two or three of these hypotheses, and others could be mentioned. None of them can be fully satisfactory to the modern social scientist accustomed to dealing with the structural features of society. They all seem to be rationalizations after the fact.

Despite the multiplicity of caste theory, the descriptive materials on caste made by authors who have seen it in operation are amazingly uniform. Without our entering into the details of the system, an analysis of the descriptive data leads us to the conclusion that the caste system is founded upon three cultural conditions: (1) the explicit concept that the whole of society is made up of necessarily interacting parts; (2) the fact that social groups, however constituted, have autonomy over their own beliefs, their own customs, and their own practices and prejudices; and (3) the arrangement of groups into hierarchies according to which intergroup affairs are regulated. It is important to note that, although castes are ranked in relation to each other, individuals are not ranked within castes. It is true that the individual's caste affiliation is determined by birth and may not be changed. But the relative position of castes may and does vary, and considerable effort has been expended in the past to raise the status of particular castes or to prevent the depression of other castes. With 2,718 castes reported in the census of 1931, there is a good deal of leeway for such action.

Recognition of the autonomy of castes in regard to their own affairs lends Hinduism its peculiar tolerance. Any group may make its own rules without interference from others, and in actuality these are often tolerated even when they interfere with smooth intergroup action. Castes on many levels in the hierarchy have often fought bitterly to protect their social, ritual, or occupational autonomy. They have even more often resorted to a flat refusal to change their practices under outside pressure. The influences of both Islam and modern Western society have been in the direction of weakening caste autonomy. Despite these influences, however, the structural aspects of caste are still strong in most of the subcontinent.

NATURE OF INDIC SOCIETY . . . The structure of a society is determined by the ways in which social groups are constituted and by the factors which knit these groups together. Whereas some world societies function through the interactions of groups defined in family terms, and others through the interplay of classes established on lines of relative wealth and position, the subcontinent embraces both of these. It further adds a third feature, caste, according to which social groups may be constituted on any basis at all but, once constituted, tend to be perpetuated. Caste in the subcontinent is not to be confused with class. The individual's caste is fixed, but although he may be hampered in his struggle by various factors inherent in his birth, his mobility in the class system of wealth and position and of personal prestige is not so fixed.

Not only, therefore, does the nature of Indic society reflect the general complexity of culture in peninsular India, but it points again to the varied sources from which it originated. The subcontinent is neither wholly of the East nor of the West. Yet nowhere does Indic culture demonstrate so clearly its genius for reworking foreign elements into its own pattern as in the intricacies of its social structure.

BIBLIOGRAPHY

Rivers, W. H. R., *The Todas* (London, 1906).

Risley, Sir H. H., *The People of India,* 2d ed. (Calcutta, 1915).

Moon, Penderel, *Strangers in India* (New York, 1945).

Hutton, J. H., *Caste in India: Its Nature, Function and Origin* (Cambridge, Eng., 1946).

Smith, Marian W., "Village Notes from Bengal," *American Anthropologist,* vol. 48, pp. 574–592 (1946).

Wernher, Hilda, and Singh, Huthi, *The Land and the Well* (New York, 1946).

Opler, Morris, and Singh, Rudra Datt, "Division of Labor in an Indian Village," in Coon, Carleton S., ed., *A Reader in General Anthropology* (New York, 1948).

Mandelbaum, David, "Family in India," *Southwestern Journal of Anthropology,* vol. 4, pp. 123–139 (1948).

Smith, Marian W., "Kota Texts, A Review of the Primitive in Indic Folklore," *Journal of American Folklore,* vol. 61, no. 241, pp. 283–297 (1948).

Mandelbaum, David, *Materials for a Bibliography of the Ethnology of India* (Berkeley, Calif., 1949).

Movius, Hallam L., Jr., *Lower Paleolithic Cultures of Southern and Eastern Asia* (Philadelphia, 1949).

CHAPTER IV BY MURRAY B. EMENEAU

Languages

THE subcontinent of India, with a population comparable in numbers to that of Europe excluding Russia, presents a linguistic picture even more diversified than that of Europe. Four language families are represented there, of which two (Indo-European and Tibeto-Burman) are found outside of India. Two others (Dravidian and Munda) are unknown elsewhere. It also has several languages of few speakers each whose affiliations are dubious or unknown.

INDO-EUROPEAN . . . Most of the inhabitants of the north of India—the Ganges, Indus, and Brahmaputra valleys, Rajputana, Gujarat, and the northern part of the Deccan—speak Indo-Aryan languages, a subfamily of the great Indo-European family, which occupies most of Europe. The history of Indo-Aryan speech falls into three periods: Old, Middle, and New.

Old Indo-Aryan.—This had several dialects, including the literary language Sanskrit (*saṃskṛta*). Old Indo-Aryan was introduced into India through the northwestern passes by invaders during the second millennium B.C. It underwent development in the course of time, and the oldest literary documents preserved already show traces of borrowing from a vernacular belonging to the next linguistic period as well as from Dravidian. Sanskrit is the classical language in which India's culture is couched, and all the other literary languages, whether Indo-European or Dravidian, contain many words borrowed from it and reflect its literary influence.

Middle Indo-Aryan.—Languages of this period are recorded in documents of various kinds; they are also called Prakrit (*prākṛta*). The inscriptions of the emperor Aśoka (third century B.C.) were written in a number of Prakrit dialects. The scriptures of southern (Hinayana) Buddhism are written in Pali (Pāli). The Jain sectarians wrote their scriptures in Ardha-Māgadhī and Jaina Māhārāṣṭrī. The old dramas are written partly in Sanskrit, partly in various Prakrits, and the Hindu grammarians describe these and still other Prakrits.

New Indo-Aryan.—The modern representatives of Indo-Aryan include a fairly large number of languages, most of them with many dialects which run into one another without well-marked boundaries. The languages of the Ganges Valley, from east to west, are as follows (the numbers of speakers are given in approximate figures according to the 1931 census of India before partition, the latest to publish an enumeration by language; about 1.5 per cent should be added for each year since then): Bengali (53 millions), Bihari (28 millions), Hindi, divided into Eastern and Western Hindi dialects (80 millions), Panjabi (16 millions). In western Punjab there is found a group of dialects called Lahnda (8.5 millions). In the southern part of the Indus Valley, Sindhi is spoken (4 millions). Rajputana is the home of a group of dialects called Rajasthani (14 millions). Gujarat is the home of Gujarati (11 millions). To the south are spoken Marathi in the west (21 millions) and Oriya in the east (11 millions). The Brahmaputra Valley is the home of Assamese (2 millions). Dialects called Pahari ("mountain dialects"; 2.75 millions) are spoken in the lower ranges of the Himalaya; Nepali is the most important. The northwestern part of the subcontinent has many tribes speaking Dardic languages and dialects; Kashmiri is the most important (1.5 millions).

The languages named, with but few exceptions, are, or have been, the vehicles of literary production. At present literatures thrive to a greater or lesser extent in Bengali, Assamese, Oriya, Panjabi, Gujarati, and Marathi. Hindi must not be omitted from this list, but is a special case. A western Hindi dialect, originally spoken in the upper Gangetic Doab, that is, around Delhi and Mathura, became in the twelfth and thirteenth centuries the speech of the soldiers and Hindu functionaries of Mogul administration at Delhi and Agra. Thence it spread to all centers of administration. When it was written, Arabic characters with the modifications used in Persia were its alphabet. It became a literary language in the sixteenth century at Golconda in the Dravidian country. Later it received the name Urdu (from *zabān-i-urdū*, "language of the camp"); otherwise it is called Hindustani (language of Hindustan). As used today by Moslems, with loan words from Persian and Arabic and written in the Persian characters, it is called Urdu. As later cultivated by Hindus (as opposed to its first cultivation by Moslems) and written in the native north Indian Devanagari script, it is often called Hindi or High Hindi. This language during a number of centuries had the role of a lingua franca in north India through association with the Mogul administration and later the British administration. As Hindi, in its Devanagari written form, it is an official language of the Republic of India. As Urdu, written in Persian script, it is an official language of Pakistan.

Iranian.—Another Indo-European subfamily, Iranian, is represented in Pakistan by the Baluchi (Balochi) language, and by speakers of Pushtu (Pashto), who spill over from Afghanistan.

DRAVIDIAN . . . The Dravidian family of languages is found only in India and Ceylon. It occupies all the peninsula south of the Indo-Aryan family and is second only to the latter in number of speakers. Four of the languages have old literatures, of which one, the Tamil, goes back to the beginning of the Christian era. The northern part of the Dravidian area is occupied by Kanarese (Kannaḍa), or Canarese, in the west (11 millions) and Telugu in the east as far south as the city of Madras (26 millions). In the Madras plains Tamil is spoken (20.5 millions). Malayalam is the language of the Malabar Coast (9 millions). Minor Dravidian languages are spoken by various small groups in the south—Tulu in Mangalore and the surrounding country on the Malabar Coast (650,000), Coorgi (Kodagu) in the Western Ghats (45,000), Toda (600) and Kota (1,000) in the Nilgiri Hills. In central India, within the Indo-Aryan area, there are several primitive tribes that speak Dravidian languages—Gondi with a number of divergent dialects (1,800,000), Kui (500,000), Kurukh (Oraon; 1 million), Malto (70,000), Kolami (28,000). Far to the northwest in Baluchistan (in Pakistan), the Brahui (200,000) speak a Dravidian language, in the midst of the Iranian Baluchi.

MUNDA . . . The third most numerously represented family in India is Munda (Kolarian). Its speakers constitute economically primitive communities scattered throughout central India in the Indo-Aryan area. They number about 5 millions. Names of languages are Kherwari (including Santali, Mundari, and Bhumij), Kharia, Juang, Kurku, Sora (Saura, Savara), and Gadaba.

TIBETO-BURMAN . . . The Tibeto-Burman language family, widespread in Tibet and Southeast Asia, is represented in India by several hundred languages, each with a small number of speakers, scattered along the Himalayan ranges (for example, Newari, spoken widely in Nepal) and in the hills of Assam (for example, the Naga dialects). The number of speakers is about 3 millions.

OTHER LANGUAGES . . . Isolated languages are Khasi, spoken in Assam by 230,000 speakers; Burushaski, spoken in the Karakorum Range (20,000); and the languages of the Andaman and Nicobar Islands. (An Austroasiatic family, connecting the Munda languages, Khasi, and Nicobarese with some of the languages of Southeast Asia, has been postulated, but so far is hardly more than a guess.)

BIBLIOGRAPHY

Grierson, Sir George A., ed., *Linguistic Survey of India,* 11 vols. (Calcutta, 1903–1928).

Chatterji, S. K., *Languages and the Linguistic Problem,* Oxford Pamphlets on Indian Affairs, No. 11, 3d ed. (London, 1945).

CHAPTER V BY MURRAY B. EMENEAU

Literature

THE oldest and most important literature of India is that composed in Sanskrit. This is the classical verbalization of Hindu culture; all other literatures of India, with minor exceptions, are derived from it.

THE VEDAS . . . The first period of Sanskrit literature is of uncertain chronology. It may have begun in the second half of the third millennium or the first half of the second millennium B.C. It ended in the first half of the first millennium B.C. There remains from this period a vast body of religious texts, called collectively the Vedas. The earliest of these texts are four ritual books, the *Saṃhitās* (or four Vedas). Their composition and editing undoubtedly occupied a long time, and the texts as they survive today show signs of much rehandling, and even of mishandling as the earliest forms of the language came to be archaic and in part unintelligible.

Of the four Vedas, the first is the Rig Veda (*Ṛgveda*), a hymnal containing 1,028 hymns in ten books. The hymns were mainly composed for use in the morning and evening rituals connected with the household fire and the preparation of the soma drink; there are also wedding and funeral hymns. Traces of other interests also are found—dialogues between mythological and historical characters, riddles, and, of great importance for later developments in Hindu thought, attempts at explaining man's place in the universe and the origin of the universe. Much of this hymnology, though in verse, is unpoetic and unexciting. At times, however, the composers were visited by inspiration and real poetry resulted. We are often enough hampered in our appreciation of the Rig Veda by the extreme archaism of the language, which the Hindus of the post-Vedic times understood only with difficulty and which present-day scholarship often labors over in vain. The stanzaic meters used in it reappear in classical Sanskrit verse in more highly developed forms. The type of composition associated with these meters is one in which each verse is almost always treated as a separate unit in subject as well as in meter; both Vedic and classical versification follows this model closely.

The Sāma Veda consists of a section of the Rig Vedic hymns with musical notations added.

The Atharva Veda, another large hymnal of 731 hymns, is chiefly a book of magic spells in verse. It also continues the Rig Vedic attempts at philosophy. Very little literary value is to be found in it.

The Yajur Veda texts are prayer books, giving both directions in prose for performing the rituals and the prose formulas and hymns to be uttered by the priests. There are in addition numerous discussions of the meaning of the rituals. These theological passages are of the same nature as the Brāhmaṇa texts that form the second major portion of the Vedic literature. In these, the rituals are discussed in all their symbolic and cosmic implications and a highly sophisticated ritualistic theory is developed. The Brāhmaṇas also present many mythological stories in explanation of the hymns and contain the crude beginnings of grammar, mathematics, and the other sciences, and further attempts at philosophy.

The last major section of the Vedas is the Upanishads (*Upaniṣad*). These advance the philosophic speculations begun in the Vedas and Brāhmaṇas, and in them we can see the main outlines of later Hindu philosophy and the germs of Buddhist and Jain doctrines as well.

The prose of the Vedas is simple in construction, probably close to colloquial usage; it abounds in repetition, both of words and of constructions, a quality permitting easy memorization, which was the method of transmission even after writing was introduced to India. At its best, this sort of prose may have an artless charm and a sinewy directness and energy, especially in narrative, but literary values other than these scarcely appear. Although it would be tempting to compare the Upanishads with Plato's *Dialogues*, it would be claiming too much for them. They have the same earnest impulse toward truth and, in addition, an urgency due to the composers' doctrine that knowledge of the truth will win the soul a blissful otherworldly existence. As literary productions, however, the Upanishads hardly rise above the level of other Vedic prose and, in fact, are at times cryptic, apparently depending upon further oral discussion for their elucidation.

THE GRAMMARIANS . . . During the last half-millennium of the pre-Christian period and the first few centuries after Christ, there was much literary activity. The grammatical studies begun in the Brāhmaṇa period resulted in a number of phonetic texts whose object was to describe the correct pronunciation of the Vedas, since rituals would have been invalidated by incorrect pronunciation. The culmination of grammatical studies is seen in the great grammar by Pāṇini (fifth or fourth century B.C.), and the two commentaries on it by Kātyāyana and Patañjali (probably second century B.C.). Pāṇini uses a prose style known as sutra (Sanskrit *sūtra*), developed from the earlier prose style but showing an extreme compression, so that much matter could be put into a short, easily memorized text. Both before and after him, the sutra is the form of many basic works on philosophy, law, ritual, and science. All these works required commentaries to make them intelligible. Patañjali shows an early type of clear and elegant prose commentary. Some later commentators developed a more highly elaborated and difficult prose style for this purpose. Still others wrote in simple verses of the epic type.

BUDDHIST AND JAIN LITERATURE . . . In this same period fall the beginnings of the Buddhist and Jain literatures. Both of them were first written in Middle Indo-Aryan languages. Buddhism came to use Pali; Jainism, Ardha-Māgadhī and Jaina Māhārāṣṭrī. Later on both were to cultivate Sanskrit in conscious competition with Hinduism. The early styles were not unlike the Brāhmaṇa prose; they seldom attained literary grace, perhaps even purposely eschewed it. The later styles, in Middle Indo-Aryan or in Sanskrit, came to strive, in a mild way, after the same literary values as those found in Hindu texts.

THE EPICS . . . During all this period there must have been epic composition. The epics that have come down to us were perhaps not completely stabilized until some centuries later, but they took their general shape at this time. The folk epic *Mahābhārata* is the story of a great interclan war of succession in the Delhi region of the upper Ganges Valley; the *Rāmāyaṇa* is the story of Rāma and his war with the demons in Lanka (Ceylon) to recover his lost wife Sītā. Both epics drew to themselves much extraneous material. The Mahābhārata especially had so much story material and so many religious and legal treatises and other didactic matter inserted in it that it runs to approximately 100,000 couplets. It became in one sense another Veda or religious handbook, in another sense an encyclopedia of Hinduism, and its influence on Hindu literature, art, and thought continues down to the present day. One of its most important sections is the famous *Bhagavad Gītā,* or *Song of the Blessed Krishna* (*Kṛṣṇa*), a religio-ethical treatise that is one of the most widely used texts of Hinduism. The *Mahābhārata*'s verses form generally a free-running narrative, which at times rises to respectable stylistic heights, marked by the same expansiveness that is familiar to the West in Homer. The didactic material is presented in verse of simple exposition, which, if it does not rise to lofty heights, yet at its best possesses earnestness and the grace of simplicity. These types of composition provide many models for later expository scientific texts and for the Purāṇas. In its final form, the *Mahābhārata* is said to have been recited by Vyāsa, a diaskeuast who heard it from earlier reciters. It is otherwise with the *Rāmāyaṇa,* whose 24,000 couplets purport to be the composition of one poet, Vālmīki. This poem shares the epic breadth of the *Mahābhārata.* Its style is somewhat more enriched than that of the *Mahābhārata,* with a greater abundance of figures of language and thought. Later literary criticism referred to Vālmīki as the Ādikavi, or first poet.

KĀVYA, OR THE FULLY DEVELOPED LITERARY STYLE
. . . This period saw also a development of verse compositions with an even richer, more elaborate style than that of the *Rāmāyaṇa.* It came to be called *kāvya,* the work of the *kavi,* or poet. All the early works have vanished except those by the Buddhist poet Aśvaghoṣa (A.D. c. 100). His *Buddhacarita* (*Life of the Buddha*) and *Saundarananda* (*Poem About the Handsome Nanda,* one of the Buddha's disciples) are works of an early but already well-developed and fully conscious literary art. At the same time there was developed a dramatic literature of mingled prose and lyric verse. The verses are of *kāvya* type. The plays are the libretti of an operalike art form in mingled Sanskrit and Middle Indo-Aryan. Again, all early examples are lost; Aśva-

ghoṣa worked in this form, but we have only a few fragments of his productions.

The next period opens with the culminating figure of all Sanskrit literature—Kālidāsa. He almost certainly belongs to the great Gupta period (fourth and fifth centuries A.D.), and perhaps he flourished in the early fifth century. Three *kāvya* works are certainly his—the *Raghuvaṃśa* (*Raghu's Lineage*), the *Kumārasaṃbhava* (*The War God's Birth*), and the *Meghadūta* (*The Cloud Messenger*); and three plays—*Shakuntala* (*Śakuntalā,* named for its heroine), *Vikramorvaśī* (*Urvaśī Won by Valor*), and *Mālavikāgnimitra* (*Mālavikā and Agnimitra,* the heroine and hero). The first named of each group is the best, in Hindu and in Western judgment, and they are the high points in Sanskrit literature. They are marked by a mature technical mastery of poetic form and figures of rhetoric, a skillful handling of situation and emotional suggestion, a classical restraint and perfection of outline. The themes are drawn predominantly from the old mythology or the epic; this is true of most of the later *kāvya* and drama. *Vikramorvaśī* depends on the Veda for its story; *Meghadūta* and *Mālavikāgnimitra* have romantic themes of the poet's own composition. Epic and romantic themes, along with the mythological, are the backbone of the later literature, with free invention less prominent than the use of stories already familiarly known.

For roughly a millennium after Kālidāsa, Sanskrit literature continued to be cultivated with some power and success. Imitative, weak productions were common also and continue down to the present day. The *kāvya* style, which culminated in poetic values in Kālidāsa's works, thereafter underwent development in a direction which is best characterized in a single word as intellectual. A highly self-conscious literary criticism grew up, one of its important traits being a minute dissection and classification of literary ornament, figures of speech. The *kāvya* came more and more to be composed in accordance with the rules of the textbooks of literary criticism. The figures of speech came increasingly to overlay the compositions, and in the end narrative and emotion were smothered by ornament. The poetical afflatus appeared again and again, and indeed was fully recognized in the theory, but if it did not operate within the rules of the textbooks, it had no chance of approval by the critics, who seem to have judged all by the rules and perhaps even to have been uncomfortable in the presence of poetical power that was unconventional and unadorned. Many of the *kāvyas* of this period show that their authors had no mean poetical gifts, but the methods of composition laid down and approved were never overthrown by a poetical revolution. Since Sanskrit was an unspoken language possibly already in Pāṇini's time, the wonder is not that no revolution took place, but that ambitious attempts at poetry continued as long as they did.

The literary critics rate as the greatest of *kāvyas* five works: the first two *kāvyas* of Kālidāsa already listed, Bhāravi's *Kirātārjunīya* (*Story of Kirāta and Arjuna*), an episode from the *Mahābhārata,* probably of the sixth century A.D.; Māgha's *Śiśupālavadha* (*Slaughter of Śiśupāla*), from the *Mahābhārata,* of the seventh century A.D.; and Śrīharṣa's *Naiṣadhacarita* (*Story of Nala*), taken from a famous interpolated story in the *Mahābhārata,* and written in the twelfth century A.D. The last is an enormously ingenious example of *kāvya* at its most learned and least poetic. Several other works are rated highly. Bhaṭṭi's *Bhaṭṭikāvya* or *Rāvaṇavadha* (*Slaughter of Rāvaṇa,* sixth or seventh century A.D.) is based on the *Rāmāyaṇa* and deliberately illustrates the rules of poetic composition and of grammar. Kumāradāsa's *Jānakīharaṇa* (*Abduction of Sītā;* probably eighth century A.D.) is also based on the *Rāmāyaṇa.* Many other works have survived, most of them imitative and pedantic. Frequently, like Bhaṭṭi's work, they are constructed to show the author's competence in literary theory and in grammar rather than his real poetic ability. This pedantry could hardly have been avoided in a culture with such predominantly intellectualizing tendencies and interests as the Hindu; even Aśvaghoṣa and Kālidāsa are not entirely free from it.

Hindu taste took great pleasure in figures of speech comparable to Western puns. Kālidāsa seldom employed them, but they became much commoner later. The learned pedants of the period of decadence go on to triumphs of ingenuity by constructing works which punningly can be interpreted in two ways throughout. Saṃdhyākara Nandin (eleventh century) is probably the earliest to produce such a work, the *Rāmacarita* (*Life of Rāma*); in 220 verses he tells at the same time the story of the *Rāmāyaṇa* and the history of King Rāmapāla of Bengal. The device is used by various practitioners to tell at the same time the stories of the *Mahābhārata* and the *Rāmāyaṇa,* the stories of Rāma and Nala, the stories of the marriages of Shiva (Śiva) and Pārvatī and of Krishna and Rukminī. One composer even succeeded in telling three stories at the same time, those of the *Rāmāyaṇa,* the *Mahābhārata,* and the *Bhāgavata Purāṇa;* he was Chidambara (Cidambara; sixteenth to seventeenth century), and the work is called *Rāghavapāṇḍavayādavīya* (*Story of Rāma, the Pāṇḍavas, and Kṛṣṇa*).

Kāvya methods were applied also to historical themes, which emerge from the treatment with little value as history or as poetry. Kalhaṇa's *Rājataraṃgiṇī* (*Stream of Kings*), on the Kashmir kings down to A.D. 1149, is the best. The Jain Hemacandra in A.D. 1163 wrote the *Kumārapālacarita,* which has as its object to tell of the reign of the Chalukya king Kumārapāla of Aṇhilvāḍa (Anhilwara; modern Patan) in Gujarat, and at the same time to illustrate the rules of Sanskrit and Prakrit grammar, in accordance with which its first twenty cantos are in Sanskrit and its last eight in Prakrit.

Kālidāsa's *Meghadūta,* a lyric, idyllic poem describing the journey of a cloud sent by a traveler as messenger to his beloved wife, also set a model for numerous imitations, all of less value than their prototype.

Moralizing *sententiae* were drawn within the *kāvya* sphere by the obvious suitability of the stanzaic meters as a vehicle for a general sentiment and a brief example. The same form was used for verses on erotic and on religious subjects. Many poets practiced verse-by-verse composition of this type, on subjects drawn from all realms of Hindu experience. The verses were often collected in groups called *śataka* (hundred; cento), such as the three by Bhartrihari (Bhartṛhari, fl. first half of seventh century) on love, asceticism, and ethics; Amaru's on love; Bāṇa's (seventh century) on the goddess Chaṇḍī (Caṇḍī), Mayūra's (early seventh century) on Sūrya, the sun god; and many others. Other collections, such as those on ethics attributed to Chanakya (Cāṇakya, fourth century), have no fixed number of verses. Many verses by different authors are preserved in anthologies, such as the *Kavīndravacanasamuccaya* (*Collection of Verses of Great Poets,* possibly prior to A.D. 1000), Śrīdharadāsa's *Saduktikarṇāmṛta* (*Great Verses Which Are Nectar for the Ears,* A.D. 1205), and numerous others. A famous early Buddhist collection of verses of this type is the *Dhammapada,* in Pali. Misplaced ingenuity results here also in works that can be read in two different ways. Rāmacandra in the sixteenth century wrote the *Rasikarañjana* (*Delight of Connoisseurs*), which is simultaneously an erotic poem and a eulogy of asceticism; it consists of 130 verses.

Kāvya compositions are not always in verse. The prose *kāvyas,* with their heavy encrustation of figures of speech, can go further than verse compositions in multiplying the ornaments, once the space limitations of stanzaic composition are removed. Subandhu (sixth or seventh century) actually boasts of a pun in every syllable. The subjects of prose *kāvya* are usually nonmythical. Their narrative substratum is sometimes an invented story of the folk tale type, as in Bāṇa's *Kādambarī* (seventh century

A.D.), Subandhu's *Vāsavadattā,* and Daṇḍin's *Daśakumāracarita* (*Adventures of the Ten Princes,* sixth or seventh century A.D.). Bāṇa's *Harṣacarita* (*Life of Harṣa*) has to do with King Harsha (Harshavardhana). The history is so submerged in poetic fancies as to be extricable only with some difficulty, but the work is important for the pictures it gives of its times.

Folk tales, when collected and recorded, sometimes underwent a mild dressing up in the ornaments of *kāvya;* the stories themselves, however, usually remained the real center of interest. Somadeva's *Kathāsaritsāgara* (*Ocean of the Streams of Stories,* eleventh century A.D.) is an enormous work in flowing, mildly decorated verses, with many shorter tales enclosed within the frame tale. It is a reworking, probably at some removes, of Guṇāḍhya's *Bṛhatkathā* (*Great Story*), which was in Paiśācī, one of the Prakrits; the loss of this early work is a serious one. Another reworking, closely allied to Somadeva's and near him in date, is Kṣemendra's *Bṛhatkathāmañjarī* (*Bouquet from the Great Story*), a dry, lifeless abstract with *kāvya* patches added at intervals. A third reworking, in a different line of transmission from the other two, is Budhasvāmin's *Bṛhatkathāślokasaṃgraha* (*Verse Abbreviation of the Great Story*), which has been recovered in a fragmentary form. Another famous collection of folk tales is the *Pañcatantra,* which has come down in a number of recensions with various names: *Tantrākhyāyika, Pañcākhyānaka, Hitopadeśa.* In the framework of the collection a teacher is represented as instructing young princes in the ways of political life by maxims illustrated by stories, which are usually animal fables. The work is a mixture of prose stories and verse maxims, with much of the *kāvya* in its verses. Another collection in the *Vetālapañcaviṃśati* (*Goblin's Twenty-five Tales*). each story of which leads up to a riddlelike problem which is solved by one of the characters in the frame story.

Both the Buddhist and the Jain literatures abound in folk tale collections. All the stories purport to be given for the sake of the morals that can be derived from them, but one suspects frequently that the monkish writers delighted in the stories for their own sakes. The Buddhist book of *Jātakas* (*Stories of the Buddha's Former Births*), containing over 500 tales, is the most famous of these collections. It dates, but in part only, from the pre-Christian period, and seems to have been finally composed in its present Pali form in the fifth century A.D. Another similar collection is found in the commentary on the *Dhammapada* (over 300 stories), slightly later than the *Jātakas*. Āryaśūra's *Jātakamālā* (*Garland of Jātakas;* third or fourth century A.D.) gives to a few stories a mixed verse and prose *kāvya* style that is almost lacking in the Pali stories. The commentaries to the Jain scriptures, in Prakrit and Sanskrit, record thousands of stories, usually in a bare narrative style with moralistic verses.

The *kāvya* style spread its influence far and wide. The lyric verses of the dramas are hardly to be separated from those of nondramatic composition and in fact are as little dramatic in character as are the arias of European opera. Important plays in the history of the Indian drama are *Mṛcchakaṭikā* (*Little Clay Cart,* prior to sixth century A.D.), by Shudraka (Śūdraka); *Priyadarśikā, Ratnāvalī,* and *Nāgānanda* by Harsha (Harṣa, probably King Harshavardhana, r. A.D. 606–647; Viśākhadatta's *Mudrārākṣasa* (ninth century A.D., or earlier); and Bhavabhūti's *Mālatīmādhava, Mahāvīracarita,* and *Uttararāmacarita* (probably eighth century A.D.). A group of thirteen dramas of some excellence, which were discovered in 1910, have been attributed to Bhāsa, who was earlier than Kālidāsa, but the ascription is still uncertain. The most important of them is the *Svapnavāsavadattā* (*Vāsavadattā Seen in a Dream*). Many late dramas survive, most of them intended to be read rather than acted and of little literary or dramatic importance.

The work that is accepted as the latest of any importance in Sanskrit literature is Jayadeva's *Gītagovinda* (twelfth century A.D.). It is in a fully formed new genre—highly emotional and dramatic lyrics connected by transitional narrative and descriptive verses, all depicting an episode of Krishna's life in the spirit of highest devotion. It undoubtedly derived much from the contemporary vernacular literatures.

PRAKRIT KĀVYA . . . Prakrit poetry, that is, poetry in the Middle Indo-Aryan vernaculars, had appeared probably as soon as these vernaculars became differentiated from Sanskrit. It must, however, soon have fallen under the influence of the littérateurs dealing with Sanskrit poetry, for the earliest Prakrit poems that survive—Hāla's *Sattasaï* (*Seven Hundred Verses*, of the first half-millennium A.D.), an anthology on love; and Pravarasena's *Setubandha* (*Rāma's Bridge*, sixth century A.D.), on a theme from the *Rāmāyaṇa*—are indistinguishable in style from Sanskrit poems on comparable subjects. The same is true of most late Jain poetry, whether in Sanskrit or in Prakrit.

NONLITERARY COMPOSITION IN SANSKRIT . . . During all this long period of literary activity, there was much other composition in Sanskrit, most of it without literary value. The philosophical and scientific works have been mentioned. The epic was continued in a jejune way by the eighteen major and many minor Purāṇas (*Narratives of Old*). These contain primarily the mythology, cosmology, and ritual of classical Hinduism, but in addition much other material, so that some of them became veritable encyclopedias of Hinduism. The Tantra literature also is an exposition of certain religious cults.

NORTH INDIAN VERNACULAR LITERATURE . . . Many of the modern vernaculars of north India have literatures of some age and standing. In general, they are dependent on the old traditions of Sanskrit literature. The epics and Purāṇas are translated or adapted frequently with some influence from the *kāvya* style. Writers of such works include Tulsī Dās (1532–1623), who composed a *Rāmāyaṇa* in the Awadhi dialect of the Eastern Hindi area; Lallūjī Lāl, author of *Prēmsāgar* (*Ocean of Love*), which is a prose rendering in High Hindi of the tenth book of the *Bhāgavata Purāṇa* (1804–1810); Jñāneśvar, who rendered the *Bhagavad Gītā* in Marathi verse about 1290; the translators into Bengali of the two epics, beginning in the fourteenth century; and others. The storybooks, such as the *Pañcatantra* and the *Vetālapañcaviṃśati,* have often been translated into Gujarati, Hindi, and other languages.

The religious and moralistic lyric, which begins in the Rig Veda and is an important strand in all Sanskrit literature thereafter, forms perhaps the richest element in the vernacular literature. It is noted for its fervor and intensity, and often possesses high stylistic qualities, both of the *kāvya* type and more untrammeled. Braj Bhākhā, a dialect of the Western Hindi area, became from the fifteenth century the accepted language in which to sing of Krishna in Hindustan; the poetess Mīra Bāī (fl. c. 1420) and the poet Bihārī Lāl (seventeenth century) are only two of the famous names in this literature. Vidyāpati Ṭhākur (fifteenth century) sang of Krishna in the Maithili dialect of Bihar. Kabīr (c. 1440–1518) composed in Hindi religious songs which embody a syncretism of Hindu and Moslem elements; Guru Nānak (c. 1469–1538), a pupil of Kabīr's, was the initiator of a line of teachers and religious poets whose compositions, mainly in Hindi, form the Granth Sahib, the sacred book of the Sikhs. In Bengali, Caṇḍīdās, a contemporary of Vidyāpati, sang of Krishna. In Kashmir the female ascetic Lallā (fourteenth century) composed songs in honor of Shiva. The Maratha poets Nāmdev (1270–1350) and Tukārām (1608–1649) are only two of this area's many mystic singers.

The chivalric ballads in the local dialects of Rajputana (beginning in the twelfth century) cannot be neglected even in a short sketch; they are a departure from the lines laid down in the older literature.

DRAVIDIAN LITERATURE . . . The literatures in the four great Dravidian languages of south India—Tamil, Telugu, Kanarese, and Malayalam—are, like those of the modern Indo-Aryan vernaculars, in general derivative from Sanskrit and predominantly religious. These literatures start earlier than those in the modern Indo-Aryan languages. Tamil has a proud literary history going back to the beginning of the Christian era, and its vast literature is second in importance only to that in Sanskrit. The earliest works preserved are a grammar, collections of sententious stanzas, and lyrics of devotion to the gods Shiva and Vishnu.

FOREIGN INFLUENCES . . . Two important foreign influences have affected Indian literature. The Persian literature of the Mogul court was the direct progenitor of an important literature in Urdu or Hindustani (see Chapter IV).

The influx of Western influences since the early nineteenth century had literary results as well as others. The vernaculars are now vehicles of such secular Western forms as the novel, essay, political speech, personal lyric, and drama of the European type. Much of the old mingles with the new; the proportion of each fluctuates with changing fashion. One literary world figure has already emerged in the person of the Bengali Rabindranath Tagore (1861–1941), whose poetry was recognized by the Nobel Prize for literature in 1913.

BIBLIOGRAPHY

Grierson, Sir George A., *The Popular Literature of Northern India,* London University, Bulletin of the School of Oriental Studies, vol. 1, part 3, pp. 87–122 (1920).

Keith, A. B., *The Sanskrit Drama in Its Origin, Development, Theory, and Practice* (Oxford, 1924).

Winternitz, Moriz, *A History of Indian Literature,* tr. by S. Ketkar and H. Kohn, vols. 1 and 2 (Calcutta, 1927–1933).

Keith, A. B., *A History of Sanskrit Literature* (Oxford, 1928).

Thomas, F. W., "Language and Early Literature," "Language and Literature," and Ghosh, J. C., "Vernacular Literatures," *The Legacy of India*, ed. by G. T. Garratt (Oxford, 1937).

Dasgupta, S. N., and De, S. K., *A History of Sanskrit Literature, Classical Period*, vol. 1 (Calcutta, 1947).

CHAPTER VI BY W. NORMAN BROWN

Dancing, Music, and Drama

DANCING and the drama are closely related in the subcontinent of India. The very words for them indicate as much. The common Sanskrit verb meaning "dance" is *nṛt,* and a Prakrit (see Chapter IV) representative of this is *naṭ.* The latter returns to Sanskrit as the base for deriving the common words indicating dramatic representation, pantomime, acting, and dancing. Accompanying the dance and drama is music, both instrumental and vocal. A drama, which contains plot, an abundance of lyric stanzas, music, and dancing—and that is the usual characteristic of the Sanskrit drama and of Indian drama generally—is commonly called nataka (Sanskrit *nāṭaka*), an actor of mime or dancer, *naṭa.* Dancing used in a drama in combination with the original plot is *nāṭya.* The dancing which is mere rhythm or graceful movement is *nṛtta;* that which is informed with aestethic and intellectual content is *nṛtya.*

The Sanskrit treatises on aesthetics indicate that the purpose of a dance or a drama is to evoke aesthetic experience in the spectators. Art is not exercised merely to entertain the spectators or to permit the artist an opportunity of self-expression. The audience has a part and must be educated in appreciation. Aesthetic experience consists in finding in a work of art a particular quality or essence called rasa (flavor or taste), which is its fundamental feature or permanent mood. There are nine of these—erotic, heroic, odious, furious, terrible, pathetic, wondrous, comic, and peaceful. In a work of art, as distinguished from a work without artistic quality, some one rasa must be dominant, though others may appear in a subordinate role. Besides these nine basic moods there are thirty-three transient moods (joy, agitation, impatience, and others), which are ancillary to the basic mood. To produce the total desired artistic effect the author contributes plot and theme, and the dancer or actor utilizes gestures or other deliberate manifestations of feeling, as well as expressions of involuntary emotion, such as trembling or horripilation.

DANCING . . . The classical Indian dance, being mimetic and meant to convey ideas and moods, is a language, and its principal means of expression is therefore gesture. Every bodily movement, however trifling, has significance as an exposition of thought, sharing that function with the vocal and the decorative (stage setting and the like) features of the performance. The dancer utilizes the limbs (defined as head, hands, armpits, sides, waist, feet, neck), the minor parts of the body (shoulders, shoulder blades, arms, back, stomach, thighs, calves, wrists, knees, elbows), and the features (eyes, eyelids, pupils, cheeks, nose, jaw, lips, teeth, tongue, chin, face); some works also mention other parts (heel, ankle, fingers, toes, palms). Every part of the body has many different uses, but the hands are the most important and may be used separately or jointly. The final number of combinations and permutations of parts of the body is almost unlimited, and the range and exactness of expression which can be attained are said by enthusiasts to equal those of speech.

Dancing has a wide and perhaps long usage in Indian religions. There are several small bronze female dancing figures from the Harappa period of the Early Indus civilizations (see Chapter XI), which suggest that dancing then served a religious purpose. The Rig Veda mentions dancing, especially by the god Indra after he has slain his enemy Vritra (Vṛtra), or by the gods as a group; this dance is the activity of creating the universe. In certain Vedic ceremonies women engage in ritualistic dancing. The Buddhists and Jains show Indra as a divine dancer. Early Indian sculpture, like later sculpture and painting, has numerous representations of dancing in many different circumstances, often exhibiting poses with meaning identifiable from the later treatises. In Hinduism the dancer par excellence is the god Shiva (Śiva), who performed a dance after slaying a fierce dwarf demon, and the south Indian bronzes which show him as Naṭarāja (King of Dancers), combining in the motions of his arms and feet all the activities of the cosmos, are among the finest products of Indian art.

There have been various schools of Indian dancing, of which the best known is that of Bharata, described in a text of perhaps the third century A.D., and illustrated by a long series of sculptures on a late eleventh-century gateway of the temple at Chidambaram in south India. Other texts of aesthetics and dancing were composed as recently as the fourteenth century. Another well-known school of dancing is that of Kathakali in Travancore, in which the story of the epic *Rāmāyaṇa* is enacted.

Besides these classical dances there are a number of varieties of folk dance in India, such as that done in Gujarat with jars in honor of Krishna, and the stave dance.

MUSIC . . . Indian music is melodic, not harmonic. The focus of interest is on singing; instrumental music is meant for accompaniment. There are many types of instruments but the commonest are drums (of many varieties) and the vina (*vīṇā*), or lute. In Indian music the octave has seven tones. There are also twenty-two microtones, which do not divide the octave into equal divisions but indicate degrees of difference from the tonic which the singer is using. In classical music the singer elects for his song a melody mold or mode called a *rāga* or *rāgiṇī*, of which there are traditionally thirty-six, though more can be cited. The *rāga* consists of a tonic and certain selected microtones —a flat, a sharp, a very flat, and a very sharp, and sometimes one or two additional. Within the limits of these the singer extemporizes. In singing there is abundant use of variation and grace notes.

In the use of time Indian music employs a variety of bars. A bar may have a single beat but with three, four, five, seven, or nine units; or it may be a two-beat bar, but with each bar having a different number of units; or a four-beat bar. Cross rhythm may be used, the singer and the accompanist employing different times, which, however, have a common factor. The climax comes at the point when the two coincide.

The first musical literature of India is the Sāma Veda (see Chapter V), which gives information on the chants (*sāman*) used in the Vedic ritual. Later data appear in the *Bharatanāṭya-śāstra*, perhaps of the third century A.D., and in works from the thirteenth century on.

DRAMA . . . The Indian drama is of obscure origin, but the Rig Veda contains a number of dialogue hymns which it has been suggested may have been recited dramatically or acted out. As we have noted, the words for actor and drama are ultimately derived from a base meaning "dance." Further, the Sanskrit drama may be interpreted as a series of lyrics dealing with the beauties of nature or personal emotions, which are connected by a slender thread of plot, and these are in fact the parts of the drama most highly appreciated by the Indian audiences. The inference is, therefore, that the dance and the song preceded the drama. That the drama has an origin in folk religious ritual is possibly inferable from the fact that the season for performing plays is particularly the spring, at the time of the festival of the god of love, and so drama appears in association with popular fertility cults. The classical Sanskrit drama is usually on a religious theme. In modern times folk plays are numerous, most of them dealing with the lives of Rāma or Krishna, who are incarnations of the god Vishnu. Another element contributing to the drama may be the puppet play, which seems to have existed in India by the sixth century B.C. or earlier and by some Western scholars is thought to have originated in India. The stage manager of the Sanskrit drama, who conventionally announces the subject of the play, is called *sūtradhāra* (string controller), and his assistant in old texts is called *sthāpaka* (arranger), both of which terms suggest the puppet play. The theory that the Greek drama may have influenced the Hindu is generally rejected today.

The Sanskrit drama is opened with a benediction (*nāndī*) spoken by the stage manager, followed by a prologue, whereupon the first actor is introduced. The play consists of acts in each of which the hero must appear; the act comes to an end when the stage is empty. An act usually does not extend over more than twenty-four hours. The action of a play is represented in prose, and the rasas most commonly depicted are the erotic and the heroic. The lyrics in the drama constitute the peak of Sanskrit poetic composition.

Different types of characters speak conventional dialects. Sanskrit is usually restricted to kings and other persons of high rank and Brahmans. Certain kinds of women (female ascetics, the chief queen, daughters of ministers, courtesans) are in theory permitted to use Sanskrit, but usually speak Prakrit, as do other women and men of lower rank. Within these groups there is further linguistic limitation; persons of one class use one sort of Prakrit, persons of another class use another. These Prakrits are stage, rather than genuine spoken, dialects.

There are several conventional characters. One is the *vidūṣaka,* a low-grade Brahman, speaking Prakrit instead of Sanskrit, who is the king's confidant, attendant, and go-between, gluttonous and stupid, and a comic figure. Another is the *viṭa,* friend of the king, a man about town. Another is the *śakāra* (one who pronounces *sh* for *s*), brother of one of the king's inferior wives, a rude, stupid, insolent, and often ridiculous upstart, whose mischief complicates the plot.

Bhāsa, the first of the important classical Indian dramatists, is of uncertain date, but earlier than Kālidāsa; the assignment of any surviving plays to him is controversial; Kālidāsa, who lived before and after A.D. 400, is the greatest Indian dramatist. He is noted above all for his *Shakuntala* (*Śakuntalā*), which dramatizes an episode of the epic *Mahābhārata* concerning King Dushyanta (Duṣyanta) and the nymph Shakuntala, whom the king discovers in a forest hermitage, weds, forgets by reason of a sage's curse, but finally remembers when he sees a ring he has left with her (this had been lost, swallowed by a fish, and found by a fisherman). Kālidāsa is also author of two other plays, *Mālavikāgnimitra* (*Mālavikā and Agnimitra,* the heroine and hero) and *Vikramorvaśi* (*Urvaśi Won by Valor,* a theme from the Veda). King Harsha (Harṣa), who ruled in northern India from A.D. 606 to 647, is the author of three plays which are sometimes suspected, but probably unjustly, of having been ghost-written by the celebrated poet Bāṇa, who lived at his court. King Shudraka (Śūdraka), of uncertain date but probably not much later than Kālidāsa, wrote *Mṛcchakaṭikā* (*Little Clay Cart*), the story of the poor but honest Brahman Charudatta (Cārudatta) and the rich and noble courtesan Vasantasenā who loves him. It is an entertaining drama with a burlesque scene on the traditional and pedantic Indian science of thieving.

Bhavabhūti, who lived about A.D. 700 or later, is considered second only to Kālidāsa. He wrote three plays, the *Mahāvīracarita* (*Early Life of Rāma*), *Uttararāmacarita* (*Later Life of Rāma*), and *Mālatīmādhava* (the story of the heroine Mālatī and the hero Mādhava). Bhaṭṭa Nārāyaṇa, who probably lived before A.D. 800, is the author of the *Veṇīsaṃhāra* (*The Braiding of the Hair*), which is based upon an episode in the epic *Mahābhārata.* It tells the story of the wicked king *Duḥśāsana* who, after the Pāṇḍavas were defeated at dicing and had lost their common wife Draupadī, dragged her off by her unbraided hair. Bhīma, one of the Pāṇḍavas, swore some day to kill Duḥśāsana and did so. Thereupon, Draupadī's hair could be braided again. Viśākhadatta, who probably lived not later than A.D. 800, is the author of a historical play, without love interest, concerning the faithful minister Yaugandharāyaṇa, whom Chanakya (Cāṇakya), minister of Chandragupta Maurya, tried to win to his master.

Rājaśekhara, who lived about A.D. 900, wrote four plays, of which the best known is the *Karpūramañjarī* (*The Camphor Garland*), written entirely in Prakrit. Krishnamishra (Kṛṣṇamiśra, fl. A.D. c. 1100) is the author of *Prabodhacandrodaya* (*Rise of the Moon of Knowledge*), an allegory of virtues set in a Vishnu milieu.

A number of treatises exist on the drama; some others, which are not extant, are mentioned by the grammarian Pāṇini (fl. fifth or fourth century B.C.). Later authors of the tenth and fourteenth centuries divide the drama into ten sorts of *rūpaka* (major types), and eighteen *uparūpaka* (minor types).

Besides the Sanskrit plays, there exist today shadow plays and plays of many sorts in the vernaculars. Very popular are plays on themes of the Krishna cycle, composed in Braj Bhākhā (Braj Bhasha), a late literary language of Mathura; so, too, the Yātrā plays in Bengal, and the plays of the Rāma cycle. In such plays the stanzas may be fixed, but the actors may improvise fairly freely in the prose portions. The modern Indian stage and motion picture industry, though affected by Western technique, still exploit the religious and heroic legends of the epics and Purāṇas, heavily interspersed with song and dance.

INDIA, PAKISTAN, CEYLON

BIBLIOGRAPHY

Ryder, A. W., tr., *The Little Clay Cart* (Cambridge, Mass., 1905).
Fox-Stangways, A. H., *The Music of Hindostan* (Oxford, 1914).
Popley, H. A., *The Music of India* (New York, 1921).
Coomaraswamy, A. K., *The Dance of Śiva* (London, 1924).
Keith, A. B., *The Sanskirt Drama in Its Origin, Development, Theory, and Practice* (Oxford, 1924).
Coomaraswamy, A. K., tr., *The Mirror of Gesture* (New York, 1936).
Garratt, G. T., ed., *The Legacy of India* (Oxford, 1937).
Daniélou, Alain, *Northern Indian Music,* vol. 1 (London, 1949), vol. 2 in preparation.
Ryder, A. W., tr., *Translations of Shakuntala, and Other Works* (New York, various dates).

CHAPTER VII BY W. NORMAN BROWN

Architecture

THE earliest architectural remains in India are at the Indus Valley sites of the third millennium B.C. (see Chapter XI). These contain an abundance of household architecture, but almost no monumental works except the so-called Great Bath. The latter is built of brick; it had an elaborate system of intake for the water, was surrounded by ancillary chambers with a puzzling passageway, and may have had a cult significance. It is not possible to relate this building to the development of Indian architecture in historic times.

For the period between the Indus civilizations and the time of the Mauryas (third century B.C.) there is no information about Indian architecture. The Rig Veda and other Vedas speak of the fortified cities of the non-Aryans, and the same works and the Brāhmaṇas ancillary to them (see Chapter V) allude to buildings, pillars, doors, and other architectural elements but give no descriptions. Except for the great walls at Rajgaha (Rājagṛha) in Bihar, there are no archaeological discoveries from pre-Mauryan times to help reconstruct any monuments.

BUDDHIST, HINDU, AND JAIN STRUCTURES . . . The Mauryan emperor Aśoka (r. c. 274–237 B.C.) built an extensive palace with floors of wood, but using stone columns and other stone elements, the whole thought to be modeled on the palace of the Achaemenian kings at Persepolis. He erected stone pillars to carry his inscriptions, and set up stupas (Sanskrit *stūpa*), or memorial mounds, to honor the Buddha—the Buddhist texts credit him with 80,000 of these—and perhaps to honor the Jain saviors as well, if the claims of the Jain texts are to be accepted. No mound survives that can definitely be assigned to Aśoka's time as now standing, but that of Sanchi, which was remade and enlarged two centuries later and is hemispherical in shape, probably gives an idea of the appearance in his day. The early form was later displaced by a loftier type, having a high, straight barrel with a rounded top. Surrounding the mound was a stone railing which consisted of tall posts pierced for the insertion of horizontal rails, a clumsy type of structure for stone but practicable in wood. The railing had one or more gateways, torana (Sanskrit, *toraṇa*), which also reproduce wooden types, and they, and sometimes the railings also, were heavily ornamented. On top was an enclosed hallowed spot surmounted by an honorific parasol or a series of superimposed parasols.

In Aśoka's reign the practice of excavating caves in rock as religious shrines began. These caves reproduced wooden structures of an elaborate character, the product of a long evolution. Some of these caves are chaityas (*caitya*) or halls of worship, others viharas (*vihāra*), or residences for monks. The oldest is a chaitya of the Ájīvika sect in the Barabar Hills in Bihar. Slightly later is the Buddhist chaitya cave at Bhaja (early second century B.C.) in western India. A long room, barrel vaulted to the roof, was supported by sloping posts. At the rear was a stupa which the worshipers circumambulated. The entrance was a horseshoe-shaped arch, repeated in miniature as a windowlike decorative motif. In the oldest specimen, however, the door is a rectangle set in a wall framed by the arch and the decorative windows are missing. In a Buddhist chaitya hall at Karli

(Karle), located near Bhaja but later than it by a century or more, the interior was provided with curved wooden beams like those of wooden structures. The cave monasteries of this period were plain, though their porches might carry decoration. Later viharas, besides having cells for monks, might also have stone benches, presumably for eating, and niches with images of the Buddha. Numerous cave temples were also excavated during the Gupta period and later, as in the series at Elura and Ajanta, both in western India. Private residences and palaces were still built of wood. Their types are exhibited in sculptures at Bharhut, Sanchi, and elsewhere.

By the end of the fourth century A.D., during the Gupta period (319–500), structural temples were built which still survive. A simple flat-roofed cell with a porch supported by pillars was a common type. In the fifth century such a temple may have a superstructure. Structural stone barrel-vaulted temples also appear in the fourth century, as in the Hindu temple at Chezarla in the northeastern part of Madras. The flat-roofed type of temple with a spire, sikhara (Sanskrit *śikhara*), over the shrine and a porch at the doorway appears in the sixth century, as in the Hindu temple at Aihole in southwestern India.

In the medieval temple architecture there is a differentiation of types. In the north the sikhara type dominates. This has a porch, an anteroom, and a cell for the main image, over which last the tower rises as a square, rarely circular, element, with curved sides, corbeled inwards until the sides nearly meet. The spire consists of compressed stories, marked by dominating vertical lines, with an amalaka (Sanskrit *āmalaka,* a cushion-shaped crown resembling the myrobalan fruit) at the top, and a finial surmounted by a vase (*kalaśa*). Especially fine illustrations of subvarieties appear in the tenth to twelfth centuries at Khajraho (central India) and at Bhubaneshwar (Bhuvaneshwar), in Orissa. Both the exterior and interior of the temple bear profuse ornamentation. The most elaborate are those of Gujarat and elsewhere in western India, whose type extended northwest through Rajputana to Delhi and Agra, and was used by both Hindus and Jains. Another type of temple, lower and more spread out, and with or without spires, appears in south India in the Hoyśala temples at Somnathpur (1268), Belur, and Halebid in Mysore State, and with spires and domes in western India in the Jain temples on Mount Girnar and on Mount Abu (thirteenth century).

In south India another style was developing. This is illustrated in monolithic temples at Mamallapuram in the seventh century, and in structural examples of the eighth century at the same place (Shore Temple) and at Conjeeveram (Kanchipuram). Horizontal lines, formed by a series of rolling cornices, dominate in place of the vertical lines of the northern spire. The successive stories are decorated with pavilions or false windows (*kuḍu*), shaped like those of the early cave chaityas. The pillars are supported by lions. The summit of the roof is a square, circular, or polygonal dome, or a long barrel vault. One of the most remarkable of all Indian temples is the monolithic Kailāsanātha Temple of the late eighth century carved in the scarp at Elura. As time goes on the spire over the shrine (vimana; Sanskrit *vimāna*) becomes higher. The outer wall assumes more importance, because within it may be housed a great number of people. The entrance (*gopuram*) through the wall eventually becomes the dominating element of the temple complex and is copiously decorated. Pillared halls (*maṇḍapam*) are added, and a tank, or artificial lake.

MOSLEM ARCHITECTURE . . . The Moslems (in India the form "Muslim" is preferred) needed religious buildings differently planned from Hindu and Jain temples. Their mosques were meant for congregational worship, not individual. They also buried their honored dead in elaborate tombs, and cultivated civil architecture on a monumental scale. Distinctively

Moslem architecture began in north India at about the beginning of the thirteenth century. The Moslems then used Hindu workmen and in building mosques adapted Hindu and Jain temple architecture by retaining parts of the forest of columns in the roofed and walled-in court surrounding the temple, but removing the temple itself, erecting a multiple-arched screen before the columns, and, generally, providing an unroofed courtyard before the screen. The ceiling of the covered part was vaulted, and the roof domed. Notable examples of such construction appear in the mosque called the Two-and-a-Half Day Hut (*aṛhāī din kā jhoṅpṛā*) at Ajmer (Ajmir) and the Quwwatul-Islām Mosque (begun in 1191) outside Delhi—beside the latter stands the Quṭb (Kutb) Minār (Tower of Victory), 238 feet high, of five stories, which was finally completed at a later time—and again at Cambay, in Gujarat.

Besides the developments at Delhi and nearby, many local Moslem styles arose during the fourteenth to sixteenth centuries. The most conspicuous were those in Ahmadabad (in Gujarat), Jaunpur (in Uttar Pradesh), Sasaram (in Bihar), Gaur (in Bengal), and Bijapur and Golconda (in the Deccan).

During the sixteenth and seventeenth centuries, Moslem architecture reached its peak under the Mogul (Mughal) emperors Akbar (r. 1556–1605), Jahāngīr (r. 1605–1627), and Shāh Jahān (r. 1628–1658). These rulers, admirers of Persian art, imported Persian architects. Their buildings retain many Indian elements, but all are blended with Iranian, especially in religious structures. Akbar's chief buildings were a tomb for his father, Emperor Humāyūn, outside Delhi; a palace fort of red sandstone at Agra; another at Lahore; and the red sandstone fort city at Fatehpur (Fathpur) Sikri, twenty-three miles from Agra. Under Jahāngīr, Akbar's tomb at Sikandra, outside Agra, was completed (1612–1613). In the gateway to the garden surrounding the tomb, the use of minarets was introduced. At Agra the remarkable white marble tomb of I'timād ud-Daulā, Jahāngīr's father-in-law, was completed at the inspiration of his daughter, Nūr Maḥall. Jahāngīr also had a mausoleum built for himself at Shahdara near Lahore.

Shāh Jahān built of marble rather than red sandstone, and is responsible for the many buildings in the Delhi fort, many others in the Agra fort, some others at Lahore, the great mosque, Jāmi' Masjid, at Delhi and similarly the Jāmi' Masjid of Agra. Above all other Indo-Moslem architecture is his Taj Mahal (Tāj Maḥall) at Agra, around a bend of the river from the fort and opposite it, which he built as a memorial to his beloved wife, Mumtāz Maḥall. Its great white dome is the dominating theme of Agra and the most distinguished symbol of Mogul rule. Shāh Jahān made use in his marble buildings of inlaid *pietra dura* ornament (previously employed in the tomb of I' timād ud-Daulā); and in many of his buildings he used foliated or cusped, instead of plain, arches. Shāh Jahān's was the golden age of the Moguls.

Under Aurangzeb (Aurangzīb, r. 1658–1707), last of the great Moguls, Indo-Moslem architecture declined; the most notable building of his period is the Jāmi' Masjid of Lahore. At this time also tombs erected in Sind, and some of the best Moslem buildings of the Deccan, such as the tomb of Sultan Muḥammad (d. 1656) at Bijapur, show Mogul influence upon local styles.

Under the British, European styles of architecture were introduced into India for government buildings and Indian styles were neglected. In the governmental buildings at New Delhi, erected in the 1920's under the supervision of a British architect, an effort was made to utilize Indian motifs of various periods.

BIBLIOGRAPHY

Fergusson, James, *The History of Indian and Eastern Architecture,* 2d ed., rev. by J. Burgess (London, 1910).

Marshall, Sir John H., "Monuments," *The Cambridge History of India* (New York): vol. 1 (1922), vol. 3 (1928).

ARCHITECTURE

Coomaraswamy, A. K., *History of Indian and Indonesian Art* (New York, 1927).

Brown, Percy, "Monuments," *The Cambridge History of India* (New York, 1937), vol. 4.

———, *Indian Architecture,* 2 vols. (Bombay, 1942).

Kramrisch, Stella, *The Hindu Temple,* 2 vols. (Calcutta, 1946).

CHAPTER VIII BY W. NORMAN BROWN

Sculpture and Painting

SCULPTURE in historic India has been devoted to the uses of the intellectual life, and hence to religion. Because the ideas which it aims to clarify are abstract, it is symbolic and ordinarily lacks naturalism, especially in medieval and modern images, which may have more than the normal number of arms, or be hybrid forms, or exhibit unusual or forced poses. Nevertheless, when Indian sculptors have wished to portray a natural subject naturalistically, they have been able to do so.

In the Indus Valley culture of the third millennium B.C., there are both kinds of presentation. Skillful naturalistic art appears on the seals in figures of the bull, but some other animal figures, though realistic, are hybrid forms and symbolic. In dancing girl bronzes, the artist achieved litheness and rhythm in dealing with the human figure, but in the portrayal of a meditative god—if it is a god—with three faces, he may have aimed to symbolize some abstract conception.

In Aśoka's time, when the historic period of Indian sculpture commences, there is both naturalism and symbolism. Aśoka erected a number of columns to honor the law, as at Sarnath, where the Buddha preached his first sermon. On top of each was a capital ornamented with naturalistic animal figures. His artists could also treat the human figure with naturalness, as in the female chowry (*chauri* or fly whisk) bearer from Didarganj, near Patna. But in representing a *yakṣa* (yaksha or fertility deity) naturalism was not a goal, since the divinity did not actually have a human form. But the *yakṣa* did have power, which the human form was used to express. Stylistically, the latter sort of figure is primitive, being frontal—that is, preferring the face focus—and giving little attention to the lower part of the body. Other objects besides the human body could serve as symbols. Aśoka's column at Sarnath had at its top not the figure of the Buddha, but a wheel, the symbol of eternal and infinite truth, which the Buddha revealed.

Similarly, the Buddha's final nirvana (Sanskrit *nirvāṇa*)—we might say death—and himself as comprising the heavens, the earth, and the hells was symbolized by the stupa (Sanskrit *stūpa*, or memorial mound). So, too, the empty seat beneath the holy pipal tree where he got enlightenment (bodhi) was not used as an icon of the Buddha, but as an ocular reference to complete and saving knowledge become available to finite humanity. Under Mahayana Buddhism a Buddha figure was created.

Symbolism is also general in Jain and Hindu sculptures. The Jain *tīrthankaras* (saviors), being emancipated and therefore incorporeal souls, must be shown symbolically; hence they are represented as kings. Ideally, the creative artist in India, before portraying a deity, must realize the deity in the deity's highest, that is spiritual and suprasensuous, character. Afterwards he should think of the deity as transmuted into a lower, physical form, apprehensible by the senses, which then becomes the symbol to be used in his sculpture.

Following Aśoka's period, in the second century B.C., comes sculpture which remains flat but develops an angularity, as on the railing which once surrounded a stupa at Bharhut, and at Bhaja in the porch of the vihara (Sanskrit *vihāra*), or monk's residence. In the next century modeled three-dimensional work appears, as between 100 and 50 B.C. at Buddh (Bodh) Gaya, the historic site of the Buddha's enlightenment, on a railing ornamented with sculptured panels and posts. The classic period of early Indian sculpture is most abundantly illustrated at Sanchi (central India) in the carving on the toranas (Sanskrit *toraṇa*, or gateways) around the great stupa, which date from about 50 B.C. to A.D. 75, with some of the work perhaps extending into the second century. The subjects come from the historical and legendary life of the Buddha, and the scenes exhibit town and country; court, village, and jungle; peace and war; heaven and earth. The Buddha himself is still represented aniconically, though gods and the Bodhisattva (that is, the Buddha in previous existences) have human form.

From about the beginning of the Christian era there was centered in the north at Mathura (Muttra) a school of sculpture executed in a mottled red sandstone, which supplied the entire northern region with its products. The characteristic Indian Buddha type develops in this school. A piece carved under the direction of a Friar Bala and discovered at Sarnath is dated in the third year of the reign of Kanishka (Kaniṣka) and is called a Bodhisattva (future Buddha) rather than a Buddha. It is a typical standing Buddha, with energy in the stance, gesture, and features, rather than repose and sweetness. The torso is finely modeled; the figure is round, though calculated for a frontal view. It was originally surmounted by a carved umbrella, now broken off, marked with lucky symbols. The seated Bodhisattva or Buddha type appears at about the same time. In an image from Katra (near Mathura) of the Buddha preaching, there appear the snail-shaped *uṣṇīṣa* (protuberance on the head) and the *ūrṇā* (curl of hair between the eyebrows). His seat is a lion throne—elsewhere it may be a lotus. A scalloped nimbus is behind him—in other figures this may be plain. The left hand rests on the thigh. In the later Kushana (Kuṣāṇa) Buddha type the robe is often over both shoulders, and more voluminously rendered than in the preceding period. In seated figures both feet are hidden; pedestals are often used. The head is covered with curls and the shaven head type disappears. This is the orthodox Indian type of Buddha, widely copied and developed, and carried to south India, Ceylon, and Southeast Asia. From these late Kushana times come numerous iconographic types of the Buddhist religion, illustrating nagas (Sanskrit *nāga*, or serpent), Bodhisattvas, *yakṣas* and *yakṣīs* (male and female fertility divinities), and others. Jain iconography of this period uses similar types.

At the same time a somewhat similar development, chiefly Buddhist, was taking place in the Andhra country of northern Madras and at a few other places in the south. The material was white marble, and the period begins about 150 B.C. The most celebrated site of this school was at Amaravati, where there was a great stupa, now demolished. The legends illustrated there and at other sites involve abundant architectural detail, walled and moated cities, palaces, stupas, toranas, bodhi trees, and temples. The Amaravati sculpture is marked by a kind of nervous irritation, contrasting with the carelessness of contemporary Mathura; there is a wide range of emotions: wild transports of joy and violent outbursts of passion, ecstatic devotion.

In northwest India, in the Gandhara region, centered at Peshawar, from the first century B.C. until about A.D. 600, there existed a variety of sculpture, as of architecture, which was largely Hellenistic. Here another type of Buddha image, with Greek and Roman characteristics of repose, developed and spread to central Asia. Many scenes from the Buddha's historical and legendary life were also illustrated in the carved stone.

During the time of the imperial Guptas (A.D. 319 to 500), Indian sculpture attains its greatest elegance. The Buddha images of that period have the greatest finish and rhythm. The great Hindu revival of this period also brought a flowering of Hindu art, and pieces illustrating it are abundant.

Medieval India continued the Gupta tradition by elaborating the number of types and character of treatment. In eastern India a celebrated school flourished in Bengal and Bihar under the Pāla kings and later (eighth to twelfth centuries); it was used by both Buddhists and Hindus. In south India there are illustrated a wide variety of Hindu themes at many sites, as at Mamallapuram, south of Madras, in the seventh century; or in the cave temples of Elura (eighth or ninth century), especially that known as the Kailāsanātha; or at Elephanta near Bombay. Other varieties are at Khajraho (tenth and eleventh century) in central India and at Bhubaneshwar (Bhuvaneshwar) and Konarak in Orissa, and on the Hoyśala temples in Mysore. Still later types appear in south India in the sixteenth century.

Bronze casting is preserved in historic India from Kushana times, and in the medieval period it was common in many parts of the country. The finest bronzes, as a group, come from south India. They represent chiefly deities and saints.

In a Moslem environment, sculpture is limited to floral and geometric design, often very intricate.

PAINTING . . . The earliest surviving paintings in India come from Ajanta and were executed on the inner walls and ceilings of the Buddhist cave temples from the second century B.C. to the sixth A.D. Some of the paintings follow story themes; others are merely decorative animal and vegetation designs. They are emotionally rich and technically proficient, showing scenes of human relationships in settings of palace, home, and city. Slightly later (fifth century) are the murals of Sigiriya in Ceylon and Sittanavasal (seventh century) in Pudukkottai State in south India. Following them are other murals at Elura and Bagh, and still later are those from temples at various places in south India.

Indian painting is especially rich in miniatures, which for many centuries were used solely as illustration to manuscripts. The tiny panels on the manuscript folios show deities or narrative scenes. The oldest known specimens come from the end of the tenth century and were made in eastern India (Bihar, Bengal, Nepal) to illustrate Buddhist palm-leaf manuscripts. The best of this early eastern Indian school were done about the middle of the twelfth century. This art is in the tradition of Ajanta painting and Pāla Buddhist sculpture. The style comes to an end in the thirteenth century. In western India (Gujarat) the Jains produced palm-leaf copies of their texts illustrated by paintings, of which the earliest known are dated at about A.D. 1100. This art has angularity of drawing and rashness of pose, and is peculiar in showing all but a very few figures with the face seen in a three-quarters view, the farther eye protruding beyond the cheek line into space. The finest examples of this early western Indian school were executed in the fourteenth century.

When paper came to India after the Moslem invasions and came to be used as a material for bookmaking at about A.D. 1400, books could be made of a different shape from the long narrow folios of palm leaves. More room was therefore available in fifteenth- and sixteenth-century paper manuscripts for the panels in which paintings were set. Most early western Indian painting of this time also was done under Jain auspices in Gujarat, but Hindus as well used this art, to illustrate both Vaishnava (Vaiṣṇava) and Shaiva (Śaiva) works. There exist also a few secular erotic works illustrated in this style at this time (fifteenth century), conspicuously the *Vasanta Vilāsa* (*Sport of Springtime*). The palette of the early western Indian school is throughout its existence (twelfth to sixteenth centuries) simple, with a red, a blue, a yellow (or gold), a white, and a green.

Persian styles of miniature painting coming to India with the paper on which they were executed blended with the early western Indian school, and probably other local varieties of Indian painting, to produce the schools known as Rajput. This process becomes prominent in the sixteenth century, at about the end of which the Rajput schools begin to appear. A similar process took place in the Deccan at the same time. Though these paintings were meant to accompany text, like early western Indian manuscript illustrations, the amount of written material on a page might be slight. By the time the blending was complete and the schools well advanced, the painting had in many quarters come to outweigh the text. The Rajput paintings flourished in Hindu courts in Rajputana, Gujarat, and the Himalayan hill states. The themes were more often than not the loves of Krishna or the whole Krishna legend. Frequently such themes were used to illustrate the *rāgas* and *rāgiṇīs*, which are musical modes. Such types of painting were made until late in the nineteenth century.

Under the Moguls (Mughals), Persian miniature painting was introduced by Akbar and Jahāngīr into their courts at Delhi and Agra, where there arose a school which is known as the Mughal, blended of Persian and Indian, but with more of Persian and less of Indian than the Rajput styles. It has landscape and sky features of Persian art, with much of Persian drawing, coloring—the palette is much more extensive than that of the early western Indian style—and other characteristics, as of movement, and the high horizon in perspective. The subject matter is often portraiture or some historic episode.

Modern Indian schools associated with cultural nationalism draw a great deal from Ajanta, Rajput, and Mughal painting. Moslems are likely to favor Mughal and Persian style; Hindus develop old themes of their faith with influences from Ajanta and the Rajput schools. Some others are influenced by modern folk art.

BIBLIOGRAPHY

Gangoly, O. C., *South Indian Bronzes* (Calcutta, 1915).

Coomaraswamy, A. K., *Rajput Painting*, 2 vols. (New York, 1916).

Brown, Percy, *Indian Painting under the Mughals, A.D. 1550 to A.D. 1750* (Oxford, 1924).

SCULPTURE AND PAINTING

Coomaraswamy, A. K., *History of Indian and Indonesian Art* (New York, 1927).

Bachhofer, Ludwig, *Early Indian Sculpture,* 2 vols. (New York, 1929).

Smith, V. A., *A History of Fine Art in India and Ceylon,* 2d ed., rev. by K. de B. Codrington (Oxford, 1930).

Brown, W. Norman, *Story of Kālaka* (Washington, 1933).

Kramrisch, Stella, *Indian Sculpture* (London, 1933).

———, *A Survey of Painting in the Deccan* (London, 1937).

Rowland, Benjamin, Jr., *The Wall-Paintings of India, Central Asia, and Ceylon* (Boston, 1938).

CHAPTER IX BY W. NORMAN BROWN

Religion and Philosophy

THE 1941 census of India, which was taken before the country was divided into the two nations of India and Pakistan, reported the total population of about 389,000,000 to be divided by religion approximately as follows: Hindus, 254,900,000; Moslems (Muslims), 94,400,000; Christians, 6,300,000; Sikhs, 5,700,000; Jains, 1,500,000; Buddhists, 232,000; Parsis (Parsees, Zoroastrians), 115,000; Jews, 22,500; animists, 25,400,000; others, 410,000. Hindus were in a majority in all the great divisions of the country except the northwest (western Punjab, Kashmir, North-West Frontier Province, Sind, Baluchistan) and eastern Bengal, in which two areas Moslems were more numerous. Since partition, the latter regions, except for Kashmir, whose status was still in dispute in 1950, have constituted Pakistan, with national boundaries corresponding roughly, though not exactly, with the boundaries of Moslem religious preponderance. Pakistan includes regions which in 1941 had about 58,000,000 Moslems and 13,000,000 Hindus and animists.

MODERN HINDUISM AND BRAHMANISM . . . This is a total way of life, including social order, law, science, literature, and art. Incorporated in it is the body of Indo-Aryan religious thought and ritual cultivated by the learned class called Brahmans (Brāhmaṇas) and stemming from the Veda (see Chapter V), altered and expanded in post-Vedic times, and constituting the higher religion called Brahmanism. It is contrasted with a mass of belief subliterate in origin, some parts of which became associated with Brahmanic culture in ancient times, others intruding into the total scheme of Hinduism very lately, and the whole coming from all the various racial and cultural elements known to have existed in India. This is the lower religion or popular Hinduism.

Hinduism countenances every shade of theological belief, starting with the most naive form of animism, passing through polytheism and monotheism, to reach at the top a rigorous philosophical monism. It has no formal creed, no standardized cult practice, no controlling ecclesiastical organization. Its adherents usually ascribe incontrovertible authority to the Veda but refer to that ancient collection less frequently than to later texts. For theology and mythology they rely upon the two great Sanskrit epics, *Mahābhārata* and *Rāmāyaṇa,* and versions of them in modern vernaculars, such as that in Hindi by Tulsī Dās (1532–1623) of Banaras (Benares); the Purāṇas (also in Sanskrit), the most important of which were probably composed between the sixth and thirteenth centuries; and a class of texts called Māhātmya (usually recent works, generally in Sanskrit), which have limited geographical provenience and purvey edifying local religious legends. For cosmogony and cosmology they accept the statements of the Purāṇas. For religious law, they refer less to the oldest legal textbooks called Sūtras (thought to be of the first four centuries B.C.), which are closely attached to the Vedas, than to the later (second to seventh centuries A.D.) Shastras (*Śāstras;* see Chapter X). In cult practice they do not employ the old rites of the Vedic ritual texts but use an infinite variety of later-developed ceremonies.

To some Hindus all phenomenal existence is only relatively

real—these are adherents to pure monism. Others may accept much simpler concepts. Probably the greatest number of those who are well read in the Hindu scriptures accept in some form, though often with considerable modification, the theory of the Purāṇas concerning the recurring dissolution (*pralaya*) of the universe and its recreation (*pratisarga*).

Conceptions of deity vary. On the medium and high intellectual levels Hindus are almost always adherents of sects or cults devoted to one of the great deities, Shiva (*Śiva*) and Vishnu (*Viṣṇu*), or to some lesser deity associated with one of them. Vishnu may be worshiped in his incarnations (avatars, Sanskrit *avatāra*), of which the two most popular are Rāma Chandra (hero of the *Rāmāyaṇa*) and Krishna (*Kṛṣṇa*). Shiva is often worshiped as the phallic symbol (*liṅga*), with which may be associated the female symbol (*yoni*) as the emblem of his wife, Pārvatī. Sectaries often wear distinguishing marks on their foreheads.

A variation of Hinduism is the Shākta (Śākta) cults, which promote adoration of the female principle or power called Shakti (*śakti*), represented as a goddess. As the creative and effective energy in the universe, this is considered by devotees to be more important than the male principle, represented in the god, which is otherwise only unrealized potentiality. This type of worship, also called Tantrism (its texts are known as tantra), is directed toward Devī (goddess), wife of Shiva, and otherwise known by many names such as Umā, Pārvatī, Durgā, Bhavānī, Kālī, and Ambikā.

On lower intellectual levels, chiefly among the illiterate portion of the population, Hindus may propitiate any of a large number of vegetation and fertility godlings, divinities of disease or misfortune, the village mother goddesses, ancestral spirits, the sun and moon. Trees, such as the variety of fig known as the pipal, and stones may be treated as sacred; also animals, such as the monkey, the peacock, the cobra, in some cases the tiger and the horse. Rivers, such as the Ganges, the Jumna (Yamunā), the Narbada or Nerbudda (Narmadā), the Godavari, the Kistna, the Cauvery or Kaveri may be holy; and so, too, mountains, such as the Himalaya and the Vindhyas. Astrology, divination, and the use of omens are common; the evil eye is feared.

On the highest intellectual level a Hindu seeks the one reality, whether conceived impersonally as Brahma (neuter) or theistically as Shiva or Vishnu.

Hinduism accepts as not requiring proof the joint doctrine of rebirth and works (karma). Every living creature, human or other, at the time of death is reborn in a different form, either higher or lower, whether as a human being, an animal, a heavenly creature, or a hell dweller. From that existence it will again be reborn, and so on endlessly. This round of rebirth is called the Sansara (*saṃsāra*). The precise form of each rebirth is always determined by the balancing, as in a mathematical equation, of the creature's deeds (karma) in previous existences. Escape from the cycle of rebirth constitutes salvation—*mokṣā,* mukti, nirvana (Sanskrit *nirvāṇa*)—and is in theory the ultimate goal of every living being, but is so difficult to attain that on the practical level the aim is almost invariably only to improve one's condition in the next existence. Rarely does anyone strive for more than a long life, perhaps lasting a few million or billion years, in the heaven of some god. Emphasis is laid upon having a guru (spiritual preceptor), who may be viewed as little less than God.

Places of worship range from the most primitive of wayside shrines, consisting of a stone set under a sacred tree and daubed with paint, symbolizing some form of divinity, to the most elaborate complex of structures constituting an enormous temple. The largest is at Srirangam in Madras, where the site, which is sacred to Vishnu, is enclosed by a wall about four miles in circumference. Certain cities are especially holy to Hindus, the most holy of all being Banaras on the Ganges. Hindus use images freely in their worship, as comprehensible symbols of a deity which has no form apprehensible by human senses. Worship may consist of offerings of flowers, fruit, grain, ghee (*ghī*, clarified butter), and money, and in some connections animal sacrifice. A worshiper may appeal to the deity directly or through the agency of a priest. Worship is usually individual, not congregational.

Religious authority vests in the Brahmans, who besides being custodians of the sacred learning constitute the priesthood. They officiate at religious ceremonies in homes or temples, and are other men's vicars in dealing with the deities. As astrologers they cast horoscopes, and then interpret them later throughout a person's life to determine auspicious and inauspicious moments and conditions for specific undertakings.

The social structure of Hinduism is embraced in the caste system. This separates mankind into many separate groups, each of which is designated by Occidentals as a caste. The word is a modification of the Portuguese noun *casta,* meaning "(pure) race, lineage," and is ultimately derived from the Latin adjective *castus* (pure); the Indian term means "group by birth" (jati, Sanskrit *jāti*). The various castes have different social precedence. At the top are the Brahmans, in traditional law constituting a highly privileged group, who have been the codifiers and formulators of the philosophy sanctioning the system, and the directors of the instrumentality for enforcing its rules. These constitute about 7 per cent of the total Hindu community. Caste is hereditary and it is not possible to transfer from the caste in which one is born to another. Neither can a non-Hindu individual ordinarily become a member of a Hindu caste, although under certain conditions a group of people can enter the Hindu system as a new caste.

The caste system prescribes strict regulations concerning marriage, which must usually be within the caste but outside the immediate family or clan; concerning eating, which is subject to taboos and complicated rules respecting the acceptance of food and drink from members of other castes; and concerning many other phases of human relationship. In its most extreme form the caste system has imposed onerous disabilities upon those lowest in the scale, known as Fifths, who are estimated at around 20 per cent of the Hindu community (49,000,000 according to the 1941 census). These perform the most degrading forms of work, such as scavenging. They have been held to pollute the higher castes through even proximity within some indicated distance and have been required to live in separate quarters in villages and towns or in separate villages. They have often been denied access to wells, roads, schools, and temples used by the higher castes, and have been forbidden by religious law to read or hear the recitation of the Hindu scriptures. In the twentieth century these rules have been greatly eased.

In Hindu theory each caste has a separate social function or occupation, different from that of any other caste, but in practice the rule does not hold. The number of castes is impossible to determine, since the criteria are not sharply separated. Endogamous groups of more than 500 members each probably exceed 1,000 in number, but most of these are of only local provenience, with but a fraction of the total number appearing in any given area.

The castes are classified by the Hindus in five groups—in descending order of social worth. Brahmans (Brāhmaṇas, or spiritual leaders), Kshatriyas (Kṣatriyas; Rājanyas, or temporal rulers), and Vaisyas (Vaiśyas; commons—that is, merchant and artisan groups) are called twice born (*dvija*), because the boys in these three groups undergo a ceremony of initiation, whereupon ideally they enter upon their religious training. The two other groups are Sudras (Śūdras, or servants); and Panchamas (Sanskrit *pañcama;* fifths) or outcasts, also known eclectically as untouchables, exterior castes, scheduled castes, depressed castes, Paraiyas (pariahs), or, in Gandhi's term, Harijan (God's folk). The last two groups have no ceremony of initiation; most of them are descendants of lowly groups at one time or another granted a place by Indo-Aryan society and religion. The fivefold classification also breaks down, since a caste may in one census assign itself to one of these groups but in the next to the group higher. Every caste, no matter how low in the scale, always knows another which it considers lower.

Man's duty (dharma) is to satisfy his caste rules and fulfill his caste functions, to honor the gods, to observe the numerous ceremonies which ideally accompany every important aspect of life from conception to after death, and to perform miscellaneous good works, such as almsgiving, the undertaking of vows and pilgrimages, often at specified times when great numbers of people gather in festivals, religious bathing, reverencing the Brahmans, and feeding the poor. Theoretically in India from the time of the texts known as Sūtras a man devoted most fully to religion, that is, especially a true Brahman, should divide his life into four periods or stages (ashrama, Sanskrit *āśrama*): (1) celibate studentship (*brahmacārin*); (2) householder (*gṛhastha*), raising a family and fulfilling his worldly duties; (3) forest-dweller, anchorite (*vānaprastha*), retiring with his wife to a remote place for religious duties and meditation; (4) wandering ascetic (*saṃnyāsin, bhikṣu*), having severed all ties with his family, living alone, subsisting on alms. This fourfold scheme is but rarely practiced today.

The center of ethics is ahimsa (*ahinsā*), the noninjury of living creatures, which Gandhi called nonviolence. The doctrine applies not only to mankind, but also to the animal world, varying in application toward the separate animal species but always demanding protection of the cow (male and female), which holds a position of peculiar sanctity in Hinduism.

Hinduism blends all its widely varying beliefs and practices into a whole by admitting, without explicit statement, that human capacities and powers are relative. It takes the position that men are not intellectually and spiritually equal. For this reason it is unrealistic to expect all human beings to believe alike, pursue the same goals, have identical behavior, attain the same spiritual heights. Absolute truth, that is, the knowledge of ultimate reality, can be achieved by only the rarest individual. Similarly, man's conduct is governed by rules that vary according to his spiritual and intellectual capacity. What is right for one man may be wrong for another. In this relative view of life lies the sanction for the social system of caste. A person is born to the status that suits his attainments in consequence of his deeds in previous existences; the functions of his status are those which he should fulfill.

EARLY INDUS CIVILIZATIONS . . . Inferences concerning the religion of the prehistoric Early Indus civilizations (see Chapter XI) are drawn from sculpture, pottery, figurines, seal designs, and other finds, especially of the Harappa period (c. 2700–1700 B.C.). No temples or indisputably religious edifices have been identified. The data give presumptive evidence for worship of a god who had characteristics similar to those of Shiva in historic times, for a cult of the Great Mother or Earth Goddess, and for phallic worship. Certain trees appear to have been sacred, including the pipal. In some representations trees have associated with them female figures which may be fertility divinities. Various animals appear to have had sanctity, including the tiger, elephant, buffalo, crocodile, rhinoceros, and mythical hybrid creatures. Symbols appear there which reappear in historic India with religious significance, among them the swastika. Small bronze dancing figures may indicate that religious dancing was practiced as in modern Hinduism.

RELIGION OF THE VEDAS . . . The religion of the Vedas, especially the Rig Veda (Book of Knowledge of Hymns; see

Chapter V), derives in part from primitive Indo-European times, but its most prominent deities and ideas seem to come from some other source. It has a class of superhuman beings known as asura, some of whom, the Ādityas, are benevolent (Varuṇa, Mitra, Aryaman, Bhaga, Dakṣa [Daksha], Ansa), others of whom, called Dānavas, are malevolent, being demons (rakshas, Sanskrit *rakṣas*). The chief god (deva) of the Vedic pantheon, Indra, is also hard to associate with any Indo-European figure. Because of his pre-eminence he is often called the sole—that is, the supreme—god.

The central theme of Vedic mythology is the conflict between Indra, the champion of the gods and their king, and Vritra (Vṛtra, the encloser), chief of the Dānavas and personification of the hard covering within which were originally contained the elements needed for creation of the existent universe (the sat). Vritra is usually described as a serpent; Indra slew him with his weapon (vajra), or, as is often said, burst open his belly. Out flowed the waters (*āpas*), often described complimentarily as cows, to fill the celestial ocean. Marvelously, they were pregnant with the sun. The universe now had moisture, light, and warmth, and creation could take place. Order (rita, Sanskrit *ṛta*) was established and put under the administration of Varuṇa, and in due time man was created. Every creature—man or god—had a personal function (*vrata*) to fulfill as part of order. When he fulfilled it, he was living in accord with the sat, and so achieving his highest good.

The Vedic cult centered about the fire sacrifice, which was personified as Agni, god of the sacrifice and the divine priest. Offerings included animals and ghee, but the most important was soma, an exhilarating drink pressed from some unknown plant, and also personified as the god Soma. This drink was especially dear to Indra. The fire ceremony, being elaborate, required a numerous and highly trained priesthood which became the source of the Brahman caste. In time the sacrifice came to be viewed as all powerful, operating as a kind of cosmic magic, which, when properly performed, could compel even the gods to the sacrificer's will.

The righteous dead went to the realm of the blessed, where lived Yama, the first man, to rejoice there with him and the gods. On the way they were protected from the demons by the two heavenly dogs, Śabala (brindled), and Śyāma (dark). The wicked, however, had no such protection, but, hobbled by their sins, were waylaid and overtaken by the demons and destroyed.

The private or household religion, covering personal matters such as love, disease, witchcraft, black magic, was provided for in the Atharva Veda (Book of Knowledge of Blessings and Curses).

In the late Rig Vedic period there are ventured various new explanations of the origin and operation of the universe. A kind of superdeism appears, centering around Prajāpati (Lord of Creatures). Or a world man, Puruṣa (Purusha, or Male), when sacrificed, provides the material of the universe. The sounds of the sacrifice, primordial and present, consisting of the crackling of the fire as the voice of Agni and the chants of the priests, are viewed as all controlling; this idea appears as the feminine deity Vāc (Voice). A strictly impersonal conception appears in Tad Ekam (Sole Principle, or neuter), from which all is evolved. These various speculations record the beginning of Indian philosophy.

UPANISHADS . . . The Upanishads (*Upaniṣad*) extend the tentative Rig Vedic philosophical inquiries about the nature of the universe and also investigate the human psyche or soul. They do not develop these topics systematically, and the explanations offered in different Upanishads are not all mutually consistent. A frequent form of Upanishadic investigation concerns the four states of the soul: waking state, dreaming sleep, deep (dreamless) sleep, and the fourth state (*turīya*), indescribable in terms of the human senses, which is the final goal in man's search for the ultimate. Other passages teach that the soul is immanent in all creation, uniform in character, and the essential part of the individual. As described by the celebrated teacher Yājñavalkya, it is pure subject, distinct from all that is material, unknowable, capable of perceiving and of knowing all, yet unmatched by any second reality to perceive or know. All else but soul is only relatively real. Duality is in the final analysis false; ultimate truth lies only in a monistic conception of the universe. The identification of the human soul (atman, Sanskrit *ātman*) and the universal soul (brahman) on these terms is the supreme achievement of the Upanishads. Besides this monism, the Upanishads contain the view that both matter (prakriti; Sanskrit *prakṛti*) and soul (purusha, Sanskrit *puruṣa*) are real, being mutually exclusive and standing in complete contrast to each other.

In the Upanishads appear the first suggestions of the doctrine of rebirth (metempsychosis, transmigration of the soul) and retribution for one's deeds (karma) in succeeding existences. The Upanishads also speak of engaging in meditation with the aid of the technique known as yoga, described below.

In the great epic, the *Mahābhārata,* in one of its sections called the *Bhagavad Gītā* (*Song of the Blessed One*), which calls itself an Upanishad, Krishna, who is an incarnation of the god Vishnu, instructs Arjuna, leader of the army fighting for the right, and, though admitting the approach to self-realization through works and knowledge, emphasizes above all loving devotion (bhakti) to God.

FORMAL PHILOSOPHIES . . . In the period of approximately a thousand years from the time of the older Upanishads—that is, roughly, from around 500 B.C. to A.D. 500—the six orthodox systems (darshana; Sanskrit *darśana,* meaning "viewing") of Indian philosophy were developed and given their classical form. These were less conflicting systems than complementary ways of viewing the universe. They provide the intellectual basis for Brahmanical Hinduism. In the order enumerated by the Hindus these systems are: (1) Pūrva (or Karma) Mīmāṅsā, "discussion of the first, or practical, part" of the Vedic religion; the formulation of its basic text is ascribed to Jaimini; (2) Uttara Mīmānsā, "discussion of the latter part" of the Vedic religion, often called Vedānta (end of the Veda); the formulation of its basic text is ascribed to Bādarāyaṇa; (3) Nyāya, "logical method," formulated in a text by Gautama (Gotama); (4) Vaiśeṣika, "differentiation," the philosophy of atomism, ascribed to Kaṇāda; (5) Sāṃkhya ("reason" or "enumeration"), which analyzes nature, and is ascribed to Kapila; (6) Yoga, which is primarily devoted to the technique of meditation, and is ascribed to Patañjali. This is the Hindu order; they are described here in another order, reflecting the relationship of ideas.

Pūrva Mīmāṅsā.—This system rationalizes Vedic fundamentalism, that is, the literal meaning and application of the Veda. It regards the Veda as authorless and self-revealed, and therefore authoritative. According to the Pūrva Mīmāṅsā, the world exists throughout eternity and is not subject to recurrent dissolution and recreation.

Sāṃkhya.—The Sāṃkhya system gets its name either from the application of reason to the analysis of the soul and nature or from the twenty-five principles or true entities (tattva) which it enumerates. The two basic contrasting entities are soul (purusha) and matter or nature (prakriti). Souls are infinite in number, and consist of pure intelligence. Each is independent, indivisible, unconditioned, incapable of change, immortal. It appears, however, to be bound to matter—prakriti, pradhana (Sanskrit *pradhāna*), avyakta. At the beginning of an eon, nature is in a state of rest, or inertia. It has three qualities (guna, Sanskrit *guṇa*) known respectively as goodness (sattva), passion (rajas), and darkness (tamas), which are in balance. But souls, because of their karma, begin to move; nature then stirs; the qualities fall out of equilibrium. From nature then evolve the other twenty-three principles. First is intelligence (buddhi); from this evolves the process or organ of individuation (ahankara; Sanskrit *ahaṃkāra,* "I-maker"). The latter differentiates itself cosmically and individually. Cosmically it produces the five subtle elements (*tanmātra*) of earth, water, fire, air, and ether, from which are produced the corresponding five gross elements (*mahābhūta*). These are the objects of sense. Individually, it produces the five senses (*buddhīndriya*) of hearing, touch, sight, taste, and smell, which make contact with the gross elements; also the mind; and also the five organs of action (*karmendriya*). This physiological psychology is common to Indian thought of all schools, with only minor variations. According to the Sāṃkhya, every individual has a subtle characteristic body (*liṅga deha*) consisting of intelligence, individuation, mind, and the ten organs of sensation and action. This is what transmigrates, being lodged in a gross body composed of the objects of sense. How soul has come to be associated with the subtle body is not made clear. Through knowledge the association may be terminated, and this separation constitutes salvation. The subtle body is dissolved and the soul exists in isolation. To obtain knowledge the best means is to pursue the technique of yoga.

Yoga.—This system of philosophy is an extension of the Sāṃkhya. It formulates systematically the techniques of meditation known as yoga, which means "harnessing" or "control" and refers to the control and suppression of the activities of the mind and the sense organs which are enumerated by the Sāṃkhya, so that these will not interfere with the soul in attaining self-realization.

The first stage of the Yoga technique is designed to cause the evolutes of intelligence (buddhi) to retract into intelligence, and this is accomplished by *kriyā yoga* (yoga of observances or physical acts) in five stages: (1) adoption of restraints (*yama*) from killing, lying, and other sins; (2) adoption of observances (*niyama*) of purity and other virtues; (3) use of posture (asana, Sanskrit *āsana*) suitable for meditation; (4) restraint of breath (*prāṇāyāma*); and (5) withdrawal of senses (*pratyāhāra*) from the objects of sense. Then comes the second, main stage of Yoga, known as superior or royal yoga (*rāja yoga*) in three phases (*saṃyama*): (1) concentration (dharana, Sanskrit *dhāraṇā*) of the intelligence (buddhi) on an object without wavering; (2) meditation (dhyana, Sanskrit *dhyāna*) as an uninterrupted mental state; and (3) trance (samadhi, Sanskrit *samādhi*), in which the individual is fully identified with the object of meditation.

Vaiśeṣika and Nyāya.—These were separate in origin but came to be combined in a common system. They both accept the idea characteristic of the Vaiśeṣika that the universe is composed of atoms (*aṇu, paramāṇu, kaṇa*), and both use a body of logic codified in the Nyāya. According to the Vaiśeṣika, the differences in the universe rise ultimately from the differences in the atoms. The idea of difference (*viśeṣa*) gives the system its name.

The Nyāya gives the rules of correct thinking. There are four ways of acquiring knowledge: (1) perception by the senses (*pratyakṣa*); (2) inference (*anumāna*); (3) analogy (*upamāna*); and (4) authority or credible testimony (*śabda*). Of these inference is the most important for acquiring philosophical knowledge. The Nyāya syllogism has five parts: (1) proposition; (2) cause; (3) illustration; (4) recapitulation of the cause, or application; and (5) conclusion. The standard example is of the mountain and the fire: (1) the mountain is on fire; (2) because it is smoking; (3) wherever there is smoke there is fire; (4) the mountain is smoking; (5) therefore it is on fire. Causation is considered to be material, or inhering, cause, which is invariable and primary for any given object; and effective, which is variable and secondary. Between these is sometimes considered to be a noninhering or formal cause. In a carpet, the threads are the material or inhering cause, the association of threads is the noninhering or formal cause, and the weaver's activities are the effective cause.

Uttara Mīmāṅsā or Vedānta.—This system is, more than any other, the lineal descendant of the philosophic speculations of the late Rig Veda and the Upanishads. A number of varying schools, however, claim the name of this system. Its basic textbook, by Bādarāyaṇa, composed possibly around the beginning of the Christian era, is called *Brahmasūtra* (treatise on Brahma), also *Vedāntasūtra, Uttaramīmāṅsāsūtra,* and *Śārīrakasūtra.* It consists of aphorisms, often no more than catchwords or mnemonic guides, in themselves unintelligible and meant to be accompanied by a commentary.

The celebrated Shankara (Śaṃkara), who lived around A.D. 800, is the author of the earliest surviving commentary on the *Brahmasūtra.* He taught unqualified monism (*advaitavāda,* doctrine of the nonsecond). His thinking starts with an examination of knowledge (vidya, Sanskrit *vidyā*). This is of two sorts: one is absolute (*nirguṇā,* without qualification); the other is relative (*saguṇa,* with qualifications). Shankara approaches the teaching of the Veda in the light of the higher knowledge. He refers to the passages of the Upanishads in which it is stated that Brahma (neuter), the supreme reality, is one only, without a second. This, other passages state, is identical with the individual reality. It cannot be described; all it is possible to say of it is that it is "not this, not this," that is, that it is nothing comprehensible to the senses and mind (using mind in the Hindu sense of the thinking organ, which is physical, as separate from the soul). It can be known only by itself, that is, by the soul in the individual, which is the universal soul. This knowledge is the higher, unqualified knowledge, coming from experience (*anubhava*), where subject and object become one, leading the individual to the realization "I am Brahma" (*ahaṃ brahmāsmi*). The world as we know it phenomenally is qualified being, which is to say, the absolute Brahma viewed by qualified knowledge or ignorance (avidya, Sanskrit *avidyā*, meaning "nonknowledge"), where maya (*māyā*, illusion or artificial construction) operates. This is Shankara's treatment of nature (prakriti). Brahma is existence (sat), consciousness (cit; chit), bliss (ananda, Sanskrit *ānanda*), completely self-sufficient. Men who live according to relative, qualified knowledge may, after death, go to the world of the fathers (as in the Veda) or the world of the gods or hell. But those who devote themselves to the higher, unqualified knowledge aim to carry knowledge up from stage to stage until it is complete and through experience one knows that he is Brahma. To this end the accepted method is yoga.

The most prominent of other Vedānta schools is that of Rāmānuja (probably fl. twelfth century, in Conjeevaram in south India), for whom God is personal, is identified with Vishnu, and has internal differences. Souls and matter both are real. The goal of man is the union of his individual soul with God. The way to release is by devotion to Vishnu. His system is characterized as qualified monism (*viśiṣṭādvaita*).

Another school originating in south India is that of Mādhva (Madhava, probably 1197–1276), who was a dualist, recognizing the reality of God, souls, and matter. No two souls are alike. Still another is that of Vallabha (1475–1531), who was born in south India but preached in north India at Mathura, the center of the Krishna cult, and afterwards moved to Banaras. He called his view purified monism (*śuddhādvaita*). He rejected the idea of maya; the way to salvation is union of the human soul with the highest god (Brahma), who is personal as Krishna and is to be reached by devotion (bhakti). Another important cult centering on Krishna was that of Chaitanya (1485–1533) in Bengal. Still another sect calling itself Vedānta (advaita, monism) is that of Nīlakaṇṭha (fourteenth century), who identified God with Shiva. The human soul is distinct from God, but its goal is to reach God, whereupon it diminishes, finally united with Him.

Some other sects have shown distinct Moslem influence. Of these one of the most important is that of Kabīr (c. 1440–1518), who came into contact with Sufism (Sufiism).

REFORMED HINDUISM . . . Nineteenth-century reform movements of Hinduism arose in part from the impact of Western ideas upon India. Among the most prominent of these is the Brahma (or Brahmo) Samāj (or Samāja), a theistic non-idolatrous movement, using a congregational form of worship and favoring social reform, founded by Rām Mohan Rai (Rām Mohan Roy, 1772/1774–1833). This was later led by Debendra Nath Tagore (1817–1905), father of the poet Rabindranath Tagore, and Keshab Chandra Sen (Keshub Chunder Sen, 1838/1841–1884). Several other Samājas grew up under the influence of the Brāhma Samāj. Another important movement was the Ārya Samāj, founded by a Brahman named Dayanand (Dayānanda) Sarasvatī (1824/1825–1883), who aimed to restore the religion and social institutions of the Veda (which he understood in his own peculiar fashion), to protect cows, to restore India's glorious past, and so to check the advance of Islam and Christianity. Still another was founded by Rāmakrishna Paramahaṅsa (born Gadādhar Chatterji or Chaṭṭopādhyāya, 1834/1836–1886), a Bengali Brahman, who taught that all religions lead to the same god and frequently experienced trance (samadhi). His favorite disciple, Vivekananda (born Narendra Nath Dutt, 1863–1902), spread the teachings of Rāmakrishna in the West, first at the Parliament of Religions in Chicago in 1893, and later in Europe. The Ramakrishna Society is active in social reform in India and in preaching in several Western countries.

BUDDHISM . . . This religion is a heterodox Indian faith in that it does not recognize the authority of the Vedic scriptures. Its founder was Siddhārtha Gautama, commonly known by the honorific title of Buddha ("the enlightened one"), son of a petty ruler of a clan called Sākya or Shākya (*śākya*) at Kapilavastu in the northeast of the present Uttar Pradesh. Buddhist tradition places his death in 544 B.C., but modern scholarship sets his dates as 563–483 B.C. (or, alternatively, 558–478 B.C.). At the age of twenty-nine, he left home to follow the religious quest. For six years he wandered from teacher to teacher and engaged in ascetic practices, all to no avail, but at last, while seated in meditation under a pipal tree near the Ganges at Gaya in the region then called Magadha, he attained enlightenment, and spent the rest of his life preaching his doctrine. He founded an order of monks (vowed to avoid unchastity, theft, taking of life, falsehood) and later admitted an order of nuns, and recognized a lay congregation. He died at the age of eighty.

The Buddha's teachings in their present form are all considerably later than the Buddha. The canon of the major division of Buddhism, which is known as Hinayana, is composed in Pali (see Chapter IV), and was preserved in Ceylon (whence it went to Burma, Thailand, and Cambodia), where it was first put into written form in the first century A.D. (or possibly first century B.C.). It is known as the Tipiṭaka (Sanskrit *Tripiṭaka*, "Three Baskets") and is in three parts: (1) Vinaya Piṭaka, rules for monks; (2) Sutta Piṭaka, collection of discourses (*sutta*), that is, texts of psalms, stories, and other edifying material, in five sections; and (3) Abhidhamma Piṭaka, collection of works of the higher religion, bearing upon psychological questions. The Mahayana division of Buddhism, which became prominent at the time of King Kanishka, first used a Prakrit for its text; later it used Sanskrit and had a canon in Sanskrit, also called the Tripiṭaka, of which many works are preserved in India and Nepal, and others, now lost, exist in Chinese versions.

In the Pali canon the Buddha's basic doctrine is considered to be expressed in his first sermon, preached at Sarnath near Banaras. In this the Buddha accepts, without offering proof, the familiar Indian doctrine of the cycle of rebirth (Sansara) and karma (retribution in future existences for one's deeds), the whole constituting a process that is painful. His message was that escape from this situation comes by avoiding the two extremes of sensual indulgence and physical self-mortification and adopting the middle path. His basic theory is enunciated in the Four Noble Truths: (1) birth, old age, sickness, death, separation from what one wants, association with what one does not want—all are painful; (2) the pain rises from the desire for gratification of the passions and for existence or for the termination of existence; (3) the cessation of pain comes from complete extinction of this desire; and (4) the way to extinguish the desire is to follow the Noble Eightfold Path of right views, right resolve, right speech, right action, right living, right effort, right mindfulness, right concentration. In various other discourses the Buddha is represented as refusing to discuss controversial metaphysical problems concerning the duration of the world, the identity of the self and the body, and the existence of the saint after death. He gives as the psychological basis of his doctrine a chain of causation or dependent origination (Pali *paṭiccasamuppāda*) of twelve members, which starts with ignorance and ends with suffering.

The Buddha did not deny the reality of things of the world though he thought ill of them. Everything about the human being is a compound of the aggregates of being (Pali *khandha*), always in a state of change and therefore impermanent and painful. The only bliss is that of the immutable absolute, which the Buddha merely describes as the state of nirvana (Pali *nibbāna*, "blowing out"). The Buddha seems to have been vague on the subject of soul; the Pali texts specifically preach that there is no soul. The scriptures advocate meditation (*jhāna*, Sanskrit *dhyāna*), with the use of methods more or less similar to those of yoga. Ethics is centered on ahimsa and *metta* (loving kindness).

The Hinayana, as taught in the Theravāda school of the Pali canon, seems to have been dominant in India until about the beginning of the Christian era. After that the Mahayana grew to prominence. The principal Mahayana doctrines, as distinguished from those of the Hinayana, are: (1) doctrine of the Bodhisattvas (beings whose essence is true knowledge), who have attained the ability to become Buddhas but elect to remain in the universe so that they may make over their acquired merit to other beings; (2) doctrine of the Buddhas, innumerable supernatural beings distributed throughout time and space; (3) worship of images; and (4) idealistic metaphysics. This is the form of Buddhism which spread to central Asia, China, Tibet, Korea, Japan, and Java. The principal Indian schools of the Mahayana are: (1) the Madhyamaka (or Mādhyamika), prominent from the first to fifth century A.D., whose best-known teachers were Aśvaghoṣa (A.D. c. 100) and Nāgārjuna (fl. second century A.D.); and (2) the Yogācāra (Vijñānavāda) school, prominent from about A.D. 500 to 1000, promulgated by the two brothers Asanga and Vasubandhu, who lived in the fifth century.

JAINISM . . . Like Buddhism, Jainism is a heterodox movement, whose historical records start in Magadha in the sixth to fifth century B.C. It was promulgated by Vardhamāna Mahāvīra, son of a petty ruler. The Jains put the date of his death at 528 B.C., but modern scholarship sets it at 468 (or 487 or 477) B.C. Mahāvīra left home at the age of thirty to follow the religious life, and in the thirteenth year of vigorous asceticism won supreme knowledge. From then until his death thirty years later he preached in the area of Magadha and nearby. Though Mahāvīra is the founder of Jainism and established his own order, he seems to have been preceded 250 years earlier by a teacher called Pārshva or Pārshvanātha (Pārśvanātha), who had established an order requiring four vows of his followers: not to injure life, to be truthful, not to steal, to possess no property. The Jain texts tell of the union of this order with Mahāvīra's during Mahāvīra's lifetime. Mahāvīra added a fifth vow for his monks, which was that of chastity. Pārshva had allowed his followers two garments, but Mahāvīra, with a strict application of the prohibition against possessing property, permitted his monks none at all. Jain tradition indicates that the question of clothing for monks remained unsolved, and at about 300 B.C. the community split on the issue into two divisions: the Śvetāmbara (White-clothed) and the Digambara (Sky-clothed, that is, naked). The division was recognized in A.D. 79 (or 82).

All Jains believe that Pārshva and Mahāvīra were not the founders of the faith, but only the twenty-third and twenty-fourth in a series of teachers all of whom are called *tīrthankara* ("fordmaker," across the ocean of existence, and "founder of a church") or Jina; modern scholarship considers the first twenty-two to be entirely mythical. The word Jina is an epithet meaning "conqueror" (of the woes of life). From this is derived the religion's own term Jaina (follower, or doctrine, of the Jinas).

The Jain canon, which was written in the Ardha-Māgadhī language (see Chapter IV) and transmitted by word of mouth, is said by the Digambaras to have been completely lost in the early third century B.C., at the time of a twelve-year famine; the Śvetāmbaras claim that a portion of it was preserved. The oral tradition is said to have been put into writing in A.D. 454. The Digambara community lives mostly in Mysore; the *Śvetāmbaras* are located chiefly in Gujarat.

Jainism accepts the common Indian notions of rebirth and karma. Salvation consists of escape from the round of existence (Sansara). The universe experiences a continuous cycle of decline and improvement, descending and ascending like the hand moving around the face of a clock. We are now very near the bottom in the present cycle. The Jains acknowledge no universal god, though they have many lesser divinities or gods who are bound in the round of rebirth. The world is eternal and consists of six substances: souls, dharma (right), adharma (wrong), space, time, and particles of matter. Souls are innumerable and are of two sorts: the perfected (siddha), who are in Iṣatprāgbhāra at the summit of the universe, enjoying perfect happiness, incorporeal, invisible; and those bound by a subtle body of deeds (karma) to the present world, sullied by contact with nonsentient matter. Jainism carries the doctrine of noninjury (ahimsa) of living creatures to an extreme not otherwise paralleled in Indian religions.

Souls in the round of rebirth are considered by Jains to be of various sorts, depending upon the number of senses and certain other qualities which they possess, as follows: first, beings called *nigoda* with none of the senses; then, (1) beings with one sense, which is touch, and with body, respiration, and an allotted span of life; these include stones, clods, minerals, water bodies, fire bodies, and vegetables growing in the ground, such as potatoes, carrots, and beets, which the strictest Jains will not eat; (2) beings with two senses (touch, taste) and having, in addition to the qualities possessed by one-sensed beings, the power of speech; these include worms; most Jains start the practice of noninjury with this group; (3) beings with three senses (touch, taste, smell), which include ants, bugs, moths; (4) beings with four senses (touch, taste, smell, sight), which include wasps, scorpions, mosquitoes; and (5) beings with all five senses (adding hearing), which include hell dwellers, higher animals, human beings, dwellers in the various heavens—of this class some have the quality of mind.

Souls suffer bondage (*bandha*) to matter (*ajīva*) by karma, which is good (*puṇya*) or evil (*pāpa*). When all karma is finally destroyed, the soul attains salvation (*mokṣā*).

The Jain lay community consists mostly of merchants. The Jains are in theory opposed to caste, but in practice they maintain close relations with Vaishnava merchant castes and intermarry with them.

SIKHISM . . . Sikhism is a reformed sect combining Hindu and Moslem elements, which was founded in the Punjab in the fifteenth century, and is centered today at Amritsar. It has drawn heavily upon the beliefs and practices of Islam. Its founder, Guru Nānak (c. 1469–1538), was familiar with Sufi (mystic Islamic) teachings; he preached monotheism, service to others, humility, self-restraint, and the mystical value of prayer. He abhorred idolatry, denied the validity of the Hindu caste system, setting up a common kitchen where all castes partook of the same food, and also opposed Moslem deistic theology.

Nānak was followed by nine other gurus. The new faith remained primarily a quietistic sect under the first five gurus, and acquired wealth. The sixth guru, Har Gobind (r. 1606–1645), rejected wealth and ease and returned to the old simplicity, but adopted militarism and armed the community to resist both Moslem aggression and Hindu intolerance. The tenth and last guru, named Gobind (Govind) Singh (r. 1675–1708), in 1699 organized the military brotherhood into a band called Khālsā (Arabic-Persian *khāliṣah,* "the pure"), whose members went through an initiation ceremony, took names ending in Singh (lion), abjured wine, the narcotic hemp, and tobacco, forbade the cutting of the hair (*keś*), imposed the carrying of a dagger (*kirpan*) and the wearing of drawers (*kach*), an iron bangle (*kartha*), and a comb (*kanga*). He was murdered in 1708. From the time of Har Gobind the Sikhs were in frequent conflict with the reigning Moslems. In the nineteenth century, Ranjīt Singh (1780–1839) established a Sikh kingdom in the Punjab and Sikh political power extended from the Sutlej River into Afghanistan. After the Sikh Wars the British annexed the Punjab in 1849 (see Chapter XIII).

The Sikh scriptures consist of a book called Granth Sahib (Revered Book), which contains a great deal of prose and poetic material ascribed by Sikhs variously to Nānak, Kabīr, and other teachers. It is regarded as the sole voice of religious authority and is held in veneration by all sects of Sikhism.

TRIBAL RELIGIONS . . . These are forms of animism or spirit worship practiced by economically backward preliterate people living in less desirable sections of the subcontinent. On contact with Hinduism, such a tribe is in time likely to become acculturated and acquire a place in the Hindu community as a low caste.

ISLAM . . . For Moslem invasions and spread in India see Chapter XIII. Islam in India has been chiefly Sunnite; Shiʿites are outnumbered eleven or twelve to one. There are a number of Moslem sects in the subcontinent, of which one of the most interesting is the Ahmadiyah, founded by Mirza Ghulam Ahmad (1839–1908), who at the age of forty became convinced that he had a divine mission, and in 1889, at the age of fifty, announced that he had received a revelation, proclaimed himself as the Mahdi, the messiah of the Moslems, and the one destined to realize similar hopes for a new savior among Hindus, Christians, Buddhists, and Zoroastrians. (See also Chapter X, section on Moslem law.)

CHRISTIANITY . . . According to legend, Christianity was brought to India by the Apostle Thomas, and the legend may have some basis in fact. In any case, by the fourth or fifth century A.D. a Christian community of the Nestorian (Syrian) sect existed at Cochin in south India, where it still survives. In the year 1542, St. Francis Xavier arrived in India and spread Christianity by preaching; in 1560 the Inquisition was introduced. Protestant missions entered south India in the seventeenth century, and became vigorous in Bengal at the end of the eighteenth century. The greater part of the Indian Christian community is Roman Catholic and is found in south India.

JUDAISM . . . Jews were settled on the west coast of south India by the fourth or fifth century A.D., and a very small community, divided three ways, still exists in Cochin. Most of India's 25,000 Jews, however, live in the large cities.

PARSIISM . . . This is the Indian form of Zoroastrianism. The Parsis (Persians) fled from Persia to India in the eighth century to avoid the Arabs and settled in Gujarat. In the seventeenth century many of them moved to Bombay where the greater part of their number now resides. They engage chiefly in commerce.

BIBLIOGRAPHY

Bloomfield, Maurice, *The Arthavaveda* (Strassburg, 1899).

———, *The Religion of the Veda* (New York, 1908).

Macauliffe, M. A., *The Sikh Religion,* 6 vols. (Oxford, 1909).

Farquhar, J. N., *A Primer of Hinduism* (London, 1912).

Avalon, Arthur (pseud. of Sir J. G. Woodroffe), *Principles of Tantra,* 2 vols. (London, 1914–1916).

Farquhar, J. N., *Modern Religious Movements in India* (New York, 1915).

Stevenson, M. S., *The Heart of Jainism* (London, 1915).

Rhys Davids, T. W., *Buddhism, Its History and Literature,* 3d ed. (New York, 1918).

Farquhar, J. N., *An Outline of the Religious Literature of India* (London, 1920).

Eliot, C. N. E., *Hinduism and Buddhism,* 3 vols. (London, 1921).

Whitehead, Henry, *The Village Gods of South India,* 2d ed. (London, 1921).

RELIGION AND PHILOSOPHY

Dasgupta, S. N., *A History of Indian Philosophy,* 4 vols., vol. 5 in preparation (Cambridge, Eng., 1922–1949).

Rādhākrishnan, Sarvepalli, *Indian Philosophy,* 2 vols. (New York, 1923–1927).

Keith, A. B., *The Religion and Philosophy of the Veda and Upanishads,* 2 vols. (Cambridge, Mass., 1926).

Hume, R. E., *The Thirteen Principal Upanishads,* 2d ed., rev. (New York, 1931).

O'Malley, L. S. S., *Popular Hinduism* (New York, 1935).

Edgerton, Franklin, *The Bhagavad Gita,* 2 vols. (Cambridge, Mass., 1944).

Archer, J. C., *The Sikhs* (Princeton, N.J., 1946).

Mackay, E. J. H., *Early Indus Civilizations* (London, 1948).

CHAPTER X BY LUDWIK STERNBACH

Law

BY PARAGRAPH 18 (3) of the Indian Independence Act (10 and 11 Geo. 6., Ch. 30) of July 18, 1947, in the two independent dominions of India and Pakistan then being created, the laws of British India and of the several parts thereof existing immediately before the appointed day, so far as applicable and with the necessary adaptations, were to continue as the law of each of the new dominions and the several parts thereof until other provision should be made by laws of the legislatures of the two dominions. On November 26, 1949, the Constituent Assembly of India adopted a new constitution, which became formally effective on January 26, 1950, and superseded the previous arrangement. In Pakistan a new constitution had not yet been drafted.

In undivided India personal law in matters of succession, marriage, divorce, adoption, gifts, and charitable endowments differed for Hindus and Moslems (Muslims), conforming in general principle to traditional law. In all other fields the statutory law applied to all persons irrespective of their religious faiths. Both systems of personal law claim divine origin and are interwoven with religion; both are based on custom and often originate from custom. But even personal law is suspended in certain agricultural tribes by customary law. A judicial decision on a customary practice is a binding authority.

HINDU LAW . . . In India, as in other countries of the Orient, law is an integral part of religion and ethics, and the books dealing with these subjects, called *Dharmaśāstras,* therefore offer us overwhelming data about religious purification and penance, prayer and sacrifice, prohibitions on food and drink, punishment in hell and rebirth, philosophy, eschatology, creation, funeral ceremonies and sacrifices to the dead, the study of the Vedas and asceticism, the manner of living and customs of Brahmans and kings, and other subjects which we do not generally expect to find treated in such books. Many of them say nothing at all about law proper, and only a few later compilations may be called purely juridical works.

According to the *Dharmaśāstras,* the Vedas (see Chapters V and IX) should be regarded as the first and foremost source of ancient Indian law. In a narrow sense, the Vedas contain much data about sacrifices, penances, and prayers, as well as ethics, which are important for the history of customs, but they refer only occasionally to legal matters.

In the older books known as the *Dharmasūtras,* so far as they have been preserved, there are always found special sections on the law of inheritance, the law of government, legal procedure, and other features of law proper as it was taught and handed down traditionally in the oldest schools of the Brahmans.

The second stage of the legal literature is represented by the very numerous metrical works which have come down to the present time under the name of *Dharmaśāstra* or *Smṛti* (*Smriti*). They differ from the *Dharmasūtras,* which are composed partly or wholly in prose, in being written entirely in verse. Yet these works, to which the *Mānava Dharmaśāstra,* the most esteemed authority, belongs, appear partly to have originated out of older

Dharmasūtras and are therefore at least connected with the Vedic literature.

The latest stage of Indian legal literature is formed by the commentaries and systematic works which have been developed from the *Dharmasūtras* and *Dharmaśāstras* since early medieval times. As the products of a new age, inspired by powerful princes and ministers, these extensive compilations gradually displaced the *Dharmasūtras* and *Dharmaśāstras* to the extent that at the time of the establishment of British rule in eastern India, the *Mitāksharā*, a law compendium of the eleventh century, was the standard work in the greater part of India. For the historical study of Indian law, for which clarification of the beginnings is of particular importance, this very large group of works is indispensable, especially since they are helpful in understanding the original sources.

In addition to the traditions contained in the Vedas, *Dharmasūtras*, and *Dharmaśāstras*, the Brahmanical authors recognize as a third source of law the way of life and teachings of pious men, such as the *Sadācāra* and the *Śishṭāgama.* In connection with law proper, particular customs and manners of various countries, castes, and families are often emphasized as standard, though of course only so far as they are not opposed to the sacred law. The important position given in this respect to customary law is thoroughly in conformity with facts and renders it obligatory for those who deal with the history of law to search for traces and survivals of Indian customary law.

The most important sources of ancient Indian law are the *Āpastamba Dharmasūtra, Gautama Dharmasūtra, Vasishṭha Dharmasūtra, Vishnu Smṛti, Mānava Dharmaśāstra, Yājñavalkya Dharmaśāstra,* and *Nārada Smṛti.*

The number of authors and works on the *Dharmaśāstras* is legion. All of them were actuated by the most laudable motives of regulating Hindu society in all matters—civil, religious, and moral—and of securing for the members of that society happiness in this world and the next. They laid the greatest emphasis on the duties of every man as a member of the whole Hindu society and of the particular class to which he belonged, and very little emphasis on the privileges of men. They created great solidarity and cohesion among the several classes of Hindu society in India in spite of conflicting interests and inclinations and enabled that society to hold its own against foreign invaders.

Today Hindu law is applied to: (1) Hindus by birth and by religion, including those who after renouncing Hinduism have reverted to it; (2) illegitimate children both of whose parents are Hindus; (3) illegitimate children in cases in which the father is a Christian and the mother a Hindu, provided the children are brought up as Hindus; (4) sons of Hindu dancing girls of the Naik caste converted to Islam, in cases in which the sons are taken into the family of the Hindu grandparents and are brought up as Hindus; (5) Jains, Sikhs, Nambudri Brahmans.

Hindus are in theory divided into four major castes: Brahmans (Brāhmaṇas), Kshatriyas (Kṣatriyas), Vaisyas (Vaiśyas), and Sudras (Śūdras). Each of these is in turn subdivided into a number of subcastes, the latter being regarded by sociologists as the true castes. The first three of the major castes are *dvija,* or twice born. Through investiture with the sacred thread they have the right to study the Vedas and perform the samskara (Sanskrit *saṁskāra*), or sacraments. All of these rights except the samskara of marriage are denied to Sudras.

Today, as in ancient times, the main sources of Hindu law are found in: (1) *Śruti,* that is, divinely inspired works, including the mass of material known as the Veda; (2) the *Smṛti;* (3) customs which are based on lost or forgotten *Śruti* and *Smṛti;* and (4) judicial decisions.

The three principal *Smṛti* texts which are still considered sources of present-day law are: (1) the Code of Manu (the *Mānava Dharmaśāstra*), compiled some time between 200 B.C.

and A.D. 100; (2) the Code of Yājñavalkya, written some time between A.D. 100 and A.D. 300 (the *Mitākshardā,* composed in the eleventh century, is the leading commentary upon this code); and (3) the Code of Nārada, written some time between 100 B.C. and A.D. 400. In addition, there are more than a hundred other *Dharmaśātras* of greater or lesser importance.

The *Smṛti* texts do not agree with each other in all respects. The conflict between them gave rise to commentaries which often have been accepted as authoritative, even if they appear to scholars to proceed by wrong interpretation. Clear proof of usage outweighs the written text of the Hindu law.

In regard to succession and inheritance, there are in principle only two schools of law, the Mitāksharā and the Dāyabhāga. (The latter is a digest of codes on division of inheritance, written between the thirteenth and fifteenth centuries A.D.) The difference between these two systems on the subject of inheritance arises from the fact that, while the doctrine of religious efficacy is the guiding system under the Dāyabhāga school, there is no such definite guiding principle under the Mitāksharā school. Sometimes, consanguinity is regarded as the guiding principle; at others, religious efficacy. Succession to stridhana (Sanskrit *strīdhana*), or property held absolutely by a female, is governed by rules different from those which govern inheritance to the property of a male. The Mitāksharā school recognizes two modes of devolution of property: survivorship and succession. The role of survivorship applies to joint family property; the rules of succession apply to property held in absolute severalty by the last owner. The Dāyabhāga recognizes only one mode of devolution: succession. It does not recognize the rule of survivorship even in the case of joint family property. The reason for this is that, while every member of a Mitāksharā joint family has only an undivided interest in the joint property, a member of a Dāyabhāga joint family holds his share in quasi severalty, so that it passes on his death to his heirs as if he were absolutely seized thereof, and not to the surviving coparceners as under the Mitāksharā law.

The joint family is a striking feature of Hindu society and Hindu law. A joint Hindu family consists of all males lineally descended from a common ancestor and includes their wives and unmarried daughters. A daughter ceases to be a member of her father's family on marriage and becomes a member of her husband's family. The joint and undivided Hindu family is ordinarily joint not only in estate, but also in food and worship. Hindu coparcenary is a much narrower body than the joint family. It includes only those persons who acquire by birth an interest in the joint or coparcenary property. The essence of a coparcenary under the Mitāksharā law is unity of ownership. Joint family or coparcenary property is that in which every coparcener has a joint interest and a joint possession; it devolves by survivorship, not by succession, and is property in which the male issue of the coparceners acquire an interest by birth. (In some cases the widow takes a share equal to that of her husband or son.) Property acquired in business by members of a joint Hindu family through their joint labor and with the aid of the joint family property becomes joint family property, and where it has been acquired without the aid of joint family property the presumption is that it is the joint property of the joint acquirers. Generally speaking the normal state of every traditional Hindu family is joint, and in the absence of proof of division such is the legal presumption. All the legal rules applied according to Hindu law depend on whether the person to which the law is being applied belongs to a joint family or not. There are therefore separate rules on alienation, debts, partition, gifts, and other subjects which are applied differently to members of a joint family and to those who are not members of such a family.

A Hindu who is of sound mind and not a minor may dispose of his property by gift or by will for religious and charitable purposes, such as the establishment and worship of an idol, feeding Brahmans and the poor, performance of religious ceremonies, and the endowment of a university or a hospital. The moment the endowment is made, all rights pass from the dedicator. Where property is devoted absolutely to religious purposes, the possession and management of the property belongs in the case of a *devasthāna* (temple) to the manager of the temple, and in the case of a math (Sanskrit *maṭha*), or abode for students of religion, to the head of the math, who is called a mahant. Temple managers and mahants form a continuous representation of the property of the idol or of the math.

Marriage is a holy union for the performance of religious duties, not a contract. In principle, a Hindu may marry any number of wives, but a woman cannot marry another man while her husband is alive. Legislation in modern times has in some provinces and states changed this general rule. The historic practice has been that the parties to a marriage must both belong to the same major caste; otherwise the marriage is invalid. But a marriage between persons belonging to different subdivisions of the same caste is not invalid. For the purposes of marriage converts to Hinduism are regarded as Sudras. Therefore, the marriage of a Sudra with a Christian woman converted to Hinduism before marriage is treated as a marriage between two Sudras and is valid. A man cannot marry a woman of the same gotra or *pravara;* that is, he cannot marry a woman if his father and the woman's father are both descendants of a common ancestor in the male line. Similarly, a man and a woman cannot marry if they are sapinda (Sanskrit *sapiṇḍa*), or persons having a common ancestor within a prescribed degree. There are two schools of thought as to who are sapinda for marriage. The wife is bound to live with her husband and to submit herself to his authority. The husband is bound to live with his wife and to maintain her. Divorce is not known in general Hindu law; a marriage creates an indissoluble tie between the husband and the wife. Judicial separation, however, is admissible.

Adoption is widely practiced and recognized in Hindu law. The objects of adoption are to secure spiritual benefits to the adopter and his ancestors, and to secure an heir and perpetuate the adopter's name. Adoption has the effect of transferring the adopted boy from his natural family into the adoptive family. In principle, it confers upon the adoptee the same rights and privileges in the family of the adopter as those of a legitimate son. On the other hand, the adopted son loses all the rights of a son in his natural family but does not sever the tie of blood between himself and the members of his natural family. For this reason he cannot marry in his natural family.

MOSLEM LAW . . . Moslem personal law has been applied in modern India to Moslems in some matters only, that is: (1) in those which have been expressly directed by the Legislative Assembly to be applied to Moslems, such as rules of succession and inheritance; and (2) to those which are applied to Moslems as a matter of justice, equity, and good conscience, such as the rules of the Moslem law of pre-emption. A Moslem is considered to be any person who professes that: (1) there is but One God, and (2) Mohammed (Muḥammad) is His prophet.

Moslems are divided into two main divisions, namely the Sunnites and the Shiʿites. The Sunnites are in turn divided into four sects: the Hanafi, the Maliki, the Shafiʿites, and the Hanbalites. The Shiʿites are divided into three sects: the Ithnaʿashariya, the Ismaʿili, and the Zaydites. Moslem law applicable to each division or sect prevails for litigants of that division or sect.

There are four sources of Moslem law: (1) the Koran (Qur'ān); (2) *ḥadīth,* that is, precepts, actions, and sayings of the Prophet Mohammed, not written down during his lifetime, but preserved by tradition and handed down by authorized persons; (3) *ijmāʿ,* that is, consensus of Moslem scholars; and (4) *qiyās,* analogical deductions derived from the comparison of the first three sources when they do not apply to any particular case.

The whole estate of a Moslem who dies intestate, or so much of it as has not been disposed of by will, devolves on his heirs at the moment of his death. The heirs succeed to the estate as tenants in common in specific shares. Each heir is liable for the debts of the deceased to the extent only of a share of the debts proportionate to his share of the estate. There is no distinction of inheritance between movable and immovable property, or between ancestral and self-acquired property.

When the members of a Moslem family live in commensality, they do not form a joint family in the sense in which that term is used in Hindu law. There is not, as in Hindu law, any presumption that acquisitions by several members of a family living together are for the benefit of the family. If during the continuance of the family, however, properties are acquired in the name of the managing member of the family, and it is proved that they are possessed by all the members jointly, the presumption is that they are the properties of the family. If after the death of a Moslem his adult sons continue their father's business and retain his assets in the business, they are deemed to stand in a fiduciary relation to the other heirs of the deceased and to be liable to account as such for the profit made by them in the business. Similarly, members of a Moslem family carrying on business jointly do not constitute a joint family firm in the sense in which that expression is used in Hindu law.

In principle, every Moslem of sound mind and not a minor may dispose of his property by will (*waṣīyah*), which may be made either verbally or in writing. He cannot dispose of more than a third of the surplus of his estate after payment of funeral expenses and debts. Bequests in excess of the legal third cannot take effect unless the heirs consent thereto after the death of the testator. The Sunnites and the Shi'ites differ widely on other more detailed rules of succession.

An important feature of Moslem law is *waqf*, the permanent dedication by a person professing Islam of any property for any purpose recognized by Moslem law as religious, pious, or charitable. The moment the *waqf* is created, all rights of property pass out of the *wāqif,* or dedicator, and vest in the Almighty. The mutawalli (Arabic *mutawallī*), or superintendent of the religious beneficiary, has no right in the property belonging to the *waqf.* In principle, *waqf* property cannot be alienated and is not liable to attachment and sale in execution of a personal decree against the mutawalli, nor can the rents and profits derived from such property be seized by execution.

The right of *shuf'a,* or pre-emption, is a right which the owner of an immovable property possesses to acquire by purchase another immovable property which has been sold to another person. The right of pre-emption is recognized by custom among Hindus of some parts of India and is governed in principle by the rules of the Moslem law of pre-emption.

Marriage is a contract which has for its object the procreation and legalization of children. Every Moslem of sound mind who has attained puberty may enter into a contract of marriage. A Moslem may have as many as four wives at the same time, but it is not lawful for a Moslem woman to have more than one husband at a time. A Moslem male may contract a valid marriage not only with a Moslem woman, but also with a *kitābīya* (that is, a Jewess or a Christian), but not with an idolatress or a fire worshiper; a Moslem woman cannot contract a valid marriage except with a Moslem. She cannot contract a valid marriage even with a *kitābī* (Jew or Christian). If such a marriage is contracted, however, it is not void, but only irregular. The husband is bound to maintain his wife so long as she is faithful to him and obeys his reasonable orders. If he neglects or refuses to maintain her, the wife may sue him for maintenance. A woman after divorce, but not after the death of her husband, is entitled to maintenance during the period of iddat (Arabic *'iddah*), or the period during which a divorced or widowed woman must remain in seclusion and abstain from remarriage.

Dower or mahr is a sum of money or other property which the wife is entitled to receive from the husband in consideration of the marriage. If the amount of dower is not fixed, the wife is entitled to "proper" dower. The wife may refuse to live with her husband and admit him to sexual intercourse so long as the dower is not paid. The contract of marriage may be dissolved: (1) by the husband at his will, without the intervention of a court; (2) by mutual consent without the intervention of a court; and (3) by a judicial decree at the suit of the husband or wife. The wife is entitled to sue for a divorce on the grounds that her husband is impotent or that he has falsely charged her with adultery.

BIBLIOGRAPHY

Hindu Law

Jones, Sir William, *Institutes of Hindu Law* (Calcutta and London, 1796).

Colebrooke, H. T., *A Digest of Hindu Law,* vols. 1–3 (Calcutta and London, 1801).

Jolly, Julius, *Outlines of an History of the Hindu Law of Partition, Inheritance and Adoption* (Calcutta, 1885).

West, Sir Raymond, and Buhler, J. G., *A Digest of the Hindu Law of Inheritance, Partition, and Adoption,* 4th ed. (Bombay, 1921).

Mayne, J. D., *A Treatise on Hindu Law and Usage,* 9th ed. (Madras, 1922).

Jolly, Julius, *Hindu Law and Custom* (Calcutta, 1928).

Kane, P. V., *History of Dharmaśāstra,* vols. 1–3 (Poona, 1930–1946); vol. 4 in preparation.

Jha, Ganganatha, *Hindu Law and Its Sources* (Allahabad, 1930).

Mulla, Sir D. F., *Principles of Hindu Law,* 9th ed. (Calcutta, 1940).

Moslem Law

Wilson, Sir R. K., *A Digest of Anglo-Muhammadan Law,* 6th ed. (Calcutta, 1930).

Fyzee, A. A. A., *An Introduction to the Study of Mahomedan Law* (London, 1931).

LAW

Mulla, Sir D. F., *Principles of Mahomedan Law,* 10th ed. (Calcutta, 1933).

Saksena, H. P., *Muslim Law as Administered in British India,* 2d ed. (Allahabad, 1940).

Tyabji, F. B., *Muhammadan Law,* 3d ed. (Bombay, 1940).

Fyzee, A. A. A., *Outlines of Muhammadan Law* (London, 1950).

CHAPTER XI BY W. NORMAN BROWN

Archaeology

MAN's residence in the Indian subcontinent, as far as present evidence indicates, begins in Quaternary (Pleistocene) times. The earliest discovered remains are of Paleolithic flake tools from the Boulder Conglomerate stage at the close of the second interglaciation, found in the terraces of the Sohan (Soan) Valley among the upper Siwalik Hills in the Potwar area of the northwestern Punjab, Pakistan. Following this industry, known as pre-Sohan, is the Sohan (Early and Late) industry proper, which is found in a large area of the northwestern part of the subcontinent, and the Madras hand-ax industry, found at widely scattered sites in peninsular India with extensions into Rajputana and central India. Microlithic industries have been discovered from the extreme northwest to the tip of the peninsula and from Sind in the west to the coast of Orissa in the east. A proto-Neolithic industry has been identified in Kashmir and adjacent Punjab, Neolithic material has been recovered from sites in almost all major sections of the subcontinent, perhaps having been diffused from north to south.

EARLY INDUS CIVILIZATIONS . . . The first remains of urban civilization in the Indian subcontinent appear at a number of sites in the Indus River system. At least four cultures have been discovered. The earliest of these is called Amri after the place where it was first identified, and is known from a poorly developed architecture, chert implements, shell, and a thin-walled painted pottery.

The second culture, discovered at Harappa and first described in print in 1924, is much the most frequently represented, endured for the longest period of time, was the most advanced, and has been well explored at Harappa, Mohenjo-daro, and Chanhu-daro. It was in contact with Sumer, Mesopotamia, as early as 2350 B.C., and possibly as late as the seventeenth century B.C. (or even a century or two later). It had well-constructed, fortified, and planned cities, chiefly of brick, provided with an excellent drainage system. Houses were usually separate and equipped with baths. It used copper and bronze extensively, and the people wore cotton clothing. They had jewelry of metal, shell, and pottery. Both cubical and tabular dice and many toys have been recovered. The thick-walled red Harappa wheel-made painted pottery has characteristic black painted decorations of foliage, animals, and geometric motifs. This culture had a system of writing, which appears abundantly on steatite stamp seals but has not been successfully deciphered. The cities were commercial, and appear to have dominated the surrounding country. In Baluchistan (both that in Pakistan and that in southern Iran) archaeological sites of the third millennium B.C. have been discovered along ancient trade routes leading to the West. A number of items of the Harappa culture reappear in later historic India and suggest that there was a continuous civilization during that time, though the connecting links have not been found. Who the people were who owned the Harappa culture is not known, though it is frequently suggested that they were Dravidians.

The third Early Indus civilization is known as the Jhukar. It was also well advanced, though less so than the Harappa, and it had cities built upon cities of the Harappa culture but of inferior architecture. Its polychrome painted pottery was different from that of the Harappa culture, and it had no writing. It appears to have belonged to a different people.

The last of the four early cultures is called the Jhangar, and is known only from a crude, handmade gray pottery with incised geometric designs. Its owners may have been nomads.

RIG VEDIC CULTURE . . . The next known period of civilization in India is that of the Rig Veda, but information about it is drawn exclusively from literary sources. No material remains have yet been identified. The people owning this culture had a language belonging to the Indo-European family and were closely related to the Iranians, forming with them a group called Indo-Iranian or Aryan. They are generally considered to have entered the Indian subcontinent through the passes of the northwest frontier at around 1500-1200 B.C. They kept herds, practiced agriculture, used metal, and perhaps had fortified settlements. They had chariots and may have introduced the horse into India. Wealth was measured in terms of cattle. Their chief weapon was the bow; they wore helmet and body armor. They gambled with *vibhīdaka* nuts for dice, raced horses, and had an intoxicating drink called sura (Sanskrit *surā*). Their society was patriarchal and divided into (1) Aryans, who were subdivided into Brahmans (Brāhmaṇas, or spiritual aristocracy), Kshatriyas (Kṣatriyas, or rulers and warriors), and Vaisyas (Vaiśyas, or commons); and (2) non-Aryans, who were Sudras (Śūdras, or serfs). Their religion (see Chapter IX) seems to have been basically different from that of the Early Indus civilizations, and it is impossible to establish any relationship between the two cultures. The ruler of a tribe or clan was a king or raja (*rājan*); there was an assembly of the folk. By 1000 B.C., the Aryans had advanced over the Punjab, and, according to literary record, seem to have reached eastern Bihar and Bengal by 800 B.C. They may also by that time have got to central India from the Ganges Valley, and have gone down the Indus to the west of the Rajputana desert, crossed Kutch (Cutch), and arrived in Gujarat. No material archaeological data exist to reveal the details of this advance. Similarly, there is no material archaeological evidence to confirm the events narrated in the great epic, the *Mahābhārata,* concerning the war between the Pāṇḍavas and the Kauravas, traditionally later than the Vedic period.

FORMATION AND GROWTH OF HISTORIC INDIAN CIVILIZATION . . . The blending of the diverse elements which formed traditional historic Indian civilization took place during the seventh to third centuries B.C. For this period archaeological exploration has revealed much of topography, history, and social conditions to supplement literary data. During these centuries the Aryan Vedic civilization, as modified by contact with non-Aryans, established itself in north India. There are presumptive reasons for thinking that a Dravidian civilization also existed in south India at this time, but there is no conclusive archaeological evidence to support the theory. During these same centuries the Persian Empire often held as satrapies areas in Afghanistan, Baluchistan, and the Punjab through which business and cultural contacts were maintained between Persia and India, especially along the great trade routes which ran from Bihar across northern India to Bactria (Afghanistan) and beyond. During the same period there was ocean-borne commerce between western Indian seaports and the Persian Gulf and Red Sea.

In these same centuries the philosophic speculations of the Upanishads (*Upaniṣad*) were formulated, and the two heterodox religions of Buddhism and Jainism rose and had their first spread. The earliest known records of these faiths are literary, but in the third century B.C., the great emperor Aśoka (r. c. 274–237 B.C.) of the Maurya dynasty, patron of Buddhism, who ruled a great empire from his capital Pāṭaliputra (modern Patna) in Magadha (part of modern Bihar), marked many sites sacred to that faith, as well as other sites, with commemorative inscribed columns. He also had edicts carved on rocks in many parts of his wide realm, somewhat in the manner of the Achaemenian kings of Persia.

The Aśokan inscriptions are not in Sanskrit, but in various spoken Prakrits (see Chapter IV) of local provenience, and are written in two scripts. One of these, known as Kharoshthi (*kharoṣṭhī*), reading from right to left, is characteristic of Gandhara in the northwest; it is a form of a script which was in use in the Persian Empire at around 500 B.C., and was employed in India until about A.D. 450. The other script, known as Brahmi (*brāhmī*), reading from left to right, was employed throughout Aśoka's empire and appears to have been derived from a western Asiatic business script which was in use during the seventh to sixth century B.C., though an unconvincing effort has also been made to derive it from the Harappa script. Brahmi is the source of all later native Indian scripts. The decipherment of these two scripts in the nineteenth century was basic to the study of Indian epigraphy and numismatics, and revolutionized knowledge of Indian history from the time of Aśoka to the Guptas (fourth to sixth century A.D.).

As the period of formation of characteristic Indian civilization was coming to a close, the contact with Persian civilization, already mentioned, assumed a special form. In the old Persian Empire, following Alexander the Great's invasion (330 B.C.), there arose a blend of the Persian culture with the classical Greek and Roman, known as Hellenistic. This entered Bactria (Afghanistan) and northwestern India, where it was cultivated under a number of Indo-Greek kings, of whom the greatest was Menander, known to Indians as Milinda (c. 150 B.C.). When the Maurya dynasty collapsed (c. 185 B.C.), these kings pushed farther into India, taking with them the Hellenistic culture. After them, in the first century A.D., the Kushanas (Kuṣāṇa), a central Asian people, came to India by way of Bactria, having been partly Hellenized on the way (see Chapter XII). Under these two sets of rulers, and their contemporaries and tributaries, both Hellenistic and native Indic civilizations existed side by side. It was thought in the nineteenth and early twentieth centuries that India owed much of her historic culture to Hellenistic influence, but it now appears that India as a whole took very little from it that endured, except in astronomy, astrology, and medicine. In architecture and sculpture Hellenistic influence still exists in Kashmir, but elsewhere in modern India traces of it can be found only with patient search. Whatever India accepted from Hellenism in literature, art, and philosophy was thoroughly assimilated by the end of the fifth century A.D., when the Huns obliterated Hellenism in India.

During this period there was a notable development of urbanization and an increase of wealth with expansion of foreign commerce. Fairly large kingdoms existed by the time of the Buddha (see Chapter IX); these were consolidated into an empire under Aśoka. Elaborate wooden houses are shown in the sculptures at Sanchi (first century A.D.). Ownership of land vested in the state; peasants rented the use of it. The caste system in a rigid form had come into existence by the time of the legal works known as the Shastras (Śāstras, starting from about the second century A.D.), and the doctrine of pollution was marking the lowest or Fifths (Panchama; Sanskrit *pañcama*) off from the rest of the community. The administration of the state was well organized, according to the Greek Megasthenes, who at about 300 B.C. visited the court of Chandragupta Maurya, grandfather of Aśoka. Further details of administration are given in the well-known *Arthaśāstra,* a work by Chanakya (Cāṇakya; also called Viṣṇugupta or Kauṭilya), Chandragupta Maurya's minister, which in its present form may be a reworking of as late a date as the second or third century A.D., but must contain a kernel of material from Mauryan times. The great flowering of Indian civilization was in the period of the Gupta dynasty, founded by Chandragupta I (r. A.D. c. 318/319–330) and lasting to the sixth century, and continued culturally until the middle of the seventh century. At this time literature, science, sculpture, painting, the dance, the drama, and music assumed their classic forms, and the religion known as Brahmanical Hinduism, with Sanskrit as its literary vehicle, acquired the major features which persist to the present. Medieval Indian history may be considered to start after the close of the Gupta period.

BIBLIOGRAPHY

Barnett, L. D., *Antiquities of India* (New York, 1914).

The Cambridge History of India: E. J. Rapson, ed., vol. 1, *Ancient India* (New York, 1922).

Macdonnell, A. A., *India's Past* (New York, 1927).

Masson-Oursel, Paul, Willman-Grabowska, Helena, and Stern, Phillippe, *Ancient India and Indian Civilization,* tr. from the French by M. R. Dobie (London, 1934).

Cumming, Sir John G., ed., *Revealing India's Past* (London, 1939).

Krishnaswamy, V. D., "Stone-Age India," *Ancient India,* no. 3, pp. 11–57 (Delhi, 1947).

Mackay, Ernest, *Early Indus Civilizations* (London, 1948).

CHAPTER XII BY WALTER E. CLARK

Two Thousand Years of History

THE first exact date in Indian history is 326 B.C., the year in which Alexander the Great invaded India, but there is some reasonably sound historical information beginning with the sixth century B.C. (For the prehistory of the subcontinent see Chapter XI.) The earliest Buddhist books describe northern India of the seventh and sixth centuries B.C. as divided into four great and twelve small kingdoms and a number of tribal republics. Since the Vedic period the center of political power had been moving eastward from the Punjab until, by the end of the sixth century, Magadha began to emerge as a great power.

Shortly before 500 B.C., King Darius I of Persia invaded and occupied northwestern India, which thereafter formed the twentieth satrapy of the Persian Empire. It is not known how long this Persian occupation lasted or how much influence it had on the development of Indian civilization. When Alexander invaded India, he found no trace of Persian rule. Northwestern India was then divided into several small, independent states.

After conquering Persia, Bactria, and Afghanistan, Alexander reached the easternmost of the rivers of the Punjab, near Amritsar, northwest of Delhi. Here his troops mutinied and refused to go farther east. After organizing four satrapies in India and one in Afghanistan, three under Greek officers and two under Indians, he was forced to retreat. He had intended to hold his conquests permanently, for he had a dream of uniting East and West. If he had lived longer the whole history of India might have been different, but he died in Babylon in 323 B.C. By 317 all trace of Greek rule in India had disappeared, but Alexander had founded eight or ten cities in Bactria and the Oxus region, and there was Greek rule in Bactria for nearly 200 years (327–135 B.C.). More and more, however, the Bactrian Greeks were cut off from the West by the rise of the Parthian Empire, and more and more did they have to struggle against increasing pressure from Scythian tribes on the north and northeast.

THE MAURYAS (322?-c. 185 B.C.) . . . Shortly after Alexander's death, Chandragupta founded the Maurya dynasty. The Maurya empire—the first great empire of India, whose capital was at Patna (ancient Pāṭaliputra) in Magadha (modern Bihar)—reached its greatest extent under his grandson Aśoka, who ruled nearly all of India except the southern tip. For Chandragupta (322?–298 B.C.) and Aśoka (c. 274–237 B.C.) there is an unusual amount of definite historical information. For Bindusāra (298-c. 274 B.C.), the son of Chandragupta, there are only a trivial anecdote given by a Greek writer and a tradition recorded by the Tibetan historian Tāranātha that Bindusāra conquered the country between the eastern and western seas. The dominant political power in India has always been in the north. The Mauryas extended their political control over central India, and later the Moguls (Mughals) and the British ruled over central India and a large part of the south. None of the central or southern dynasties was ever able to occupy and control northern India.

The organization of Chandragupta's empire is better known

than that of any other Indian king down to the time of Akbar. Much information has been preserved in a Greek book written by Megasthenes and in a Sanskrit text called the *Arthaśāstra*. About 302 B.C., Seleucus I Nicator, Greek ruler of western Asia, sent to the court of Chandragupta an ambassador named Megasthenes, who lived for several years at Pāṭaliputra and wrote, in Greek, a book giving a detailed account of the country and people. The book itself is not extant, but substantial fragments have been preserved in quotations by later writers. The *Arthaśāstra* gives us a glimpse of a world of thought and action utterly different from that which we get from the older religious Vedic literature. There are some minor discrepancies with Megasthenes, but very great agreement. The work is traditionally ascribed to Chanakya (Cāṇakya; Kauṭilya), Chandragupta's prime minister. The final redaction of the text in its present form may date from the beginning of the Christian era, but its essentials are corroborated by Megasthenes and may be taken as giving a fair picture of life and government in early Mauryan times. The *Arthaśāstra* is probably the oldest extant work of secular Sanskrit literature and one of the most important works of Indian antiquity that have come down to us. It deals with government as regulating all matters of daily life, with practical worldly affairs, and with technical matters, economics, government, and politics rather than religion and philosophy.

In form, the government was an autocracy, tempered by reverence for the Brahmans, who were exempt from taxation and, as a general rule, from capital punishment except for treason. State was superior to church. There was some regard for the religious sanctity of the priesthood, but government was essentially free from priestly domination. There was a constant struggle for existence between kingdoms. In general, might was right. The spy system was highly organized, and the whole machinery of government seemed to depend on secret information as a safeguard against rival states, as a means of instigating revolution in rival states, and as a means of maintaining a check on officials. Hence the frequent comparison of this book with Niccolò Machiavelli's *The Prince*. There is much on taxation (normally one sixth of the produce), on irrigation, on state control of butchers, liquor sellers, gamblers, and courtesans, on shipping by river and ocean, and on mining and metallurgy. Much attention was paid to meteorology, pastures and grazing grounds, and medicine, and to the taking of a regular census and the registration of travelers. The vigorous attitude toward life, and the efficient state organization of and control over innumerable practical details, surprises us after the almost exclusively religious texts of the Veda and the world-renouncing philosophy of the Upanishads. It is probable that a more energetic spirit was always present outside of Brahman religious and philosophical circles.

Aśoka, after waging one war in Kalinga, was converted to Buddhism and zealously proclaimed Buddhism in a number of inscriptions carved on rocks and inscribed on pillars in various parts of his great empire. The earliest inscriptions in India, they form one of the most remarkable series of public documents in world history. Aśoka preached the sanctity of animal life, the noninjury of any living creature, and the sin of the old Brahmanical animal sacrifices. He inculcated the virtues of truthfulness, of reverence for parents, elders, and teachers, of tolerance for the beliefs and practices of others, and of almsgiving. He emphasized inward piety rather than rituals and festivals. Officials were appointed who went through the country convening the people and preaching the Buddhist faith (dharma). Buddhist missions were sent abroad and to the far south of India. Aśoka was also a great builder of Buddhist stupas. He had roads constructed, and gardens for medicinal herbs planted. It has been suggested that his mildness and tolerance and his pacific tendencies in the midst of a turbulent world contributed to the rapid collapse of the Maurya empire after his death.

NORTHERN INDIA, SECOND CENTURY B.C.—FOURTH CENTURY A.D. . . . The Mauryas were succeeded at Pāṭaliputra by the Śungas (c. 185–73 B.C.) and the Kanvas (73–28 B.C.), who ruled over a much-diminished empire. Under the Śungas there seems to have been a Brahmanical reaction to the Buddhism of Aśoka, and there are reasons for thinking that the period was of great importance in the development of secular Sanskrit literature.

After Aśoka's death the Maurya empire began to break up as the Bactrian Greeks pushed into India from the northwest and as central India became independent under the Andhra dynasty, which lasted from about 230 B.C. to about A.D. 225. For over 450 years the thirty kings of the Andhra dynasty ruled over the whole of the Deccan. This is the longest dynasty in Indian history. There are some inscriptions, but the history of the period is still obscure. It seems to have been an important period in the development of literature, art, architecture, and religion.

Early in the second century B.C. the Bactrian Greeks pushed over the Hindu Kush into the Kabul Valley and India. They won control of the whole of northwestern India and maintained themselves there until early in the first century, when they were overwhelmed by the coming of the Sakas and Kushans.

Some time between 170 and 165 B.C. a tribe called by the Chinese Yüeh-chi (Yuechi), which dwelt in eastern Turkestan and western Kansu, was attacked and defeated by the Hsiung-nu, who lived north of them in what is now known as Mongolia. The Yüeh-chi were probably Iranian; the Hsiung-nu were probably the ancestors of the Huns. Defeated, the Yüeh-chi moved to the west, where they met the Iranian nomadic tribes called Sakas. These, driven out of their homeland by the Yüeh-chi, pushed off by the Bactrian Greeks, and blocked by the Parthians, moved southward through eastern Persia to Sakastan (modern Seistan). Many of these Sakas pushed eastward into India and then moved up the Indus Valley, through the Delhi gap, and down the Ganges Valley or the Indus Valley, across Kutch (Cutch), into Gujarat, and even into the northwestern part of the Deccan. We have coins and inscriptions of Saka kings from the first century A.D. until after A.D. 400. They rapidly became Hinduized.

The Yüeh-chi crossed the Oxus into Bactria and completely swept aside Greek rule there. For a century or more the Yüeh-chi, divided into five branches, dwelt in Bactria. At the end of the first century B.C. (or early in the first century A.D.) they were united by one king who belonged to the Kushan branch. Under the name Kushana (Kuṣāna), they pushed into India and founded an empire which covered most of northwestern India, Afghanistan, Bactria, and the western part of Turkestan. This empire lasted until about A.D. 220. The last of the Kushan kings bore an Indian name, a clear indication that the Kushans had gradually become Hinduized as had the Greeks and the Sakas.

THE GUPTA EMPIRE, A.D. c. 318–500 . . . Again there is a dark period in Indian history until the formation of the Gupta empire, founded by Chandragupta I about A.D. 318–319, and lasting to about A.D. 500. Its capital was Pāṭaliputra, where the Mauryas also had ruled. The Guptas ruled most of northern India, while the Deccan remained independent under various dynasties.

The 160 years covered by the reigns of the five great Gupta kings—Chandragupta I, Samudragupta, Chandragupta II, Kumāragupta I, and Skandagupta—were the golden age of Hinduism and classical Sanskrit literature. Literature, sculpture, painting, music, architecture, and science reached a high level of excellence. The country was rich and prosperous; the administration was tolerant and efficient. A series of important inscriptions makes it possible to reconstruct the history of the Gupta period with a fullness not possible since the time of Aśoka.

Much light is cast on the Gupta period by the account left by the Chinese pilgrim Fa-hsien, who came to India to visit the Buddhist holy places and to procure manuscripts. He left China in A.D. 399, traveled across central Asia, reached Magadha in 405, stayed there for six years, and returned to China by sea by way of Ceylon and Java, reaching home in 414.

By the time of the Guptas, Hinduism (see Chapter IX) had become well established. The old sacrificial system of Brahmanism, with its emphasis on fire sacrifices and external ritualistic acts, had been replaced by temple and image worship. Sacrifice had been replaced by an attitude of worship and devotion (bhakti) to new gods or to gods who were of small importance in the Vedas—Vishnu, Shiva, Krishna, Rāma. Philosophical Brahmanism with its tendency to pantheism and monism continued as the higher theology and philosophy of Hinduism, aiming at salvation beyond that of the heavens of the personal gods. Popular Brahmanism was modified into the dharma of Hinduism, a traditional code of social customs.

At this time a new spirit had arisen in Buddhism which fundamentally changed its whole character. The old Buddhism of the Hinayana variety had been superseded by the Mahayana (see Chapter IX). Mythology had begun to weave wonderful stories of the past lives of the Buddha when he was a Bodhisattva on his way to Buddhahood. The monks had begun to take up permanent residence in monasteries, to become lax in discipline or to plunge into metaphysical and logical speculation and scholastic wrangling. They lost their hold on the people and became merely monastic communities. Buddhism merged into the main stream of the popular religion, Hinduism.

By this time or somewhat earlier the Indians were using nine numerals with zero and place value. These were adopted by the Arabs in the eighth century and soon spread to western Europe, being called Arabic numerals only because they were transmitted to the West by the Arabs. Our numerals of the present day are very similar to those in Indian inscriptions of the sixth century.

India was not cut off from the rest of the world. We now know that the Indians were one of the greatest navigating and colonizing peoples of antiquity. From the first century of the Christian era, and probably from three or four centuries before that time, Indian culture had been spreading eastward to Indochina, from Burma to China, and through the islands from Sumatra and Java to Borneo and the Philippines. For more than a thousand years the whole of southeastern Asia was closely connected with India by trade and colonization. There were Indian colonies, Indian dynasties of kings, Indian architecture and art, Indian religions, and Indian codes of law and government in Southeast Asia. From the ninth to the fourteenth century Angkor in Cambodia was one of the most magnificent and flourishing cities in the world. Its civilization was largely Indian. The Buddhist stupa of Borobudur in Java is one of the most remarkable buildings of the ancient world. Indians traveled freely to Egypt and Arabia and there was a large amount of trade with Egypt (from the third century B.C.) and with the Roman Empire. Many Roman coins from the first two centuries A.D. have been found in southern India.

NORTHERN INDIA, FOURTH TO TWELFTH CENTURIES A.D. . . . The Gupta empire was destroyed by invasions of the White Huns during the latter part of the fifth century. These were probably Iranian and mixed tribes who were uprooted and shoved southward by the Huns as they moved westward toward Europe. They occupied northwestern India until about A.D. 528. The Indians describe them as fierce and cruel, and say that wherever they went their coming was marked by massacres and devastation.

Order was brought out of chaos by Harsha (Harṣa) of Kanauj (r. A.D. 606–647) in a brilliant period of renaissance which did not survive his death. The Chinese pilgrim Hsüan-tsang (Yüan Chwang) gives an invaluable description of the India of Harsha's time. He started on his travels in 629, came across central Asia, traveled over a large part of India, spending eight years in Harsha's dominions, and returned to China in 645 through central Asia with a large collection of Buddhist manuscripts. The rest of his life was spent in correlating the results of his expedition and in translating Buddhist texts into Chinese.

The books of Hsüan-tsang, Fa-hsien, and other Chinese pilgrims, and of Megasthenes and other Greek visitors to India, are of great importance because there is practically no historical literature in Sanskrit. Scattered inscriptions, some genealogical lists, some semihistorical novels, dramas and epics which are so overlaid by romance that history is almost lost sight of, and a mass of highly romantic fables and stories make it impossible to reconstruct more than the bare bones of history except for a few periods where the narratives of more historically minded foreigners help to fill out the skeleton. In contrast to the Chinese and Greek travelers, none of the hundreds of Indians who traveled to Egypt, China, and the Far East have left records.

For over 500 years after Harsha the history of northern India is dominated by Rajput tribes who moved over the country and formed rapidly shifting kingdoms. Some of these tribes may have been descendants of old Hindu Kshatriyas (Kṣatriyas), but most of them seem to be tribes which came into India with the White Huns and became Hinduized.

CENTRAL AND SOUTHERN INDIA, FIFTH TO FOURTEENTH CENTURIES A.D. . . . Central India and southern India went their own way, little influenced by the happenings in the north. In the Deccan the most important kingdoms were those of the Western Chalukyas of Badami (A.D. 550–753), the Eastern Chalukyas of Vengi (seventh to twelfth centuries), the Rashtrakutas of Malkhed (A.D. 753–973), the Western Chalukyas of Kalyani (A.D. 973–1190), the Hoyśalas of Halebid in Mysore (A.D. 1190–1327), and the Yadavas of Deogiri (modern Daulatabad, A.D. 1190–1318). In the south the earliest empire was that of the Pandyas. During the first three centuries of the Christian era a large literature grew up in Tamil, the language of the Pandya country. The Pandyas were succeeded by the Cholas, who also quickly absorbed the Cheras, another early dynasty.

The Pallava dynasty of Kanchi (Conjeeveram) played a large part in the history of south India, where it was the dominant power from the fifth to the ninth centuries, during the period between the two Chola empires. It has left many remarkable buildings. The Pallavas were succeeded by the great empire of the Cholas (A.D. 907–1310). Southern India was rich and prosperous because of foreign trade, especially with the Roman Empire. The influence of Brahmanism had already spread to the far south. By the eleventh century all of southern India had become a part of the great Chola empire. All of these kingdoms in central India and the south were swept away by the great Moslem invasions of that region in the early fourteenth century, except for Vijayanagar (A.D. 1336–1565), the last great Hindu kingdom in India.

THE MOSLEM CONQUEST, EIGHTH TO FOURTEENTH CENTURIES . . . After Mohammed's death in A.D. 632 the Arabs spread out of Arabia both westward and eastward. They conquered Mesopotamia and Persia in the seventh century and Sind in the beginning of the eighth century. Beginning about A.D. 1001, with Mahmud of Ghazni (971?–1030), there came a long series of Moslem plundering expeditions from Afghanistan into India, which gradually overcame Rajput resistance and occupied most of northern India.

In A.D. 1206, Delhi became the capital of a Moslem Indian empire which lasted until A.D. 1707. Gradually, Moslems occupied the greater part of central India (the Deccan) and much of southern India. In 1347, a rebellion established the Bahmanis at Gulbarga (1347–1526) as an independent Moslem power in central India. This empire eventually broke up into five parts, of which the most important were Bijapur, Golconda, and Ahmadnagar. These three were defeated and annexed by the great Moguls of Delhi, Shāh Jahān and Aurangzeb.

The result of the Moslem conquest was a great stagnation of Hindu literature, learning, and culture. Indian civilization had absorbed all the earlier invaders, but Hinduism has never been able to absorb Islam nor has Islam been able to suppress and absorb Hinduism. The two centuries of the Moslem conquest resulted in a great destruction of Indian art and architecture and of Hindu and Buddhist manuscripts, and in the virtual annihilation of the old Hindu nobility and ruling classes, except in the fastnesses of Rajputana. The five centuries of organized Moslem rule (A.D. 1206–1707) left little that was constructive except a remarkable Moslem art and architecture. The positive achievements of Islam in India must be left to Moslem historians. From the Hindu point of view the occupation was disastrous.

MOSLEM RULE, A.D. 1206–1707 . . . William H. Moreland, in *From Akbar to Aurangzeb,*[1] describes the first half of the seventeenth century as a period in which the masses of the people were forced by the administrative system to live on the borderline of starvation or rebellion. Stanley Lane-Poole, in *Mediaeval India,*[2] remarked that the most important effect of Moslem rule was the formation of a new vernacular, Urdu (see Chapter IV), a new architecture and art, a few provinces still under Moslem rule, and a large Moslem minority which has formed a difficult element in the modern political situation of the subcontinent.

---

[1] London, 1923, p. 245.

[2] New York, 1903, pp. 422–423.

Between 1206 and 1526 there were thirty-four kings at Delhi. Eleven were deposed, assassinated, or killed in battle. It was a turbulent period of gradual consolidation of Moslem rule over northern India and its expansion into central India.

A more stable government began with the foundation by Baber (Babur, real name Zahir ud-Din Muhammad) in 1526 of the dynasty of the great Moguls, which lasted until 1707. Baber is one of the most romantic and attractive figures in Indian history and the author of delightful *Memoirs.* Descended from Tamerlane on his father's side and from Genghis Khan on his mother's side, he was king of Ferghana. Driven thence by his uncles he took possession of Kabul (1504) and started upon the conquest of India. He died in 1530. Humāyūn (r. 1530–1542; 1555–1556) succeeded his father but continually fought to retain his position in upper India and was finally defeated by Sher Shah (1542–1545), an Afghan chief. He became a homeless wanderer, and it was during this time that his son Akbar was born. Humāyūn found refuge in Persia, and in 1555 he was able to regain India.

The reigns of Akbar (1556–1605), Jahāngīr (1605–1627), Shāh Jahān (1628–1658), and Aurangzeb (Aurangzīb, 1658–1707) mark the high point of Moslem rule in India. The reign of Akbar, who was one of the greatest rulers of India, was marked by firmness and benevolence and by a policy of toleration and conciliation of Hindus. He organized a durable empire. He had an inquiring and receptive mind that tried to understand all creeds and doctrines; he went so far as to give up Islam and tried unsuccessfully to found a new eclectic religion. His administrative system is known in great detail through the encyclopedic work *Aīn-i Akbarī* (*Institutes of Akbar*), written by his close friend, confidential secretary, and adviser, Abu-l Fazl.

Jahāngīr and Shāh Jahān were much weaker men. The empire continued unimpaired under the impetus given by Akbar's organizing genius, and under the two rulers Moslem art and architecture reached its zenith in India. Jahāngīr was arbitrary and fitful, a patron of painting and architecture who considered that attention to administrative details was derogatory to royal dignity, and therein he was quite different from Akbar, who said that every minute spent in the comprehending of small things is a minute spent in the service of God. It was in the reign of Jahāngīr that the British first established themselves in India and sent their first embassy to the Mogul court. It has been said of Shāh Jahān that he was a strange compound of tenderness and cruelty, of justice and caprice, of refinement and brutality, of good sense and childishness. His health was finally undermined by drink and opium. The best-known building in India, the marvelous Taj Mahal, was erected by Shāh Jahān as the mausoleum of his favorite wife, Mumtāz Maḥall. Under Jahāngīr and Shāh Jahān there was a great increase of taxation to support extravagant nobles and luxurious courts and to pay for magnificent buildings. This was a crushing burden on agriculture and industry.

Aurangzeb was a stern puritan and religious bigot who persecuted Hindus and everywhere substituted Moslems for Hindus. He ate no animal food and drank only water. He allowed himself no self-indulgence in pleasures, fasted much, and tried to suppress singing and dancing. He knew the Koran by heart and spent much time in copying manuscripts. He was a man of the utmost physical and mental courage with a stern sense of justice, but he was respected rather than loved. Most of the latter half of his reign was spent in the Deccan waging long, fruitless wars against Bijapur, Golconda, and the Marathas, in an attempt to defeat the Shiʿites and set up an orthodox Mohammedanism in the south. His successors were feeble rulers, had short reigns, and spent much of their time in fratricidal wars. The great empire soon broke up into independent kingdoms.

BIBLIOGRAPHY

Lane-Poole, Stanley, *Mediaeval India* (New York, 1903).

Rhys Davids, T. W., *Buddhist India* (New York and London, 1903).

Watters, Thomas, *On Yuan Chwang's Travels in India* (London, 1905).

Shamasastry, Rudrapatha, *Kautilya's Arthaśāstra* (Bangalore, 1915).

Rawlinson, H. G., *Intercourse Between India and the Western World* (Cambridge, Eng., 1916).

Smith, V. A., *Akbar, the Great Mogul* (London, 1919).

Moreland, W. H., *India at the Death of Akbar* (London, 1920).

Smith, V. A., *Asoka*, 3d ed. (Oxford, 1920).

Leyden, John, and Erskine, William, trs., *The Memoirs of Babur*, ed. by Sir Lucas King (Oxford, 1921).

The Cambridge History of India (Cambridge, Eng.): vol. 1 (1922), vol. 3 (1928), vol. 4 (1937).

Giles, H. A., tr., *The Travels of Fa-hsien* (Cambridge, Eng., 1923).

Moreland, W. H., *From Akbar to Aurangzeb* (London, 1923).

Smith, V. A., *Early History of India*, 4th ed. (Oxford, 1924).

Mukerji, Radhakumud, *Harsha* (Oxford, 1926).

Edwardes, S. M., and Garrett, H. L. O., *Mughal Rule in India* (Oxford, 1930).

Smith, V. A., *A History of Fine Art in India and Ceylon*, rev. by K. de B. Codrington, 2d ed. (Oxford, 1930).

Dodwell, H. H., ed., *The Cambridge Shorter History of India* (Cambridge, Eng., 1934).

Rawlinson, H. G., *India: A Short Cultural History* (London and New York, 1938).

CHAPTER XIII BY HOLDEN FURBER

British Conquest and Empire, 1707-1947

THE 240 years between the death of the last great Mogul (Mughal) emperor, Aurangzeb (Aurangzīb, r. 1658–1707), and the inauguration of independent governments in India and Pakistan saw the European intrusion into the Indian subcontinent culminate in complete foreign conquest and then give way to a reassertion of power by Indian leaders determined to shape their countrymen's own destiny. These years may be conveniently divided into three periods. In the first, 1707–1815, European commercial penetration was supplemented by a military struggle between the British and French (assisted by their Indian allies) which left Britain unchallenged as mistress of India; in the second, 1815–1885, Britain built her Indian Empire; in the third, 1885–1947, a nationalist movement developed to whose leaders British power was finally surrendered, but not until many changes had been made in the Victorian bureaucratic regime and all efforts to preserve Indian political unity had failed.

BRITISH CONQUEST (*1707–1815*) . . . The progressive disintegration of Mogul central authority which characterized the early decades of the eighteenth century gave rise to struggles between Indian princes to which the European powers, already firmly entrenched in trading posts called factories, could not be indifferent. Doubtless, increased European commercial activity tending to turn the more important factories into fortified enclaves outside Indian control played its part in weakening the Mogul Empire. Nevertheless, the directors of East India trading enterprises in Europe did not embark willingly and deliberately upon the course of embroilment in Indian disputes from which the building of a British empire in India was to follow. Their chief concern was trade, at this period the purchase of Indian goods—that is, chiefly cotton and silk hand-woven cloth, raw silk, pepper, saltpeter, and sundry drugs—with the proceeds of cargoes of silver, base metals, and woolens exported from Europe. It was not without significance that the European powers which held almost entirely aloof from Indian disputes were the smaller trading nations—Portugal, the Netherlands, and Denmark. Britain and France were unable to do so primarily because of their involvement in wars with each other over European and American issues. The conditions under which Europeans lived and traded in eighteenth-century India also helped to make it impossible for the subjects of the two foremost European powers to forget national rivalries in the pursuit of individual gain.

However much the directors of the British and French East India companies might wish to neutralize their shipping and their Indian factories from the consequences of war in Europe or in North America, they were defeated by the impossibility of confining the arena of Anglo-French naval conflict to the Atlantic and by the extensive opportunities open to their servants in India for the acquisition not only of wealth but of power. In the early 1740's the materials for empire building were already at hand. Internecine strife was clearly apparent in southeast India and latent elsewhere. Each contestant for Mogul administrative office or local lordship was eager to acquire European military skill and weapons in exchange for cash, credit, or grants of land. A few Europeans were aware of the possibilities of fashioning armies of European-officered Indian mercenary sepoys and Eurasian artillerymen. More Europeans were anxious to supplement profits from country trading within the Indian seas with profits from military and political activity. The arrival in India of the news that France and Britain, since 1741 *de facto* combatants in the War of the Austrian Succession on behalf of their respective allies, had at last officially declared war upon each other (March 1744), was but a spark to this tinder. Thenceforth, European initiative, enterprise, and greed, armed with powerful European weapons and assisted by Indian disunity and treachery, completed the destruction of the Mogul Empire and laid the foundations of British ascendancy.

The first theater of Anglo-French conflict in India lay in the southeast. Here, in a bewildering series of intrigues, the men on the spot supported their respective candidates for the subahship of the Deccan and the nawabship of the Carnatic. In the first phase the honors were distinctly with the French, not only because of Admiral Bertrand Mahé, comte de Labourdonnais', capture of Madras (1746), which the diplomats restored to Britain in 1748 at the Treaty of Aix-la-Chapelle, but because of the skill of Marquis Joseph François Dupleix (governor general, 1742–1754) in buttressing his Indian allies' position and initiating in the Deccan the system of a French-officered subsidiary force paid with the revenues of lands especially assigned for the purpose. However, with young Robert Clive's renowned exploit in storming and holding Arcot (August 31–November 15, 1751) to relieve the pressure on the British-sponsored candidate for the nawabship in Trichinopoly, the tide began to turn against the French. Dupleix' dismissal (1754) by a government stung by serious military reverses, and under pressure from directors who had never approved Dupleix' policy, may be said to presage French failure in India. Nevertheless, to contemporaries the French in India appeared for many years afterwards to have the advantage of the British in military skill and in the arts of Indian diplomacy.

Far more significant for the future were the events which took place in Bengal upon the death of its nawab, Ali Vardi Khan, in April 1756. His young and dissolute successor, Siraj-(Suraj-) ud-Daula, perhaps prompted by a desire to prevent the Europeans from behaving in Bengal as they had in the south, rashly drove the British out of Calcutta and thus brought down upon himself the full force of a retaliatory expedition from Madras led by Clive. Bengal then lay exposed both to the exercise of European military skill marshaled by a "heaven-born general" and to the practice of the arts of fomenting treachery by an experienced coterie of Europeans and Indians. The recapture of Calcutta (1757), supplemented by a few months of intrigue, sufficed to undermine Siraj-ud-Daula's authority. Plassey, fought on June 23, 1757, was not so much a battle as the essential military climax of a carefully prepared coup d'état which ensured that future nawabs of Bengal would be mere puppets of the British. Despite its bizarre qualities as an engagement in which 2,000 sepoys and 1,000 Europeans defeated a vast Indian army honeycombed with treachery, Plassey may quite appropriately be regarded as the symbol and portent of European domination of India. The ease with which it laid open to conquest and spoliation one of the great Mogul viceroyalties invested it with glamour during the period of British rule. It came to epitomize the curiously complex web of European and Indian interests from which a new order in India was fashioned in the ensuing half century. In 1763, by the Treaty of Paris, French interests in India were reduced to Pondichéry (Pondicherry), Chandernagor, and a few other small posts.

By 1770 the outlines of the system on which British power was to rest in India began to be clearly discerned. In taking control, with the nominal consent of the almost powerless Mogul emperor at Delhi, of the revenue of Bengal, through the emperor's so-called grant of the dewanee (Persian *dīwānī*) in 1765, the British East India Company stood forth as a country power in its own right. Its advantages over other country powers in any contest for supremacy were three: its corporate immortality, its control of naval power, and its possession in Bombay and Madras of subsidiary bases of operations. Its disadvantages lay in its alien character and in the reluctance of its directors to sanction a policy of conquest and expansion.

For an understanding of the manner in which some hundreds of its servants were able in a few decades to secure it recognition as the most powerful of Indian powers, it is necessary to bear in mind the almost constant interaction of European and Indian events. In the London of the 1770's, the return of many a nabob with a fortune, and the prospect of avoiding the export of silver by purchasing homeward cargoes with the surplus revenue of Bengal, convinced both the government and the company that the Indian possessions were of immense and increasing benefit to the British nation. Henceforth, the company's affairs were subjected to ever-closer scrutiny and regulation by Parliament. No one doubted the chaotic and precarious state of the company's finances, but it was felt that, once the company's servants had been prevented from cheating their employer, Indian wealth would flow to Britain in an ever-broadening stream. In India, the newly arrived writers, factors, and military cadets were learning of the multifarious ways in which they could become wealthy as a consequence of the company's expanding political activities. Military campaigns, whether connected with the Anglo-French wars in Europe or not, gave opportunity for collusive supply contracts of many kinds. Assumption of governmental functions of any sort usually meant that a company's servant was in a position to bestow favors—for example, exemption from customs duties—for which the Indian mercantile community was willing to pay. Profits from such transactions could be reinvested directly or indirectly in ventures of various kinds, not the least of which were ever-expanding British country trading voyages in the Far Eastern seas.

It is against this background that the wars and annexations of the years 1765–1815 should be viewed. An era of frank spoliation under Clive gave way to a period of more subtle penetration under Warren Hastings (1772–1785). Of Hastings it may be said that his difficulties arose primarily from too great familiarity with Indian institutions and ways of life. To him, the company was an Indian power strengthening its influence vis-à-vis other Indian powers. By his opponents, India was seldom thought of apart from its place in British politics. Hastings infused with vigor an administrative machine still largely dependent on Indian personnel. He developed a subsidiary alliance system. Although he did not crush the power of the Moslem sultans of Mysore, Haidar (Hyder) Ali and Tipu (Tippoo) Sahib, in the First and Second Mysore Wars, he made the company's sword respected from Delhi to Cape Comorin. Fortunately for Hastings, the American War of Independence ended before France could follow up the naval victories which Admiral Pierre André de Suffren had won for her in the Indian seas. By the time Hastings left India, the bases of British economic and political dominance were firmly laid and all was ready for the march of British power.

A dramatic personal vendetta between Warren Hastings and Philip Francis had during the 1770's brought India more and more into the public eye in Britain. As a consequence of renewed financial embarrassments growing largely out of the American War of Independence, the affairs of the East India Company were drawn into the vortex of British politics in the early 1780's. The prospects of drastic reforms envisaged by Charles James

Fox and his friends alarmed the most powerful among the India interests. After the direct intervention of King George III had caused the defeat of Fox's India bill in the House of Lords, the India interests helped greatly to consolidate William Pitt the Younger in power in 1784. Pitt's India act, which set the pattern of Indian government from 1784 to 1858, subjected the company's political activities to control by the state but left the company's patronage and commercial activities comparatively undisturbed. After the removal in 1786 of a clause requiring an investigation into the private fortunes of company servants upon their return to England, nearly every European intimately concerned with India was satisfied. British and foreign investors in the company were sure of their dividends. Europeans who had supplied the company in India with funds acquired in devious ways were certain that their bills of exchange on London would be paid. British and foreign agents concerned with remittances from India through non-British channels were sure that if the whole edifice of British power in India did not crumble, no law of the British Parliament could completely destroy their profits. Fixed salaries, supervision by governors no longer closely identified with the company's service, and other reforms were inevitable, but India could still offer attractive opportunities to enterprising Europeans.

To effect a policy of reform and meet the growing public criticism which was soon to culminate in Edmund Burke's orations against Hastings, the Pitt ministry chose as governor general the first Marquis Cornwallis, who was to redeem in India a reputation tarnished by the American disaster. Cornwallis, during the years 1786–1793, more than justified the government's choice. Personally incorruptible, he developed in Bengal an administrative policy which resulted in the efficient professional bureaucracy of the Victorian era. From his day dates the policy of Europeanizing all but the lesser ranks of the civil service which was to prevail throughout the next century. From his day, too, dates the beginning of the transformation of the company's Madras, Bombay, and Bengal armies into something more than mere mercenary forces without any tradition or *esprit de corps*. It was, however, thirty years before the pay and conditions of service in India were such that disaffection among the company's European military officers was not to be feared, and even longer before military efficiency ceased to be impaired by ill feeling between the company's army and the king's regiments stationed in India.

Lord Cornwallis' most lasting achievement, and the one which in the Indian mind has overshadowed all his efforts at reform, was the celebrated permanent revenue settlement in Bengal (1793). This arrangement, with which his name is always associated, though others both in India and Britain bore much of the responsibility for it, had the effect of making the Bengal zamindars not only landlords of the soil in the European sense, but landlords obligated to pay the government a fixed rent which could not be altered under the vastly changed circumstances of the next century.

Though a faithful adherent to the policy of no aggrandizement enjoined by both company and government, Cornwallis was drawn, largely through the complex machinations of European merchants and company servants, into a full-scale conflict with Tipu, sultan of Mysore (Third Mysore War, 1789–1792). In this contest, Cornwallis had the support of the two other strong country powers—the Marathas and the nizam of Hyderabad. Even after this war, which deprived Tipu of an immense treasure and half of his territory, there was some prospect that the company might be able to forego further territorial expansion. Many of the men most influential in directing policy sincerely wished the company to remain *primus inter pares*, holding the balance among the important country powers and acting, whenever necessary, in the name of a subservient and completely cowed Mogul emperor. The French Revolution, however, extinguished such hopes. Napoleon's Egyptian expedition of 1798 thrust India into the arena of world politics. In the person of the first Marquis Wellesley, governor general from 1798 to 1805, there came out to India a great proconsul who turned the company's ally, Nizam Ali, into a feudatory (1798); destroyed Tipu (Fourth Mysore War, 1799); took the first and most decisive steps in the conquest of the great Maratha chieftains; and paid no attention to the company's concern over its ever-mounting Indian rupee debt.

Meanwhile, British mercantile interests outside London, newly strengthened by the then imperfectly perceived consequences of the Industrial Revolution, were preparing for the final attack on the company's monopoly of the India trade. Although the true economic benefits to the British nation from the increasingly complex process of empire building in India at this period were in all probability of quite modest proportions, few contemporary Europeans doubted that they were enormous. Few of the merchants who so ably marshaled their influence in Parliament to open the trade with India to all British subjects in 1813 realized that the trade thus opened would soon differ profoundly from the India trade carried round the Cape of Good Hope since the days of Vasco da Gama. Nor did they realize that the new trade in which export of machine-made textiles and other consumers' goods was to be the dominant element would provide a far firmer base for empire than the old. Thus, as the company was ceasing to be a merchant in India and was concentrating its energies on the administration of its growing raj (Sanskrit *rājya*, rule), the machine had already begun the reduction of India's old handicraft industries to a shadow of their former selves. India, for centuries a workshop for Europe, was about to fall completely under the domination of the new workshop of the world. Nowhere was the peace of 1815 more of a *Pax Britannica* than in the lands bordering the Indian Ocean.

BRITISH RAJ, 1815–1885 . . . Political and Military History. —In considering the process by which the great bureaucratic Victorian Indian Empire was built, it is perhaps well to summarize the political and military history apart from other aspects of the story. After 1815 there was no turning back. As governor general succeeded governor general, the British color crept over the map—extinction of Maratha power under the first Marquis of Hastings (1813–1822) by 1820; conquest of Assam, Arakan, and Tenasserim (First Burmese War, 1824–1826), under Earl Amherst of Arakan (1823–1828); annexation of Coorg and strict control over many renowned and ancient Rajput houses under Lord William Cavendish Bentinck (1828–1835). With British power unchallenged from the Bay of Bengal to the eastern edge of the Indus basin, it was only natural that the prospect of Russian expansion to the confines of India should begin to agitate more and more British minds.

In 1838 there were inaugurated profitless and unhappy policies which, in aiming to secure Afghanistan from Russian penetration, brought in their train defeats, military and diplomatic, which helped prepare the way for the Indian Mutiny of 1857. In brief, without sufficient attention to the slender potentialities of Russian policy or power in this region, without constant and unremitting adaptation to the ever-changing military situation among Pathan tribesmen and along the Perso-Afghan frontier, an attempt was made in the First Afghan War (1838–1842) to thrust British power beyond the Indus in support of Shah Shuja (r. 1803–1810; d. 1842), an unpopular Afghan chieftain. The war was, moreover, undertaken before the Sikh power in the Punjab was itself subdued (1845–1849), such was the measure of British confidence in the invincibility of the Anglo-Indian military machine under the administration of George Eden, Earl of Auckland (1835–1841). There ensued the utter military defeat of 1842, when a faithful pony brought into Jalalabad the exhausted Dr. William Brydon as the sole survivor of an army of more than 4,000 troops and 12,000 camp followers which had sought safety by retreating through the passes from Kabul.

Although the conquest of Sind (1842–1844) and of the Punjab (1845–1849) were in a sense by-products of Afghan disaster, neither these operations nor the marching of armies back and forth in southern Afghanistan could obliterate the consequences of the ill-starred First Afghan War. The spell of British invincibility was broken. Afghanistan was evacuated. The raj had lost face at a time when the Indian masses were becoming dimly conscious of the impact of such new forces as the nonofficial European merchant and plantation owner, the Christian missionary, the steamship, the telegraph, and the railway. Moreover, James Ramsay, the first Marquis of Dalhousie (1848–1856), a young and masterful administrator, pressed on in the 1850's with a policy of annexing the territories of Indian princes who were either without heirs or peculiarly impervious to admonitions of reform from the company's government. This policy culminated in 1856 in the annexation of Oudh, perhaps the worst governed of the premier states, but the one from whose domains most of the sepoys in the Bengal Army were recruited.

Upon Lord Dalhousie's successor, Earl Canning (1856–1862), the storm burst on May 10, 1857. Vexed as are the problems of the origins of the Indian Mutiny, there is no question but that the decisive factor was the widespread belief that the cartridges issued with the new Enfield rifles were greased with animal fats abhorrent to both Moslems (Muslims) and Hindus. Careful study of the first weeks of the mutiny shows no widespread conspiracy, concerted planning, or well-thought-out objectives. This does not mean, however, that various native princes and influential landlords did not join the movement for political motives or that it did not evoke vague stirrings of national consciousness among some of those chiefly concerned. Nevertheless, it was primarily a military revolt of one of the company's three armies. The Bombay and Madras armies were unaffected, as was most of the subcontinent outside the regions near Delhi in which the fighting took place.

The mutiny was suppressed with great severity in 1857–1859. The heroic, moving tales of the blowing up of the Delhi magazine, of the siege of Cawnpore (now Kanpur), and of the relief of Lucknow, on which Rudyard Kipling's generation was reared, form only the more colorful side of the story. The mutiny left a legacy of bitterness which persisted for at least a generation, but, even more important, wherever it may not have fostered hatred, it fostered the type of aloofness in the ruling race which the increasing number of Western-educated Indians most resented. In government the mutiny caused the dissolution of the East India Company and brought British efforts to modernize and reform the great Indian princely states to an abrupt and unnatural halt. The India Act of 1858 transferred all the East India Company's authority to the crown and provided for the administration of India through a secretary of state for India in the British Cabinet.

With British dominance throughout the subcontinent assured after the suppression of the mutiny, the officials concerned with India's foreign policy became more preoccupied with the problem of the northwest frontier. Here the persuasiveness of the forward school and the belligerent imperialism of Benjamin Disraeli combined to produce a Second Afghan War (1878–1880) almost as inglorious as the first. The first Earl of Lytton (viceroy, 1876–1880), unable to readjust his Afghan policy quickly to Disraeli's diplomatic triumph over Russia at the Congress of Berlin, became involved in a war which did little to pacify the frontier, greatly increased the Indian debt, and left on the Afghan throne in Abd-er-Rahman (Abd-ur-Raḥmān) Khan (r. 1880–1901) a chief who had every reason to prefer Russian to English influence.

Social and Economic Developments.—In Lord Lytton's day the men who staffed the great bureaucracy which had been built up during the two previous generations were of a somewhat different stamp from those who had served Lord Hastings. In 1815 the company's patronage system was still vigorous and a young man's hopes of an Indian career depended upon his connections. In the next sixty years there occurred a gradual extension of the Indian services beyond the coterie of families connected with East India interests in the eighteenth century. Among such families, varying social backgrounds had been represented—chiefly London merchant and shipping families, lesser country gentry, and younger sons of Scottish nonnoble houses—but by the early nineteenth century all were characterized by close association with India and Indians. Furloughs in those days were infrequent, keeping a European wife and children in India was a hazardous venture, and it was difficult to cut oneself off from Indian life. By 1880 all this was profoundly changed. The introduction of competitive examinations for the Indian services in 1853 tended to confine them to the best brains of the English university world, a world which can hardly be described as other than socially select. Improvements in communications and sanitation made it possible for nearly all British officials to keep British wives and children in India. Inevitably, the European station with its club grew up beside the military cantonment, its life divorced from the surrounding Indian world.

Improvement in communications led to the perfection of the bureaucracy. The most remote post office came into immediate contact with headquarters. A subordinate army of Indian clerks and messengers was available to copy and move the mountains of official papers which made the wheels of government revolve. At the top stood the viceroy, struggling desperately not to be buried under the ponderous files, and unquestionably the most hard-worked official in her majesty's dominions. Disraeli's action in 1877 in making Queen Victoria empress of India was criticized as out of keeping with British tradition, but it effectively symbolized the transformation which had taken place in Indian government since the days when the East India Company had a personality of its own.

In 1833 began the social and educational changes which were to lead to the first meeting of an Indian National Congress in 1885. This was the time when the effects of the Reform Bill of 1832 and the reform and free trade movements in Britain began to be felt in India. The company lost its monopoly of the China trade and became merely a vehicle for governing India, dominated largely by men who had served in India. The home government, however, was controlled by Whig politicians immersed in the Reform Bill struggle who had little experience of India. It was hardly extraordinary that they should stand for an ever-wider extension of Christian missionary enterprise and the introduction of an educational policy favoring the teaching of English and the dissemination of European rather than Oriental learning. Missionary policy had long been settled on the understanding that the government would continue its policy of neutrality with respect to all religions. Active controversy in the early 1830's concerned educational policy. The older generation of company servants, who knew something of the values of Indian learning both ancient and modern, were no match for the brilliant Thomas Babington Macaulay, future historian of the English Revolution of 1688. Macaulay, who came out to make his fortune as the new law member of the governor general's council in 1834, wrote in February 1835 the famous minute which was decisive in determining the English character of higher education in India.

With respect to elementary education, decisive action was not taken until 1854, when the dispatch of Sir Charles Wood (later the first Viscount Halifax) declared that both English and vernacular languages should be used in diffusing European knowledge. The officials who drafted this dispatch, realizing the impossibility of securing enough persons qualified to teach English in the elementary schools, were inaugurating a policy of extensive government support to vernacular education for the masses. There had thus evolved by the postmutiny period the educational policy which was to become typical of modern India: stress on European learning, instruction in the vernacular at the elementary level, higher education on a British model, government grants-in-aid to all properly managed schools willing to accept government inspection, and equal treatment of each school accepting the conditions, irrespective of communal or other affiliations.

By 1885 civil and military government servants, businessmen, missionaries, and schoolmasters had built in India an empire very different from that over which the East India Company had presided. In 1815 the company's domain was still a country power, pre-eminent among country powers, and ruled by men whose outlook was often as much Indian as British. Most of these men believed in a policy of noninterference with Indian life and society and in limiting India's contacts with Europe to those arising from the commercial and administrative activities which ensured their own well-being. In 1885 India had become the greatest modern colony, a vast domain ruled by a *corps d'élite* sent out for that purpose by an alien European power.

INDIAN NATIONAL DEVELOPMENT, 1885–1947 . . . Although one or more Indian nationalist bodies met annually from 1885, the general history of India and the histories of Indian nationalist movements were not closely intertwined until after World War I. The Victorian bureaucratic machine moved ponderously on, paying hardly any heed to nationalist agitation except when moved to action by some overt act. Liberal-minded viceroys like George Frederick Robinson, the first Marquis of Ripon (1880–1884), were the exception, not the rule. The raj occupied itself with the perfection of antifamine programs, with army unification (1893), and with irrigation schemes. British rule was assumed to be permanent. The storm raised by Lord

Ripon's attempt to deprive Europeans of their privilege of being tried always before European judges (Ilbert Bill) enjoined a continued policy of caution as far as Indianization of the civil services was concerned. Nevertheless, Indianization was begun on a modest scale, and was accepted as an inevitable goal of future policy. Before 1906, however, there was no serious consideration of extending self-government beyond very modest dimensions.

In the first Marquis Curzon of Kedleston (1899–1905), India received a proconsul of Wellesleyan stature exactly a century after Wellesley. Though not a century behind the times, Curzon was peculiarly blind to Indian sensibilities. His partition of Bengal into two provinces, made in the interests of bureaucratic efficiency, exasperated the rapidly increasing number of politically conscious Indians both within and outside Bengal. This action was perhaps the most important single factor which ushered in the period when peaceful nationalist agitation was occasionally embarrassed by the commission of political crimes of various sorts. It was greatly to the credit of the philosophic Liberal, Viscount Morley of Blackburn, who became secretary of state for India in 1905, that he did not allow himself to be diverted by sporadic acts of violence from his plans for drastic Indian political reform.

Lord Curzon's departure, hastened by his dispute with the first Earl Kitchener of Khartoum over the latter's proper functions as commander in chief in India (1902–1909), prepared the way for the first major step toward Indian self-government. The Morley-Minto reforms (Indian Councils Act) of 1909 introduced the elective principle for some seats in the governor general's Legislative Council and greatly increased the elective element in the provincial legislative councils. All this, however, was done on a basis of representing various communities, chambers of commerce, and other similar groups. In accordance with this principle, Moslems, who had sent a special deputation, led by the Aga Khan, to the viceroy, Gilbert Elliot-Murray-Kynynmond, the fourth Earl Minto (1905–1910), in 1906, received separate representation. This granting of separate electorates to minorities, though later vehemently criticized by Indian nationalists, was quite in keeping with the most advanced and liberal British thought of the day with respect to broadening the base of Indian government. Nearly every Briton who studied the subject intimately at that time held that the British parliamentary system was entirely unsuited to Indian conditions. Not only was anything like universal suffrage for India regarded as unthinkable, but everyone assumed that the problem was to give the intellectuals and the propertied and influential segments of Indian communities a feeling that they had a share in the government of their country.

Consequently, by 1910 the autocratic nature of Indian government was hardly changed at all. The Morley-Minto reforms, however, did have the effect of causing many of the intellectual moderates prominent in nationalist bodies to feel that they had not labored in vain. Psychologically, the appointment of one distinguished Indian to the governor general's Executive Council, coupled with the association of many others in the high administrative and legislative spheres, marked a sharp break with the Victorian past. For this the Indian National Congress was largely responsible. It had met annually since 1885, when Allan Octavian Hume, a retired civil servant, and a few of his friends assembled about a hundred people in Bombay with the benevolent acquiescence of the government. Year by year the organization had grown. Europeans, Parsis, and Moslems were prominent in it from its earliest years, but inevitably the majority of its members were Hindus, among whom lawyers from Calcutta and Bombay predominated. Its continued existence and the success it achieved in bringing pressure to bear upon the government caused Moslem religious leaders and landlords to realize how far the Moslem community had lagged behind the

Hindu in producing an English-educated minority eligible for high government posts. The Moslem League was therefore formed in 1906.

The success of the great imperial durbar (*darbār*) of 1911, when the capital was moved to Delhi and the partition of Bengal was reversed, on the occasion of the coronation of King George V, was in itself a testimony to the strength of the British raj. All that nascent nationalism had accomplished was to associate with durbar government a handful of distinguished Indians, most of whom were out of sympathy with the National Congress. In Gopal Krishna Gokhale and Bal Gangadhar Tilak, Indian nationalism had produced its first great figures, the one a moderate, the other an extremist who was thought of as the inspiration of the increasing number of political assassinations. In 1913, however, the raj seemed more stable than ever and would doubtless have been capable of resisting change for many years had it not been for World War I.

World War I profoundly disturbed the placid currents of Indian political and administrative life. Not only did Indian troops fight in France and the Middle East, but the best of the British civil and military administrators were drawn away from India. Nationalists had a practical demonstration of the ability of Indian government to function without the accustomed quota of British personnel. When it appeared toward the end of the war that British officialdom was intent on returning to the old order of things, great resentment and frustration spread over India. Racial bitterness reached a climax with the Amritsar massacre of 1919, when General Reginald Dyer ordered troops to fire on an unarmed mass meeting in an enclosure with only one very narrow exit. Nearly all politically conscious Indians felt that India's great efforts in the war had been betrayed, and that the Montagu-Chelmsford reforms (named for Edwin Montagu, secretary of state for India, and Frederic Napier Thesiger, the first Viscount Chelmsford, viceroy 1916–1921), then being framed into the Government of India Act (1919), were very inadequate as an implementation of the solemn British wartime promise (August 20, 1917) of ". . . the gradual development of self-governing institutions with a view to the progressive realization of responsible government in India as an integral part of the British Empire. . . ."

Nevertheless, the Montagu-Chelmsford reforms of 1919 definitely broke with the idea that India must follow some other path than that leading toward parliamentary self-government. The reasons for this change are complex, but it was a natural consequence of the attainment of a separate international position by the British self-governing Dominions during the war and at the peace conference. India, despite her juridically dependent status, could hardly be denied many of the privileges accorded to the Dominions, notably the privilege of signing the peace treaty separately and of becoming in her own right a separate member of the League of Nations. She was also accorded much more independence in fiscal policy than had been customary before the war. Moreover, the phrase "responsible government" used in the declaration of 1917 was, in view of its history in the Dominions, generally interpreted as meaning responsible cabinet government of the British parliamentary type.

The Montagu-Chelmsford reforms set the pattern which was to determine the actual administration of India from 1919 until the eve of independence. The central government at New Delhi underwent almost no change between 1919 and 1946; the system by which the British crown's paramountcy over Indian princely states was exercised changed slightly in form but not in substance. In the provinces, there was change: full autonomy on April 1, 1937 (when the Government of India Act of 1935 went into effect) replaced the partial autonomy granted in 1919, but World War II supervened so quickly that full provincial autonomy was to a large extent stillborn. In brief, what the Montagu-Chelmsford reforms did at the center was to set up a bicameral legislature—the upper house (Council of State) chosen by an electorate of approximately 80,000 and the lower (Legislative Assembly) by an electorate of approximately 1,000,000 (registration, about 5,000,000). Nominated members were still an important element in both houses; in choosing elected members communal electorates were used extensively. Legally, the executive remained authoritarian and bureaucratic, not responsible to the legislature and buttressed by extensive emergency powers. Practically, the central legislature was a fairly effective forum for the ventilation of grievances, accomplished much useful work, and, paradoxically, despite its powerlessness attracted some of the ablest Indian politicians, especially at times when nationalists were not boycotting the government and refusing to take their seats. In the provinces, the reforms introduced dyarchy—that is, the turning over of certain departments, such as those dealing with education and other "safe" subjects, to Indian ministers responsible to majorities in the lower houses of the provincial legislatures. Naturally, the system did not work well. The India Act of 1935 granted full provincial autonomy and expanded the provincial electorates to cover approximately 33,000,000 voters, but provincial governors retained ample emergency powers, including that of assuming full powers of administration in the event of political deadlock.

Within a decade after the end of World War I serious Hindu-Moslem differences in the nationalist movement began to appear. Among the causes for the disappearance of the earlier atmosphere of harmony, dating back to 1916 when the Congress had reluctantly acquiesced in the existence of Moslem electorates, must be listed the new revolutionary fervor imparted to the Congress movement by Mohandas K. Gandhi; the fiasco of the caliphate agitation (protest by Indian Moslems against the Treaty of Sèvres) of 1920–1922; Mohammed Ali Jinnah's emergence to leadership among the Moslems in contrast to Gandhi, as leader in the Congress; and increasing fear among Moslems of Hindu domination of any centralized parliamentary government. In his philosophical nonviolence, Gandhi developed a technique difficult for Moslems to understand and he further baffled Moslem nationalists by calling off a civil disobedience movement, because of outbreaks of violence (at Chauri Chaura), in 1922 when it seemed to be succeeding. At the time of the caliphate agitation, Mustafa Kemal (later Kemal Atatürk), by setting up a nonreligious Turkish state, and the Moplas (Moplahs, Moslem peasants of Malabar), by killing Hindus in southern India, greatly embarrassed the Moslems and Hindus who were attempting to mitigate the terms of the Treaty of Sèvres. As Gandhi developed the peculiar religious quality of his hold over the Indian masses, it was natural that Moslems, especially those of the more conservative and less revolutionary types, should turn to Jinnah or to other Moslem leaders.

The immediate occasion, however, of serious Hindu-Moslem rift was the Nehru report of the Indian National Congress of 1928, resulting from the challenge of British conservatives that Indians had many criticisms of the existing government but were never willing to draw a blueprint for a new one. Under the chairmanship of Pandit Motilal Nehru, a distinguished committee drew up a constitution for India on a dominion-status basis. Since it was not a federal constitution and made no concessions to Moslem susceptibilities, Moslem opinion was alienated. An all-India Moslem conference gathered at Delhi under the aegis of the Aga Khan. Representatives of the Moslem League, now solidly behind Jinnah, and of nearly all other Moslem organizations, proclaimed in 1929 the Moslem fourteen points, which insisted on separate Moslem electorates, a federal government with residual powers in the provinces, a three-fourths majority rule in legislatures on all communal questions, and appropriate Moslem representation in both provincial and federal cabinets.

During the decade 1929–1939, the Moslem-Hindu rift steadily widened. Each of the great parties—the Congress and the

Moslem League—perfected its organization under its own high command and gradually reduced to insignificance the smaller nationalist organizations, whether moderate, such as the liberals led by distinguished Indians who tried to find a compromise in a nonrevolutionary program, or extremists, such as the Hindu Mahasabha, which desired a Hindu raj. Henceforth the communal question was in the forefront of all Indo-British political discussion.

British officialdom, realizing the futility of a further approach through an all-British parliamentary commission, assembled the leading Indian princes and political leaders in London in 1930–1932 for three round-table conferences after publication of the report of the Simon Commission (named for Sir John Simon, later Viscount Simon). Gandhi, who had in the spring of 1930 dramatized the Congress struggle by a no-rent campaign and by a march to the sea against the government salt monopoly, was persuaded to make an appearance at the second conference. Nothing, however, could break the communal deadlock. Prime Minister Ramsay MacDonald found himself compelled, much against his will, to authorize a British communal award, allocating seats to the different Indian communities in the legislatures of the proposed new federal Indian constitution.

Six years of discussion (1929–1935) at last produced in the India Act of 1935 a new Indian constitution. Nothing, however, could get the federation, so laboriously worked out on paper, into being. The princes, at first willing to accede to the federation, shied off in such numbers that the federal part of the act remained a dead letter. The Congress Party, which had always inveighed against the scheme as being too heavily weighted in the princes' favor, was not loath to see it die. The Moslem League, with its fears of a Hindu raj, was also not displeased with the result. Thenceforth, the political struggle shifted to the provinces, where, under the act, full autonomy was to be tested for the first time. Following much searching of heart, the Congress

Party decided upon a policy of accepting office in the provinces after receiving assurance that the governors' special powers would not be frequently or unreasonably used.

Soon after the act of 1935 went into effect (April 1, 1937), Congress ministries took office in seven of the eleven provinces of British India, all of them Hindu-majority provinces except the North-West Frontier Province, where Khan Abdul Gaffar Khan, the "Frontier Gandhi," and other Congress Moslems had built up a strong following. (Later a Congress ministry also took office in Assam.) During the ensuing two prewar years, the Moslem League accused the Congress of establishing Hindu tyrannies in the six Hindu-majority provinces (Madras, Bombay, United Provinces, Bihar, Orissa, Central Provinces) which denied Moslems their legitimate rights, especially in educational and cultural matters, and precluded the possibility of their ever wielding any political influence in these provinces. On its side, the Congress Party insisted that it did endeavor to give Moslem interests their due weight and that the Moslem League distorted every Moslem grievance for propaganda purposes.

World War II thus found the two great Indian communities more deeply divided than ever. The Congress Party proclaimed itself a noncommunal organization striving to achieve India's freedom through nonviolent revolution. The Moslem League frankly professed its communalism and sought support as a protector of 94 million Indian Moslems (1941 census) against the prospect of Hindu domination. Such was the situation when the Congress Party leaders ordered all the Congress ministries out of office in October 1939 on the ground that they could not participate in an imperialist war thrust upon India without her consent. This course naturally had the effect of placing the Moslem League in a stronger position than the Congress during the war. When much of Indian political life was necessarily suspended, whether or not wartime emergency measures were in force, Jinnah and other Moslem leaders were out of jail and free to develop for propaganda purposes the plan for a separate Moslem state called Pakistan, first suggested in 1933 by some Moslem students at Cambridge University. In 1940 the League adopted its famous resolution that "the areas in which the Moslems are numerically in a majority, as in the northwestern and eastern zones of India, should be grouped to constitute independent states in which the constituent units shall be autonomous and sovereign."

In March 1942, at a very dark period of the war, Prime Minister Winston Churchill's coalition government sent Sir Stafford Cripps to India with an offer which has since been the occasion of much controversy. Its main purpose was to gain the cooperation of both the Congress and the League with the existing government by transferring to Indians on a *de facto* basis all power save that of the command of military operations and by emphasizing dominion status with consequent option of secession from the British Commonwealth as the immediate postwar British program. Negotiations broke down mainly as a consequence of the difficulties inherent in the plan for ensuring effective British control of military operations. In the postwar part of the offer, however, the prospect of partition was hinted at in the provisions whereby dissatisfied provinces could stay out of the proposed union and form a union of their own on a dominion-status basis. The Congress Party therefore publicly condemned the offer for too great indulgence toward the Pakistan idea, while the Moslem League condemned it for precisely the contrary reason.

In the Quit-India campaign which followed the rejection of the Cripps offer, Gandhi, Jawaharlal Nehru (who had long been recognized as the nationalist figure next in importance to Gandhi), and all the other Congress leaders were arrested along with several thousands of their followers in August 1942. Each side accused the other of precipitate action; the viceroy Victor Alexander Hope, second Marquis of Linlithgow (1936–1943), insisted that widespread violence was planned, while Gandhi insisted that his arrest precipitated the violence. While Indian troops and resources made their contribution to victory and bureaucratic government prevailed not only in New Delhi but in most of the provinces, all political progress was at a standstill. Despite Gandhi's release on medical grounds in May 1944, the deadlock continued until, with the assurance of victory in Europe, more and more of the Congress leaders were freed in the first half of 1945. Gandhi's conversations with Jinnah in September 1944 had frustrated the hopes of those who believed that the two men could agree on some formula that would reconcile their differences on the Pakistan issue.

While the first Earl Wavell, viceroy from 1943 to 1947, was releasing political prisoners, planning to broaden the Executive Council, and preparing for the new elections scheduled for the winter of 1945–1946, the whole scene was changed by the overwhelming victory of the Labour Party in Britain in July 1945. The election tended to remove the Indian nationalists' reluctance to believe that Britain was really determined on a full transfer of power untinged by imperialism. Within ten months, a conference attended by all political leaders was held at Simla in an unsuccessful effort to set up an interim national government (June 1945); new elections were held (in the winter of 1945–1946); and a British Cabinet mission came out of India to form a plan of breaking the Congress-League impasse (March 1946).

The Cabinet mission's scheme, announced in a white paper on May 16, 1946, endeavored to keep India united while permitting Moslem-majority provinces to group themselves together with a great deal of autonomy. It set up a feasible procedure for the election of a Constituent Assembly by the 1,585 newly chosen (January–April 1946) members of the provincial legislatures, with ninety-three seats to be awarded to nominees of the princely states. Moreover, it gave assurance for the first time of

Britain's readiness to abandon paramountcy over all the princely states. Neither Congress nor the Moslem League felt it wise to refrain from ultimate acceptance of the plan, but before the summer was out both parties were engaged in a dispute as to various points of interpretation. In September, Lord Wavell brought matters to a head by allowing a newly appointed Executive Council to function as an interim government led by Jawaharlal Nehru. This speedily caused the Moslem League leaders to review their decision and brought about an agreement to enter the government despite nonrecognition of the League's contention that it was the only body representing Indian Moslems. For a fleeting moment foreign observers thought a Hindu-Moslem accord would be reached, but it soon appeared that the government seldom if ever functioned normally. Ministers of the opposing groups seldom met face to face and most Cabinet business was done by correspondence. Moreover, the Moslem League let it be known that League members elected to the Constituent Assembly would not take their seats.

This situation remained virtually unaltered in December 1946 after Lord Wavell had succeeded in inducing Nehru and Jinnah to fly to London for conferences on the clarification of the Cabinet mission's plan. When such clarification had accomplished nothing in making the interim government workable, the British government decided (February 1947) to replace Lord Wavell with the first Earl Mountbatten of Burma and to announce that Britain would withdraw from India by June 1948 in any event, transferring power preferably to one government, but not hesitating to transfer it to more than one government if such action proved unavoidable. This fateful announcement caused intense political activity behind the scenes at both London and New Delhi. On June 3, 1947, came the announcement of the plan for the partition of India into two independent dominions—India and Pakistan. The Indian princely states, no longer under British suzerainty, would be left free to accede to either dominion or not, as they chose. Both the Congress and the Moslem League accepted the plan.

An Indian Independence Act was passed through the British Parliament with very little debate in July, and on the appointed day, August 15, 1947, the British Indian Empire ceased to be. In its stead, after great communal disturbances in the Punjab and Bengal, which took a toll of many thousands of casualties and involved the migration of at least six million people, there appeared two new nations, the one, India, covering most of peninsular India, since nearly all the princely states fell within its orbit; the other, Pakistan, with its 70,000,000 population (1947), the most populous Moslem state in the world, composed of two disparate blocs of territory—in the northwest, Baluchistan, Sind, the North-West Frontier Province, and the western Punjab up to a line drawn just east of Lahore; in the northeast, the Moslem-majority districts in eastern Bengal and the Sylhet district of Assam. Despite the continued membership of both countries in the Commonwealth of Nations, all politically conscious Indians hailed the end of the era of European rule which had so imperceptibly begun two centuries before.

BIBLIOGRAPHY

Muir, Ramsay, *The Making of British India, 1756–1858* (New York, 1915).

Dodwell, H. H., ed., *The Cambridge Shorter History of India* (New York, 1934).

Thompson, E. J., and Garratt, G. T., *The Rise and Fulfilment of British Rule in India* (London, 1934).

Andrews, C. F., and Mukerji, Girija, *The Rise and Growth of the Congress in India* (London, 1938).

Rawlinson, H. G., *India: A Cultural History* (New York, 1938).

Brailsford, H. N., *Subject India* (New York, 1943).

Moon, Penderel, *Strangers in India* (New York, 1945).

Moreland, W. H., and Chatterjee, A. C., *A Short History of India*, 2d ed. (New York, 1945).

INDIA, PAKISTAN, CEYLON

Coupland, Sir Reginald, *India: A Restatement* (New York, 1946).
Majumdar, R. C., Raychaudhuri, H. C., and Datta, Kalikinkar, *An Advanced History of India* (New York, 1946).
Nehru, Jawaharlal, *The Discovery of India* (New York, 1946).
Smith, W. C., *Modern Islam in India,* rev. ed. (London, 1947).

CHAPTER XIV BY HOLDEN FURBER

India and Pakistan, 1947-1950

INDIA

THE larger of the two dominions into which the former British Indian Empire was divided on August 15, 1947, was called the Union of India. Its status was changed to that of a republic on January 26, 1950, when a constitution, drawn up by an indirectly elected Constituent Assembly and adopted on November 26, 1949, was formally introduced. The seat of government is at Delhi, which has a population (1941 census) of 521,849. The total area of the territory claimed by the Union of India is 1,221,-880 square miles (the status of some of this area is disputed by Pakistan), and the population, as estimated in 1951, is 347,340,-000, giving a density of 260 to the square mile. The country has a railroad system of about 33,984 miles. The principal ports are Calcutta (1941 population, including Howrah, 2,488,183), Bombay (1,489,883), Madras (777,481), and Cochin (26,320). The largest inland cities, with their 1941 populations, are Hyderabad (739,159), Ahmadabad (Ahmedabad, 591,267), and Kanpur (Cawnpore, 487,324).

The Union of India includes the following political divisions:

(1) nine states which until August 15, 1947, constituted, in whole or in part, provinces of British India, and with which have been merged a number of minor princely states: Assam, Bihar, Bombay, Madhya Pradesh (formerly Central Provinces and Berar), Madras, Orissa, Punjab (East Punjab), Uttar Pradesh (formerly United Provinces), and (West) Bengal (including Cooch-Behar); (2) eight states formed of former major princely states or of unions of states: Hyderabad, Jammu and Kashmir (status disputed by Pakistan), Madhya Bharat, Mysore, Patiala and East Punjab States Union, Rajasthan, Saurashtra, and Travancore-Cochin; (3) ten states of lesser size and rights formed of former lesser princely states or unions, or chief commissioner's provinces of British India: Ajmer (formerly Ajmer-Merwara), Bhopal, Bilaspur, Coorg, Delhi, Himachal Pradesh, Kutch (Cutch), Manipur, Tripura, and Vindhya Pradesh; and (4) the Andaman and Nicobar Islands.

The unit of currency is the rupee, divided into sixteen annas; as of June 1950 it was valued at twenty-one cents in United States money. The flag has three horizontal stripes of equal width, the top saffron, the middle white, and the bottom dark green. In the center of the white stripe is Aśoka's wheel. The coat of arms, derived from a pillar erected by Aśoka at Sarnath near Banaras (Benares), also shows the wheel.

GOVERNMENT (AUGUST 15, 1947—JANUARY 26, 1950) . . . The Indian Independence Act, passed by the British Parliament in July 1947, provided for the setting up in India of two independent dominions—India and Pakistan—effective from August 15, 1947, and announced that the paramountcy hitherto exercised by the British crown over the Indian princely states lapsed as of that date. When boundaries had been fixed, the Dominion of India consisted of: (1) six governors' provinces with boundaries unchanged—Madras, Bombay, Central Provinces and Berar, Uttar Pradesh, Bihar, and Orissa; (2) three governors' provinces formed as a consequence of dividing predominantly Moslem from predominantly non-Moslem areas—(East) Punjab, (West) Bengal, and Assam (without the Moslem-majority district of Sylhet); (3) areas administered directly by the central government through chief commissioners—Delhi, Ajmer-Merwara, Coorg, Panth Piploda, and the Andaman and Nicobar Islands; and (4) such princely states as acceded to the Dominion. By 1949 the process of accession within the orbit of India as distinct from Pakistan could be said to be complete, the only unsettled issue being the future of Kashmir.

In form, the government of the Dominion of India resembled that of the other dominions of the Commonwealth of Nations. The governor general (the first Earl Mountbatten of Burma, until June 1948; Chakravarti Rajagopalachari, from June 1948 to formal application of the new constitution on January 26, 1950) was appointed by the king on the advice of the Indian Cabinet led by Pandit Jawaharlal Nehru, which was responsible to a majority of the Constituent Assembly acting as an interim central legislature. In practice, all Indian politicians and officials realized that the situation was exceptional. Lord Mountbatten, in the first months of transition from the old order to the new, could not possibly confine his role entirely to that of a ceremonial head of state, nor could the Constituent Assembly, admittedly an interim body, possess all the attributes of a normally elected parliament.

The machinery set up by the British Parliament in the India Act of 1935 lay ready to hand for the purpose of effecting the transition to independence with a minimum of disturbance of administrative and legal functions. The Indian Independence Act gave an Indian executive the power to adapt the 1935 act to the new situation by the simple process of order in council. Pandit Nehru and his colleagues were thus able to bring to life the federal portion of the 1935 act, which had lain in abeyance, and to use the procedure for princely accession provided in that act as a framework within which to develop their own policy for the integration of former princely India with former British India. Consequently, the federal, provincial, and concurrent lists in the act of 1935 were the basis for determining which legislative subjects fell to the Constituent Assembly as an interim central legislature, which remained to the provincial legislatures of the nine governors' provinces, and which were shared between them.

The whole structure of provincial government, in which full responsible cabinet government had been inaugurated on April 1, 1937, remained virtually unimpaired. The provincial legislatures, newly elected in the winter of 1945–1946, continued as before; in cases in which a former historic province was partitioned, as in the Punjab, the members for the districts within the new India became the legislature of the new province. In a few cases, British officials were permitted to remain as governors for many months; in others, Indians were immediately appointed. Provincial legislatures were the popular base on which the new Dominion of India might be said to rest during the interim period. It was the members of these legislatures who elected the majority of the Constituent Assembly in which all *de facto* power actually resided. In February 1949, the Constituent Assembly contained 235 members so elected, plus 68 chosen by the governments of princely states, making a total of 303. The effect of all these measures was to give the leaders of the Indian Congress Party an administrative machine able to cope with the vast problems of partition without being unduly preoccupied with questions as to the constitutionality of its procedure or the legal validity of its acts.

By assigning the task of constitution making to a distinguished drafting committee, the Constituent Assembly during 1947–1948 was able to devote its almost undivided attention to its work as an interim legislature. Meanwhile, the new Dominion's Ministry of States and Home Affairs, under Nehru's second-in-command, the late Sardar Vallabhbhai Patel, attacked the main problem which could simplify the work of constitution framing. Three methods were used to substitute, for the jumble of more than 500 princely states which acceded to India, a small group of administrative units comparable to governor's provinces and capable of becoming along with them the states of a new republic of India. Most of the smaller nonviable princely states were merged with adjacent provinces. These lost their administrative identity and their rulers accepted pensions on varying terms. Many middle-sized and large states were grouped into administrative unions, each of sufficient stature to be a state of the future republic. In these cases, new regimes based on responsible cabinet government were introduced; the chief prince became a rajpramukh, or the executive head of the union, and had a fixed privy purse; the other princes of the union retained a position of dignity within their own states but were virtual pensioners. In some instances it was planned to rotate the office of rajpramukh among a group of princes. The relationship of these new princely unions to the new government of India was governed by instruments of accession which gave the central government as much power over them as it exercised over the governors' provinces. Finally, a group of former Punjab hill states were merged into a union and placed directly under the central government; that is, they were put on an equal footing with such centrally administered areas as Delhi or Coorg and were not thought of as areas capable of possessing any states' rights within the future republic.

By 1949, when these processes were completed, there were only a handful of former princely states retaining separate administrative identities. Of these, Hyderabad and Kashmir were special cases. Hyderabad, the largest Indian state, refused to accede to either dominion and was the scene of disturbances which led to Indian military occupation in September 1948. In Kashmir, when the truce agreement between India and Pakistan took effect on January 1, 1949, the capital, Srinagar, and adjacent regions recognized the authority of the government acting in the name of the maharaja, who had acceded to India in 1947; the western and northwestern portions of the region were under the so-called "Azad (Free) Kashmir" government sponsored and militarily supported by Pakistan. In December 1948, Mysore, Travancore, Bhopal, and Cochin were the only other major states left unaffected by the integration program of the Ministry of States and Home Affairs. In April 1949, Cochin was merged with Travancore and Bhopal's administration was taken over by the central government. The constituent units of the new Indian republic became the nine former governors' provinces plus a half dozen princely unions and three individual princely states: Hyderabad, Mysore, and Kashmir.

It was also decided in April 1949 that the new Indian republic would remain associated with the British Commonwealth. The Constituent Assembly approved the following declaration issued as a consequence of the meeting in London of the Commonwealth prime ministers:

> . . . The Government of India have informed the other Governments of the Commonwealth of the intention of the Indian people that under the new constitution which is about to be adopted India shall become a sovereign independent republic. The government of India have, however, declared and affirmed India's desire to continue her full membership of the Commonwealth of Nations and her acceptance of the King as the symbol of the free association of its independent member nations and as such the Head of the Commonwealth.
>
> The Governments of the other countries of the Commonwealth, the basis of whose membership of the Commonwealth is not hereby changed, accept and recognize India's continuing membership in accordance with the terms of this declaration.
>
> Accordingly, The United Kingdom, Canada, Australia, New Zealand, South Africa, India, Pakistan, and Ceylon hereby declare that they remain united as free and equal members of the Commonwealth

of Nations, freely cooperating in the pursuit of peace, liberty, and progress.

This meant, in effect, that India would continue to take her full share in intra-Commonwealth consultations with respect to defense, finance, and other economic and political matters and that her citizens would not be foreigners in other Commonwealth countries. Her position would differ from that of the others only in the republican form of government and absence of formal allegiance to the king as the sovereign in whose name all governmental acts are performed.

The Constituent Assembly, which began debate on the draft of a republican constitution in November 1948, completed discussion and amendment of the draft a year later. The new republican constitution took effect on January 26, 1950, but the Constituent Assembly remained as an interim legislature until elections could be held throughout India on a basis of adult suffrage.

CONSTITUTION OF THE REPUBLIC OF INDIA . . . Form of Government.—India is a sovereign democratic republic and a union of states. The term state is broadly defined: it is applied to all centrally administered areas except the Andaman and Nicobar Islands as well as to former governors' provinces of British India, former Indian princely states, and new unions of such princely states. Centrally administered areas, though called states, possess no states' rights whatever. The structure of the government is federal, but its spirit is unitary. The states which do possess any degree of states' rights have very limited powers as compared with the states composing such other federal unions as the United States of America, Canada, and Australia. As in Canada, residual power rests expressly in the central government. For the sake of clarity, the term state is not here used to refer to any centrally administered area.

Central Government.—EXECUTIVE: All executive action is

taken in the name of a president who is a ceremonial head of state acting on the advice of ministers responsible to a majority in the lower house of the central legislature. The president is a citizen over thirty-five years of age elected for a five-year term; he may be re-elected. He is chosen by an electoral college formed of the elected members of both houses of the central legislature and of the elected members of the legislatures of the states. Each member of the college casts a large number of votes, the exact number being determined by an elaborate method of calculation based on census figures for the population of each state. The problem of succession in the event of the president's death or disability is handled by the provision for a special presidential election within six months thereafter. A vice president, elected at a joint sitting of both houses of the central legislature, presides over the upper house; he acts as president only during the short interval prior to the special election. The provisions concerning the Cabinet introduce no novelty into the normally accepted conventions of the British cabinet system except for the provision of a professional attorney general, a portfolio obviously intended for an eminent lawyer whose tenure need not be affected by the vicissitudes of parliamentary politics.

LEGISLATIVE: The central legislature consists of 750 members, 500 in a lower house called the House of the People, and 250 in an upper house called the Council of States. The 500 members of the House of the People are chosen by universal adult suffrage in such a way that there is not less than one member for every 750,000 persons, or more than one for every 500,000. The lower house is subject to dissolution in accordance with usual British practice; it is considered dissolved at the expiration of five years unless a proclamation of emergency is then in force. A Cabinet minister may not hold his post more than six months without a seat in either house. He may speak, but not vote, in the house of which he is not a member. Of the 250 members of the upper house, twelve are eminent citizens appointed by the president because of their achievements in literature, art, science, and other fields. The other members are elected by the elected members of the lower houses of the state legislatures according to a scheme based on population which restricts the princely states to less than 40 per cent of the seats. The upper house is not subject to dissolution, but the terms of the members are so arranged that one third expire every two years. Provisions for a joint sitting of both houses obviate the possibility of legislative deadlock.

JUDICIARY: There is one national judiciary depending on appointment by the central government and protected by the usual safeguards which ensure the independence of judges in Great Britain. Salaries cannot be reduced. Removal cannot be effected except by an address voted by two thirds of both houses of the central legislature on the grounds of proved misbehavior or incapacity. The Supreme Court of seven justices is the guardian and interpreter of the constitution. There is no limitation on the power of the central legislature to increase the number of Supreme Court justices.

State Governments.—EXECUTIVE: In states formerly governors' provinces of British India, the governor is appointed by the president (that is, by the national Cabinet). The governor's dependence on the central government is designed to be close and intimate. He is not merely a ceremonial head of state who acts always on the advice of a state cabinet responsible to a majority of the lower house of the state legislature. There is provision made for such a cabinet, but the governor has power to reserve bills for the president's consideration and is given authority to act in his discretion to a considerable extent.

In states formerly Indian states or unions of such princely states, the prince serving as rajpramukh is executive head of the government of the state. Because of his hereditary position and the financial guarantees given to him by the terms of the relevant instrument of accession, his constitutional position is not precisely the same as that of a governor of a state which was formerly a governor's province of British India. Responsible cabinet government, however, is established in these states and their position vis-à-vis the central government is intended to be in nearly all respects the same as that of the former governors' provinces.

LEGISLATIVE: The state legislative structure may be bicameral or unicameral. All state legislatures, with the concurrence of a majority of the central legislature, may decide to change from a bicameral to a unicameral system or vice versa. The powers exclusively within the state legislative sphere are limited to such matters as education, public order, and police. State legislatures would, however, exercise in practice many of the powers listed on the concurrent list of powers shared with the central legislature, such as criminal and civil procedure, marriage and divorce, probate, trusts, and contracts. It was expected that state legislatures deriving from the former legislative councils in certain princely states would exercise in practice greater powers than other legislatures.

JUDICIARY: There is no state judiciary.

Bill of Rights.—The list of fundamental rights enforceable in the courts is comprehensive and follows a United States, rather than a British, model. Its most significant provisions may be summarized as follows. No titles may be conferred. "No person shall be deprived of his life or personal liberty except according to procedure established by law." There are specific provisions against double jeopardy, *ex post facto* laws, and bearing witness against oneself. The prohibition of untouchability is absolute. No citizen on grounds only of religion, race, caste, or sex may be denied access to stores, hotels, restaurants, and places of public entertainment or to any well, tank, road, or place of public resort supported wholly or in part by public funds. Freedom of worship and equality of treatment of all religions by the state is provided for, but the state may regulate any "economic, financial, political, or other secular activity" associated with religious practice and may effect social welfare or reform by such measures as the opening of Hindu religious institutions of a public character to any class or section of Hindus. Citizens may assemble peaceably and without arms. The right of freedom of speech is qualified by the government's right to make any law relating to matter which "offends against decency or morality or which undermines the security of or tends to overthrow the state." The central legislature may by law prescribe the circumstances under which, and the class or classes of cases in which, a person may be detained for a period longer than three months under any law providing for preventive detention.

Citizenship.—The central legislature possesses full powers with respect to all matters concerning citizenship. Pending exercise of such powers, the following are citizens:

(1) Persons of Indian domicile born in India (or either of whose parents were born in India) or with five years' residence in India.

(2) Refugees from Pakistan who have entered India before July 19, 1948, and who have remained there and who were born in (or any of whose parents or grandparents were born in) the former British Indian Empire.

(3) Refugees from Pakistan who have entered India after July 19, 1948, and have registered with the authorities after six months' residence in India.

(4) Persons who were born in (or any of whose parents or grandparents were born in) the former British Indian Empire, but who are ordinarily residing abroad may be registered as citizens of India on application to the appropriate consular or diplomatic representative of India, but no person who has voluntarily acquired citizenship of a foreign state shall be a citizen of India, and no person who migrated to Pakistan after March 1, 1947, and remained there shall be a citizen of India.

Amendment.—The following matters are protected against

hasty constitutional amendment: (1) the allocation of legislative powers between the Union and the states; (2) the representation of the states in the central legislature; (3) the powers of the Supreme Court and the high courts; and (4) the rules for amending the constitution. An amendment touching these matters must be ratified by one half of the states, as well as by the central legislature (a majority of the total membership in each house and a majority of at least two thirds of members present and voting being necessary for ratification). Amendments touching other matters may be effected by the central legislature voting as described above.

Emergency Provisions.—Faced with war or domestic violence (actual or potential), the president may issue a proclamation of emergency which enters into force at once but must be laid before the central legislature within two months. The central legislature may by resolution of both houses extend the period of emergency beyond the period of two months. While such a proclamation is in force, the central government may exert any degree of control over state governments, and the guarantees to individuals in the bill of rights may be largely suspended. If, upon receiving a report from a state governor or rajpramukh, the president is satisfied that the peace and tranquillity of a state is threatened, he may proclaim an emergency in such state, whereupon he may virtually take over the state, suspend the legislature, and legislate for the state through the central legislature. Such a regime, if ratified within two months by the central legislature, and every six months thereafter, may continue for as long as three years. This provision is analogous to Section 93 of the British India Act of 1935, which empowered the British governor of a province, confronted by political deadlock or abstention which made government under the other provisions of the act impossible, to take over the administration of the province.

Policy Toward Minorities.—On May 12, 1949, the Minorities

Committee of the Constituent Assembly rejected provisions which accorded, for a ten-year period, reserved seats in the lower houses of the central and state legislatures to scheduled tribes, scheduled castes, Moslems, Anglo-Indians, and Indian Christians (in Madras and Bombay only). The constitution, however, retained for a ten-year period provisions for reserved seats in the lower houses of the legislatures for certain scheduled tribes and scheduled castes (depressed classes, untouchables). Moreover, the scheduled tribes of primitive peoples, numbering approximately 10,000,000, retain their special status with adequate guarantees against exploitation. Authority was given to the president and the governors and rajpramukhs to nominate to the lower houses of the central and state legislatures a few representatives of the Anglo-Indian (Eurasian) community. Not more than two such representatives may sit in the central legislature.

Provisions Concerning Language.—According to Article 343, "The official language of the Union shall be Hindi in Devanagari script" but ". . . for a period of fifteen years from the commencement of this Constitution, the English language shall continue to be used for all the official purposes of the Union for which it was being used immediately before such commencement." The central legislature may by law provide for the use, after fifteen years, of English for such purposes as it may think fit. The president may, during the fifteen-year period, authorize the use of Hindi in addition to English for such official purposes as he thinks fit. After five years, the whole position with respect to language would be reviewed by a commission which would make recommendations to the president. The power to make other languages than English official languages of a state (for state purposes only) rests with the state legislature, and the president, if satisfied that a substantial portion of a state's population wish any language spoken by them to be recognized as an official language within that state, may require the official recognition of such language by the state government.

Directive Principles of State Policy.—A list of these principles is a unique feature of the constitution. They are simply admonitions and are not enforceable in the courts. The Cabinet is expected to bear them in mind in shaping its policy. These principles reflect the social philosophy of the Congress Party as it has developed under Nehru's leadership. Most notable perhaps is the emphasis on an "economic system which does not result in the concentration of wealth and means of production to the common detriment"; on the desirability of equal pay for equal work for both men and women; on old-age, unemployment, and disability benefits; and on the desirability of fostering village panchayats (local assemblies). Also noteworthy is the setting up of free and compulsory education for all children under fourteen years of age as a goal which should be reached within ten years after the constitution comes into force.

FOREIGN POLICY AND DEFENSE . . . On more than one occasion since August 15, 1947, the government of India defined its foreign policy as one of "aloofness from power blocs." Pandit Jawaharlal Nehru and his colleagues did not wish India to be thought of as aligned with the signatories of the North Atlantic Treaty. Nevertheless they desired to make India a bulwark against communism. With the eclipse of China, India stood in 1950 as the foremost Asian country, the natural leader of other Asian countries in the task of liquidating imperialism and colonialism. The great break with the past consisted in the direction of India's foreign policy from Delhi and not from London. Instead of being an adjunct of British policy, Indian policy was to be based on exclusively Indian considerations.

Among India's objectives in 1950 were: (1) the integration into India of Portuguese and French India; (2) the setting up of independent nationalist regimes in Southeast Asia; (3) the stabilization of such regimes, as in Burma; and (4) the protection of Indian minorities living outside India. None of these objectives were being sought in 1950 by aggressive, unilateral, or belligerent methods. The method for furthering the annexation of the tiny remnants of the Portuguese and French Indian empires to India was that of fostering plebiscites in these foreign enclaves and persuading the governments concerned to relinquish control. Should difficulties ensue, it was expected that India would advocate that the problem be considered by the United Nations. On June 19, 1949, Chandernagor voted overwhelmingly for union with India. The freedom of nationalist regimes in Southeast Asia was sought in 1947 and 1948 through Asian conferences held at Delhi and through vigorous advocacy of the nationalist cause in the Security Council and General Assembly of the United Nations. In 1948 and 1949, India consulted with the other interested Commonwealth countries on the means of helping the government of Burma to pacify that country. Through continuing membership in the Commonwealth, India expected to be in a better position to bring the utmost pressure to bear on the Union of South Africa with respect to South Africa's policy toward the Indian minority in the Union. In the United Nations since its inception, India has vehemently opposed South Africa both on the Indian minority issue and on the problem of the future government of the mandated territory of South-West Africa.

In 1949 it was not clear whether failure to settle the Kashmir issue promptly and peacefully would overshadow all other issues confronting India and Pakistan. The furtherance of all India's foreign policy objectives and all plans for defense based on continuing membership in the Commonwealth depended upon the maintenance of peace between India and Pakistan. Were India to be obliged to undertake military expenditures on a scale comparable to that of the first year of the fighting in Kashmir, 1947–1948, the whole attention of the government would necessarily have to be given to preserving peace and stability in the Indian subcontinent. General relations between the two dominions improved during 1950, and in April a pact was signed on the treatment of minorities in their respective territories. Meanwhile the question of Kashmir remained under consideration by the United Nations; in the summer of 1950 mediation by the United Nations through the person of Sir Owen Dixon ended in failure.

India's defense plans in 1950 were based on continuing membership in the Commonwealth and on the maintenance of peace with Pakistan. Attention was concentrated on making the portion of the British Indian Army and Air Force allotted to India an ever more efficient military instrument staffed by wholly Indian personnel. The government decided in 1949 to increase the size of its small navy, but recognized that the substitution of Indian for British officers in the Indian Navy would require a much longer period of transition. Continuing Commonwealth membership was expected to give all the advantages of interchange of information and equipment which had characterized the period before independence.

PAKISTAN

Pakistan is the smaller of the two nations into which the former British Indian Empire was divided on August 15, 1947. The name Pakistan (*pākistān*) was coined from the Persian *pāk* (pure) and *stan* (place), and means "Land of the Pure." It is also interpreted as an acrostic: *P* for Punjab, *A* for Afghan (Province)—that is, North-West Frontier Province, *K* for Kashmir, S for Sind, and (*s*)*tan* for the last syllable of Baluchistan. The word was first used as the symbol of a political ideal in 1933 by some Moslem (Muslim) students at Cambridge University. The idea was adopted, though not by name, by the Moslem League in 1940 (see Chapter XIII).

The seat of government is at Karachi, which has a population

(1941 census) of 349,492. The total area claimed by the Dominion of Pakistan is 370,311 square miles, and the population, as estimated in 1949, is 75,100,000, giving a density of 202.8 to the square mile. The country has a railroad system of about 8,000 miles. The principal ports are Karachi and Chittagong (1941 population, 92,301). The chief inland city is Lahore, with a population (1941) of 671,659.

In general, Pakistan was formed by separating from prepartition India areas in which the population was preponderantly Moslem. The Pakistan Constituent Assembly, in defining the objectives of its constitution (to be completed some time in 1951), declared its adherence to the principles of Islam.

Geographically, Pakistan is in two parts—West Pakistan, which has an area of 312,302 square miles and a population (1949 estimate) of 30,000,000; and East Pakistan, with an area of 58,009 square miles and a population of 45,100,000—lying on opposite sides of the subcontinent of India nearly 1,000 miles apart, separated by the great width of the Union of India. Politically, the Dominion includes: (1) five provinces which until August 15, 1947, constituted, in whole or in part, provinces of British India: Baluchistan, East Bengal (including the Sylhet District of Assam and constituting East Pakistan), North-West Frontier Province, Punjab (West Punjab), and Sind; and (2) various princely states, notably Kalat, Bahawalpur, and Khairpur.

The unit of currency is the rupee, divided into sixteen annas; as of October 1950 it was valued at approximately thirty cents in United States money. The flag is dark green with a white bar at the pole end and a white crescent and star in the center.

GOVERNMENT . . . The Indian Independence Act, passed by the British Parliament in July 1947, provided for the setting up in India of two independent dominions—India and Pakistan —effective from August 15, 1947, and announced that the paramountcy hitherto exercised by the British crown over the Indian princely states lapsed as of that date. When boundaries had been fixed, the Dominion of Pakistan consisted of: (1) two governors' provinces with boundaries unchanged—North-West Frontier Province and Sind; (2) two governors' provinces formed as a consequence of dividing predominantly Moslem from predominantly non-Moslem areas—West Punjab and East Bengal; (3) an area administered directly by the central government through a chief commissioner—the former British Baluchistan; (4) tribal territories on its frontiers outside the administrative boundaries of any province; and (5) a few contiguous princely states which acceded to the Dominion. By 1949 the process of accession of the handful of princely states within the orbit of Pakistan as distinct from India could be said to be complete, the only unsettled issue being the future of Kashmir. An "Azad (Free) Kashmir" government, sponsored and militarily supported by Pakistan, exercised authority throughout part of the sparsely settled region of northern and western Kashmir.

In form, the government of the Dominion of Pakistan resembled that of the other dominions of the Commonwealth of Nations. The governor general (Mohammed Ali Jinnah, until his death in September 1948; Al-Haj Khwaja Nazimuddin after September 1948) was appointed by the king on the advice of the Pakistan Cabinet led by Liaqat Ali Khan, which was responsible to a majority of the Constituent Assembly acting as an interim central legislature. In practice, every Pakistani politician and official realized that the situation was exceptional. Mr. Jinnah was the Qaid-i-Azam ("Great Leader") of the Moslem League. Pakistan was the fruit of the unrelenting campaign waged by the League. Mr. Jinnah's appointment, forced by his own refusal to accept the first Earl Mountbatten of Burma as governor general of both new dominions, was quite out of keeping with the long-standing British tradition that the governor general of a dominion should be a ceremonial head of state standing above local and party politics. Moreover, the Pakistan Constituent Assembly, made up largely of Moslem League members who had refused to take their seats in the Constituent Assembly planned for a united India, was hardly the equivalent of a normally elected Parliament.

Unlike the new India, Pakistan had to build a completely new central government. It inherited neither a capital nor an administrative machine. Conditions in Karachi, the natural choice for a capital, were chaotic for many months. Added to the problems of setting up ministries with neither adequate personnel nor equipment were those of devising a system of administration for a nation consisting of two disparate blocs of territory hundreds of miles apart. The framing of a new constitution was thus thrust into the background. In September 1950, the constitution was still in the drafting stage. The Pakistan Cabinet was apparently quite content with the prospect of a long interim period during which government would be based on the India Act of 1935.

The Indian Independence Act gave the Pakistan executive power to adapt the act of 1935 to Pakistan by the simple process of order in council. The Moslem League leaders were therefore able to model their central government on the federal government projected in the 1935 act, which had never come into existence. They could also use the procedure for princely accession provided in that act as a framework for integrating with Pakistan the handful of contiguous Moslem princely states. As in India, the federal, provincial, and concurrent lists in the act of 1935 were the basis for determining which legislative subjects fell to the Constituent Assembly as an interim central legislature, which remained to the provincial legislatures of the four governors' provinces, and which were shared between them.

The whole structure of provincial government, in which responsible cabinet government had been inaugurated on April 1, 1937, remained virtually unimpaired. The provincial legislatures, newly elected in the winter of 1945–1946, went on as usual; in cases in which a former historic province was partitioned, as in the Punjab, the members for the districts within Pakistan became the legislature of the new province. Provincial legislatures were the popular base on which the Pakistan government might be said to rest. It was the members of these legislatures who had originally elected the majority of the Constituent Assembly in which all *de facto* power actually resided.

In practice, the Pakistan government appeared stronger than that of India vis-à-vis the provinces and less strong vis-à-vis the princely states. The small size of Pakistan, as compared with India, facilitated a closer central control of the provinces. Moreover, provincial politics in Sind and the North-West Frontier Province became so chaotic in 1948 that the Pakistan Cabinet had to show a firm hand in dealing with them. There seemed to be no prospect that the Pakistan provinces would possess a large degree of states' rights under the projected constitution. To enhance Karachi's prestige as a national capital, plans were made to make the city a centrally administered area and to move the provincial capital of Sind elsewhere.

Pakistan's policy toward the half dozen princely states on its borders differed from that of India. Before partition, Jinnah publicly announced a hands-off policy with respect to the princes. This meant that the important states (other than Kashmir) with which Pakistan was concerned, such as Bahawalpur, Kalat, and Khairpur, were left pretty much alone during the first few months after partition. Assured of control of their foreign affairs, defense, and communications, the Pakistan government regarded the problem of remodeling their domestic regimes as a matter which could well be deferred until the new constitution was framed.

Similarly, the Pakistan Cabinet was in no hurry to transform Pakistan formally into a republic and to define its relationship to the British Commonwealth in new terms. One reason for this was that Pakistan had, during 1948 and 1949, far greater need of British personnel in its services, both military and civilian, than had India. A British governor remained in the North-West Frontier Province, British Army officers in considerable numbers continued to serve in the Pakistan Army, and British civilians did not disappear entirely from Pakistan government offices.

It was expected that the transition from the old political order to the new would take longer in Pakistan than in India. Until its new constitution was evolved, Pakistan's government would correspond in form to that of a federal dominion within the Commonwealth of Nations. Its governmental institutions would be primarily those of British parliamentary democracy, in which the chief repository of power is a Cabinet of ministers headed by the leader of the majority party in the lower house of the legislature. In practice, however, the state would in many respects resemble a one-party authoritarian bureaucracy during the interim period.

FOREIGN POLICY AND DEFENSE . . . The government of Pakistan since August 15, 1947, has riveted its attention on the three problems of most importance to it: (1) Kashmir, (2) the northwest frontier, and (3) Palestine. Apart from support of the United Nations and the general cause of world peace, Pakistan has not concerned itself very much with broader world issues. The attention of Pakistan's leaders has inevitably been concentrated first upon self-preservation. The immediate objective has been to maintain the viability and territorial integrity of their new and admittedly unique state. They have been unable to forget that the very concept of Pakistan was anathema to many persons prominent in the government of India. They have realized that they must keep a half dozen of their ablest men on duty in world capitals to put Pakistan on the map and to build up its prestige as the most populous Moslem nation.

To Pakistan, the Kashmir issue has been of great importance. If it was settled in such a way as to deprive Pakistan of the whole of Kashmir, the repercussions in the adjacent Moslem tribal frontier areas would be bound to be serious even if war between Pakistan and India were somehow avoided. The Pakistan leaders, therefore, conscious of the grave risks involved, agreed to a truce in Kashmir on January 1, 1949. They based their policy on the idea that if a plebiscite could be held in this predominantly Moslem area uninfluenced by outside considerations the decision would favor Pakistan. Until this issue was settled, the formulation of a long-range foreign policy based on friendship and co-operation with India had to be postponed.

Since the Kashmir and the northwest frontier issues are interlocked, the governments of Pakistan and Afghanistan have not been able to settle the future of the tribal areas on a permanent basis. By 1950, the Pakistan government had introduced few modifications into the traditional British policy of controlling the frontier. Much of the British personnel remained to serve the Pakistan government. Subsidies to tribes, though perhaps to a lesser extent, continued to be paid. Concessions to demands for an autonomous "Pathanistan" of Pushtu-speaking peoples were regarded as out of the question. On the whole, the Pakistan government seemed disposed to resist any pretensions of the Afghanistan government to exercise authority beyond the historic frontier of the British Indian Empire.

Preoccupation with these crucial problems, almost domestic in character, prevented the Pakistan government in its first three years of existence from developing the peculiarly close co-operation with other Islamic countries which had been expected. In this field, Pakistan was able to do little more than give special attention to its diplomatic contacts with Iran, Turkey, and the Arab states, and to give strong support in the United Nations to the Arab cause in Palestine.

Pakistan's defense forces consist of that part of the former

British Indian Army allocated to Pakistan in the summer of 1947. Little attention was paid to naval defense in 1947–1950, and equally little to the defense of East Bengal, which was presumably regarded as defensible only by the pen and not by the sword. All military effort had perforce to be expended in Kashmir and on the northwest frontier. Since British officers early in 1948 were strongly enjoined not to become involved in the support of the "free" Kashmir forces, their activities were more confined to the northwest frontier, while Pakistani officers concerned themselves with the direct and indirect support of the Azad (Free) Kashmir government. Pakistan's defense policy could not be definitely settled until the outcome of the Kashmir dispute determined whether relations with India were to be amicable or not. In 1949–1950, it was based on continuing membership in the Commonwealth of Nations and on the maintenance of peace with India.

CHAPTER XV BY WILLIAM F. CHRISTIANS

AND G. P. MALALASEKERA

The Dominion of Ceylon

CEYLON, a large island of the Indian Ocean, lies off the southeast coast of India between latitudes 5°55′N. and 9°50′N. and longitudes 79°42′E. and 81°53′E. It is separated from the mainland by Palk Strait in the north and the Gulf of Mannar in the west. Between the strait and the gulf is a ridge of sandbanks, known as Adam's Bridge, which nearly joins the island to the mainland and interferes with navigation except for small boats. In 1796 the British captured Dutch settlements on the island. They administered the area from Madras until 1798, when it was made a crown colony. In 1802, under the Treaty of Amiens, Ceylon was formally ceded to Great Britain. Since February 4, 1948, Ceylon has been a dominion of the Commonwealth of Nations. The flag is that of the Sinhalese kings, with a standing yellow lion against a red background, to which have been added a green stripe symbolizing the Moslem population and a saffron stripe for the Tamils.

Roughly pear shaped, with the broad end to the south, the island extends 270 miles from Point Pedro (Point Palmyra) in the north to Dondra Head in the south. Ceylon's greatest breadth, from Colombo to Sangamankanda, is approximately

140 miles. The total area is 25,332 miles, or a little over half the size of New York State. The principal cities are Colombo (1946 population, 353,374), the capital, largest city, and principal seaport; and Jaffna (estimated 1946 population, 63,000), Dehiwala-Mount Lavinia (56,900), Kandy (51,200), Moratuwa (50,700), and Galle (49,000). Kandy, a former capital, is noted for its Buddhist temples, including Daḷadā Mālagāwa, the most sacred of all Buddhist temples.

THE LAND . . . Topography.—Structurally, Ceylon is an extension of the south Indian plateau. The major portion of the island is composed of very ancient Archean gneisses overlain in many sections with thick metamorphosed sediments, such as quartzite, granulite, and crystalline limestone, which together make up the Khondalite system. The Khondalite series is folded into a complex syncline with a general north-northwest, south-southeast axial trend. The only other important rock type is a sedimentary Miocene limestone which fringes the northwest coast and covers the Jaffna Peninsula. The island is divided into three fairly distinct levels or zones. The highest level or terrace appears at 6,000 feet; the intermediate level, at around 1,600 feet; the lowest terrace, at 100 feet. Rising above the highest terrace, where local relief is considerable, are the highest peaks of Ceylon, the sacred Adam's Peak (7,365 feet), said by Moslems to contain the footprint of Adam, and Pidurutalagala (8,292 feet), the highest point on the island. The drop from the highest terrace to the 1,600-foot level is quite abrupt. Here there is considerable local relief with ridges and isolated hills rising from the terrace floor. The lowest terrace covers the northern two thirds of the island and is generally overlain with alluvial material. The average elevation of this plain is about 100 feet, though isolated hills rise to 200 or 300 feet above sea level.

The rivers form a radial pattern from the central highland core. Streams are generally short and swift; the longest, Mahaweli Ganga, a little over 200 miles in length, empties into Trincomalee Bay. Waterfalls, one of the major scenic attractions, are characteristic where the rivers drop from one terrace level to the next. The typical coastline is low with offshore coral reefs and sandbanks topped with dunes behind which lie both fresh- and brackish-water shallow lagoons. Coral flourishes all around the island, and most of the sand deposited on the beaches and dunes is composed of comminuted coral. Occasionally rocky headlands reach the water's edge, as at Galle on the southwest tip of the island. Although there are frequent inlets, the harbor facilities at Colombo itself are largely artificial, breakwaters having been constructed to afford protection from the open sea on both the north and west sides. Trincomalee, however, on the northeast coast, is reputed to be one of the finest natural harbors in the world.

Climate.—Ceylon's location and its local relief features are the two chief determinants of its climate. Proximity to the equator gives the island a generally uniform tropical climate, but local elevation modifies the intensity of the heat. The lowlands are uniformly and continuously hot at all seasons, with average temperatures around 80°F. Seasonal variations generally amount to only 3° or 4°F., but they are slightly greater in the extreme north. Diurnal ranges are much greater than seasonal ranges. On clear days at Colombo it is not uncommon for day and night temperatures to differ by 15°F. In the highlands temperatures decrease in almost exact ratio to elevation. At Nuwara Eliya, above 6,000 feet, the average January temperature is 54°F., while in May, the hottest month, the average is 62°F. These differences between highlands and lowlands determine the kinds of crops which are raised at various elevations. While these average temperatures do not seem excessive, they are accompanied at all times by a high humidity which makes the heat feel more intense.

Rainfall on the island, as in India, is dominated by the monsoon winds. The seasonal change in wind direction causes a change in the location of the area of heaviest rainfall. In addition to rainfall resulting from the monsoons, local thunderstorms and tropical cyclones, especially during the intermonsoon periods, bring some rain to the island. The rainiest section is in the southwest. Here the rainfall everywhere is over 75 inches per year; on the windward slopes of the mountains it is in excess of 200 inches. The wettest period is in summer, during the southwest monsoon, but the balance of the year is by no means dry. The monsoon rains are generally heaviest in May. In the northern plains and in the extreme southeast, rainfall is everywhere less than 75 inches per year and many places receive less than 50. Moreover, rainfall here is much less reliable than in the southwest; it is primarily associated with the northeast (winter) monsoon winds; and there is a marked dry season with drought periods of up to sixty days in many sections, especially in the extreme north. Here irrigation is needed if agricultural production is to attain maximum yields. As a result of the marked contrast both in amount and in reliability of rainfall, this portion of Ceylon is agriculturally less productive than the southwest.

POLITICAL DIVISIONS AND POPULATION . . . A census taken on March 19, 1946, gave the population of Ceylon as 6,693,945; of the total 36,606 were nonresidents; residents were 6,657,339. The density was 262.8 persons per square mile. (In mid-1949 an official estimate placed the total population at 7,288,000.)

Ceylon is divided into nine provinces, which are subdivided into nineteen districts. A government agent is in charge of each province, and an assistant government agent of each district. Provincial areas and population figures are given in Table I; birth, death, and infant mortality rates, in Table II.

TABLE I. PROVINCIAL AREAS AND POPULATIONS, 1946

Province	Area (in square miles)	Population	Percentage increase over 1931
Western	1,432	1,876,904	29.9
Central	2,290	1,135,290	19.1
Southern	2,146	961,418	24.7
Northern	3,429	479,572	20.2
Eastern	3,840	279,112	31.4
North-Central	4,009	139,534	43.4
North-Western	3,016	667,889	22.1
Uva	3,278	372,238	22.8
Sabaragamuwa	1,893	745,382	28.9
Total	25,332 *	6,657,339 †	25.4

* Corrected addition. † Resident population.

THE PEOPLE . . . The permanent population of Ceylon comprises Sinhalese (now, preferably, called Sinhalas); Tamils; Moors and Malays, together grouped as Moslems; Burghers, descendants, mixed and pure, of Portuguese and Dutch colonists of the sixteenth and seventeenth centuries; Eurasians; and

TABLE II. BIRTH AND DEATH RATES; INFANT DEATHS (1941–1948)

Year	Birth rate per 1,000 population	Death rate per 1,000 population	Infant deaths per 1,000 live births
1941	36.5	18.8	129
1942	36.7	18.6	120
1943	40.6	21.4	132
1944	37.1	21.3	135
1945	36.7	22.0	140
1946	38.4	20.3	141
1947	39.4	14.3	101
1948	40.5	15.2	92

Veddas (Veddahs), the remnant of an aboriginal stock. There is an Indian community of merchants and a larger group, mainly from south India, of estate laborers. There are also small communities of Europeans, Chinese, and Baluchis (commonly termed Afghans). In 1946 the number of immigrants was 282,-925, of whom 95 per cent came from India; estate laborer Indian immigrants numbered 78,593. Emigrants numbered 226,135, of whom 97 per cent went to India; estate laborer emigrants numbered 75,939. The division of the permanent population by ethnic groups and religions is given in Table III.

TABLE III. ETHNIC GROUPS AND RELIGIONS, 1946
(in thousands)

Ethnic groups		Religions	
Low-Country Sinhalese	2,903	Buddhists	4,295
Kandyan Sinhalese	1,718	Hindus	1,320
Ceylon Tamils	734	Christians	603
Indian Tamils	781	Moslems	437
Ceylon Moors	374	Others	3
Indian Moors	36		
Burghers and Eurasians	42		
Malays	23		
Veddas	2.4		
Europeans	5.4		
Others	41		

The Sinhalese are the descendants of a north Indian people, who are believed to have colonized the island in the sixth or fifth century B.C. They are generally divided into two groups, Low Country and Kandyan. The former inhabit the western and southern coastal areas, the latter the north central plain and the mountains. The division is not ethnic, but originated in the administrative cleavage caused by European occupation of the littoral. The Sinhalese are a handsome people, slender and well proportioned, with fine features and smooth black hair. The women, particularly, have a fine carriage and possess large, lustrous eyes. Skin color varies from light olive to dark brown. The Sinhalese are highly civilized, with a culture over 2,000 years old and four centuries' contact with Western thought. They are gentle and hospitable. The Ceylon Tamils, who live mainly in the arid north and the east, are an alert, industrious people who came to political notice about the fourteenth century. Conservative descendants of south Indian colonists and invaders, they have largely retained their Indian way of life, unlike the Sinhalese, who early developed a civilization distinct from that of the subcontinent. The Moors engage chiefly in small-scale trade; the Malays, in services like the police and the fire brigade. The Veddas occupy the almost inaccessible forest regions of Uva and Eastern provinces. Once completely wild, they now cultivate dry crops, though they prefer hunting, for which they use a primitive firelock instead of the ancestral bow and arrow. They are a very dark people with pronounced Negroid features, speak a patois, and practice animism. They do not easily make friends with strangers. The Veddas are kin to the wild tribes dotting the forest patches of the arc extending from Borneo westward to India through the south Asian land mass. The Burghers have the lightest complexions of the permanent inhabitants. By endogamy a minority of the Dutch Burghers have preserved the European blood upon which they pride themselves, and they are striving to retain their individuality. The rest of the Burghers are merging into the other racial groups, notably the Sinhalese. Not long ago the Burghers filled the learned professions, such as law, medicine, and the church, or were prominent in European merchant firms. Their interests are becoming more diversified. The small Chinese community consists mainly of peddlers. The Baluchis are exclusively money lenders.

NATURAL RESOURCES . . . Natural Vegetation.—Forests cover some three fourths of Ceylon. Because of marked contrasts in rainfall and elevation the types of plants vary widely from place to place. The lower slopes of the mountains and the wetter portions of the lowlands, where the land has not been cleared, are covered with a thick, broadleaf evergreen forest composed of many species. Parasitic vines and creepers are common in the plant associations of these areas. On some of the higher plains where rainfall is scant, coarse grass is typical. In the highlands, where wetter conditions exist, temperate zone species prevail, and climbing plants are much less common. In those parts of the plains where a marked dry season is characteristic, thorn forest is typical. Elsewhere on the plains a dry zone forest with a great variety of trees, generally with small leaves and thick bark, is most frequent. It is from this type of forest that the slow-growing ebony and satinwood are obtained.

Animal Life.—Most of the animals found in India, except the royal tiger, are also native to Ceylon. Leopards and various types of small cats are common. In the northern and eastern provinces elephants are numerous, although their numbers have been greatly reduced by hunting. Bears, monkeys, wild hogs, and several species of deer are all found on the island. The bandicoot is a familiar garden pest, as it is in India. Great numbers of birds, many with bright plumage, are common. Especially numerous are pheasants, peacocks, partridges, and pigeons.

Mineral Resources.— Mineral wealth is neither extensive nor varied. The chief mineral industry, graphite (plumbago) mining, is subject to wide fluctuation both in the amount produced and in numbers employed. In 1940 about 18,000 were engaged in graphite mining; in 1946, only 1,785. Production dropped from a high of 27,734 tons in 1942 to a low of 4,623 tons in 1946, but rose again to 14,194 tons in 1948. Commercial deposits occur in veins, lenses, and pockets in the Khondalite series. The principal markets are the United States and the United Kingdom. Good-quality mica occurs in the hill country, but mining has been haphazard and production erratic. Precious and semiprecious stones, including sapphires, rubies, beryl, topaz, garnet, zircon, and many varieties of quartz, are obtained from the alluvial gravels derived from the Khondalite rocks. Since all gems are bought through auctions or private sales, no annual production figures are available; conservative estimates place the value at around $500,000 per year. Iron ore sufficient to meet local needs is available, but coal is lacking, and cheap electric power is not yet a possible substitute. Although the island has considerable amounts of potential hydroelectric energy, relatively little had been developed by 1949. Colombo was, with one exception, the only city which provided electrical energy for other than domestic use and street lighting. Here an ever-increasing volume was used for industry. In Galle power was provided for a plywood factory at Gintota. In 1948 the island's electric power capacity was 21,000 kilowatts. Plans were under way in 1949 to develop hydroelectric energy; when completed, the projects were expected to give the island a total in excess of 100,000 kilowatts.

AGRICULTURE . . . Agriculture occupies a paramount position in the economic life of Celyon. Fully 60 per cent of all gainfully employed persons are engaged directly in farming, and agricultural products account for well over 90 per cent of all exports. Despite this great emphasis on crop production, there is an inadequate supply of food for local needs. Food imports normally constitute one third or more of all imports; in 1948 they amounted to 52 per cent. Food supplies could be augmented considerably through the expansion of irrigation facilities in the dry portions of the north and in the southeast; in 1949 a three-year project to irrigate 120,000 acres in the Gal Oya Basin was begun.

Agricultural production falls into three major types: (1) the rice-coconut complex, (2) rice-vegetable-tobacco farming, and (3) plantation agriculture. The first two types are characterized by small-scale operations, intensive hand cultivation, and small capital investment. Plantation agriculture is generally carried on in large units, capital requirements are great, and financial success is geared to world market conditions. In terms of numbers employed, by far the most important is the rice-coconut type, localized in the southern three fourths of the island. It is the Sinhalese who practice this system. Rice is grown primarily as a subsistence crop; the coconut supplies some food, household articles, and a major cash crop. Some coconuts are grown under plantation methods, but the bulk of the island's production is derived from small-scale native plots. The rice-vegetable-tobacco form of agriculture is localized in the relatively unproductive soils of the Jaffna Peninsula and adjacent areas of the extreme north. This area is occupied predominantly by Tamils. Rice and vegetables are the chief food crops. Tobacco is grown on a commercial basis. Rainfall here is light (twenty-five to fifty inches) and comes in the northeast monsoon period. Consequently irrigation is essential. The relatively infertile soil requires heavy fertilization. Plantation agriculture is confined primarily to the hilly regions of the south. Tea (140,000 metric tons in 1948) and rubber (90,800 metric tons in 1949) are the dominant crops. Tea is grown from sea level to 6,000 feet, but the best qualities are obtained from the higher elevations; rubber is confined to elevations under 2,000 feet. (During the Portugese and Dutch periods cinnamon was the chief plantation crop; in the nineteenth century coffee led all others, but in the 1870's a blight attacked the coffee tree, and cinchona was dominant for a brief period. It is only since the early twentieth century that tea and rubber have achieved first place.) Although rubber occupies a greater acreage than tea (573,243 in 1946 as compared with 533,830 in tea), its export value is far less: 14 per cent of the value of all exports in 1948, compared with 59 per cent for tea. World War II stimulated rubber production; its future seems less secure than that of tea.

An interesting agricultural system of Ceylon is chena cultivation. Under this system, practiced primarily in the dry zone, crops are grown on burned-off jungle land. As soil fertility decreases, the cultivator migrates to new areas. Fortunately this type is declining as lands are permanently cleared with government co-operation.

Acreage in principal crops, other than tea and rubber, in 1946 was as follows: rice (912,500), coconuts (920,093), vegetables and related crops (140,000), areca nuts (69,000), palmyra (50,000), cinnamon (33,077), citronella (30,107), cacao (19,700), cardamoms (6,000), and tobacco (2,656).[1]

Animal husbandry has occupied an unimportant place in the economy of Ceylon. After World War II four large cattle farms were started and attention was being given to the development of animals suited to the climate and to the production and processing of disease-free milk products. In 1946 there were 1,577,327 horned cattle, 296,151 goats, and 63,301 swine.

INDUSTRIAL DEVELOPMENT . . . Manufacturing is relatively unimportant in Ceylon, although shortages during World War II and attendant high prices and limited shipping space did much to stimulate industrial expansion along certain lines. Much of the war and postwar development was aided by government ownership and control. In 1939 the government built a coir factory to make such articles as camouflage material and bags for coal, tea, and salt. In 1946 some 5,000 workers were employed in the government-controlled machine phase of this industry. In addition, probably 50,000 were employed in cottage-type, small-

[1] These figures do not in many cases include holdings of less than one acre, of which there are many. The tobacco figures are inadequate, since they represent only the crop for one season and not for the entire year.

scale coir spinning and weaving, some entirely under private control, some aided by the government. In 1941, a government plywood factory was built to supply tea chests, decorative panels, and furniture, and a shoe factory and a tannery were begun. In December 1942 a steel rolling plant using scrap metal was completed. Other government plants of wartime origin include a paper mill, a quinine factory, and a ceramics factory producing crockery and utility ware. The war also stimulated private development of such industries as those producing glass, matches, soap, hosiery, paper, twine, lacquered ware, and ink. The government assisted in the expansion of many cottage-type industries, especially in such fields as textiles, pottery, rattan goods, mats, and handmade paper.

In the early postwar period the trend of industrialization was difficult to predict in detail, but certain features seemed fairly clear. First, there seemed little doubt that Ceylon would remain essentially an agricultural nation producing commercial crops. Second, the government would probably find it necessary to continue to play a major role in financing and controlling industrial expansion in such fields as power, heavy industry, fertilizer manufacture, cotton spinning, and certain pharmaceuticals. Third, for a considerable time private enterprise would probably be limited to consumers' goods for which processes are relatively simple, capital requirements small, and technical requirements at a minimum. Fourth, the cottage-type industry would continue to provide a source of income and supply many local necessities.

TRADE . . . The foreign trade of Ceylon consists primarily in the exchange of agricultural products for manufactured goods and food. While World War II had little effect upon the general character of the island's trade, it did modify it in detail and alter the direction of its movement, especially in imports. War-stimulated industries made the island less dependent on foreign sources for certain manufactured products than was true before the war. Disturbances during the war and in the postwar period cut off trade with Japan and interfered with the movement of rice from Southeast Asia. The total value of both import and export trade increased manyfold—imports, for example, from 236 million rupees to 985 million rupees between 1938 and 1948; exports, from 284 million rupees to 1,009 million rupees in the same period—but because of the very high prices that Ceylon had to pay for her imports (in 1948 the import price index was 525, on a base of 100 for 1934–1938, while the export price index was 344), there was relatively little real gain resulting from the increased value. In 1948 the major groups of import items and the percentage for each group included: food, drink, and tobacco, 52 per cent; manufactured products, 36 per cent; raw materials, 11 per cent. During the war there was a marked decline in the import of rice and a marked increase in the import of wheat and wheat flour, mostly from Australia, and bread has become an important item in the diet of many people in Ceylon. A marked increase in the import of preserved milk and milk foods was also noted. Tea, rubber, and coconuts dominated the export field in 1948, as they had for many years, tea accounting for 59 per cent, rubber for 14 per cent, and coconut products for about 13.5 per cent of the total export trade. A large portion of Ceylon's trade is with Commonwealth countries: 45 per cent of imports, and 52 per cent of exports, in 1948. In that year the chief sources of Ceylon's imports were the United Kingdom (17.4 per cent), Burma (17.4 per cent), India (12.8 per cent), Australia (12.7 per cent), and the United States (7.6 per cent). Exports in 1948 went primarily to the United Kingdom (29.8 per cent), the United States (16.3 per cent), Australia (8.3 per cent), Egypt (6.3 per cent), and the Union of South Africa (4.3 per cent).

TRANSPORTATION AND COMMUNICATIONS . . . All railways in Ceylon are government owned. The system, which comprises 806 miles of broad-gauge (5½ feet) and 106 miles of narrow-gauge (2½ feet), focuses on Colombo and serves the southwest coast and the southern highlands, with two lines extending to the north, and two to the east coast. Large sections of the south and southeast are without rail service. There are over 17,500 miles of road and cart tracks in the island; 6,364 miles can be classed as main through arteries, of which 5,457 miles are surfaced and generally suitable for all-weather use. A series of canals along the southwest coast provides a water route of about 120 miles between Kalutara and Puttalam. Air transport is available to India, Pakistan, the United Kingdom, and Singapore. Colombo, one of the world's great entrepots, has extensive wharfage facilities.

The telegraph and telephone systems are operated by the Post Office Department. As of September 30, 1947, there were 1,046 post offices. In 1948 there were 11,110 miles of telegraph lines and 70,445 miles of telephone wires. The government maintains a broadcasting service with programs in English, Sinhalese, and Tamil. A great many newspapers and periodicals are published in Ceylon in all the major languages.

ECONOMIC AND FINANCIAL FACTORS . . . The standard unit of currency is the rupee; in May 1950 it was valued at 20.8 cents in United States money. The primary units of weights and measures are identical with those in Great Britain. There are some fifteen banks doing business in Ceylon, many of them branches of Indian and British concerns. In addition, the post-office savings banks, the State Mortgage Bank, and the Agricultural and Industrial Credit Corporation carry on limited and specialized banking functions. In 1950 the new Central Bank of Ceylon began functioning. Revenue was estimated at 565 million rupees in 1948–1949; expenditures at 532 million. In 1948 national income was about 2,272 million rupees. Between 1937 and 1950 the cost of living index rose from a base of 100 to 319.

GOVERNMENT . . . The island as a whole first came completely under foreign control in 1815, and until 1931 was administered as a crown colony of Great Britain. In that year, the Donoughmore Constitution gave the island a great measure of self-government and almost entire control of finance. It also established universal suffrage. It provided government by ministers, of whom seven took office as chairmen of the executive committees into which the legislative assembly, the State Council, was divided. The broad model was the London County Council. In 1945 the Soulbury Commission made further changes, and on February 4, 1948, Ceylon became a fully self-governing dominion in the Commonwealth of Nations. The postwar changes in Southeast Asia, particularly those which established the Dominions of India and Pakistan in 1947 and led to the republican Union of Burma in 1948, doubtless accelerated the pace of Ceylon's progress to free nationhood.

The king is represented by a governor general. Parliament, on the British model, consists of two houses, the House of Representatives, with 101 members, and the Senate, with 30 members. The governor general nominates 6 members to the former, and 15 to the latter, to which the House of Representatives elects the balance. The interests of unrepresented minorities are safeguarded by nominations. The prime minister presides over a Cabinet of 14 members, whom he chooses. The first parliamentary elections, held in September 1947, gave a plurality of 42 seats to the United National Party, which came into power with its chairman as prime minister. The opposition consisted mainly of Left-wing elements: the Communist (Stalinist) Party, and the Bolshevik Sama Samaja and Lanka Sama Samaja parties (both Trotskyist). The Ceylon Tamils allied themselves with their Indian brethren in the Tamil Congress Party. The Ceylon Indian Congress formed its own group. All of these joined in opposition to the United National Party. There were 21 Independent members. Subsequently, the government was strengthened by the accession of a number of Independents, by differences among the Left-wing parties, and by a major split in the Tamil Congress ranks, the leader of that group accepting a Cabinet appointment. The government in 1949–1950 was therefore a coalition. Complete executive power is exercised by the Dominion, which also controls all legislation. Certain appeals are allowed to proceed to the British Privy Council. The Supreme Court is the highest tribunal; it is presided over by a chief justice and several puisne judges. Of similar status are the commissioners of assize. There are a court of criminal appeal and other appellate courts presided over by one, or a board of, puisne judges. District, magistrates', requests', and rural courts exercise restricted powers. Civil law is based on the Roman Dutch law introduced by the Dutch in the seventeenth century. Criminal law is on the British model. Moslem marriages and divorces are governed by Koranic laws administered by boards of Kathis. The Ceylon Tamils have their own property law, known as Thesa Walamai. The police force operates under an ordinance of 1865, amended by later ordinances. At its head is a senior civil servant.

The prime minister is also minister for defense and external affairs. The island is represented by an ambassador in the United States, by a minister plenipotentiary in Burma, and by high commissioners in the United Kingdom, Australia, and India. In unrepresented countries its interests are served through the British government. India is also represented by a trade commissioner; Pakistan, solely by a trade commissioner. A citizenship law safeguards the island's position vis-à-vis nationals of other countries but enables them to be domiciled under conditions meeting the island's requirements. The law has had doubtful reception in India and Pakistan, but the influx of their nationals necessitated some restriction. The law also clarified the island's attitude toward countries seeking to discriminate against its nationals. The Ceylon Naval Volunteer Reserve and the Ceylon Army are the chief instruments of defense. Officers are trained in England. Defense is co-ordinated with British strategy and machinery.

Public health and welfare services and social legislation are advanced. The network of hospitals in the chief towns has been extended to remote areas, where numerous rural hospitals, maternity homes, and prenatal clinics have been established. Curative and preventive treatment is available at specialized clinics. In areas distant from transportation lines there is a system of outdoor dispensaries. There are also milk feeding centers for infants. Social legislation is administered largely by the Ministries of Health and Local Government and of Labour and Social Services.

Government service is controlled by the Public Services Commission, which recruits candidates for higher government posts. The commissioners hold competitive examinations for young graduates seeking to join the civil service. Senior civil servants are appointed government agents. Each ministry is administered by a permanent secretary, generally a senior civil servant. Rural administration is under divisional revenue officers, aided by village headmen. Local government service covers the most remote areas. Cities and large towns are administered by municipalities, and smaller units by urban and town councils, while villages have village committees. Members are popularly elected. A local government commission unifies the service.

WAY OF LIFE . . . The people of Ceylon are peace loving, law abiding, and gentle. They are tolerant of and receptive to new ideas. As a result, early Christian missionaries were welcomed warmly, although Christianity has made little headway since its introduction in the sixteenth century. Most Sinhalese are Buddhists; Tamils are Hindu by religion. The Buddhist Sabbath is reckoned by the four lunar phases. On these days Buddhists visit temples, offer flowers in memory of the Buddha, and listen to a sermon by a monk. The monks are celibate, eat but one meal a day, and live withdrawn from ordinary affairs. Religious ceremonies have comparatively little ritual, worship being individual. The Hindus are more ritualistic. Their priests are Brahmans, members of an exclusive priestly caste. Buddhist monks have no caste restrictions to prevent them from adopting a spiritual life, and they can renounce their religious calling at will.

Residents of towns live in semi-European style, but rural folk lead more natural and simpler lives. British law imposed monogamy except in the case of the Moslems. The Moors segregate their womenfolk, but there is a movement toward freedom. Malay women are not segregated. Tamil women are conservative, but neither the Sinhalese nor members of the other ethnic groups have imposed restrictions upon women. Family life is patriarchal, younger members being respectful toward their elders. Children are affectionately regarded. Marriages are arranged by parents, and the dowry system prevails. Property is inherited equally by all children in a family. The average meal consists of a large dish of boiled rice with several vegetables separately made into curries. Although meat and fish are eaten, the diet is mainly vegetarian. Most village folk chew betel leaf mixed with slices of areca nut, a pinch of burnt lime, and sometimes spices such as cloves and cardamoms. Persons educated in English, as well as those employed in government and other modern services, wear European clothes, but the majority of the population wear a cloth falling to the ankles and held at the waist, topped by a loose calico shirt or coat. In the villages many people normally are bare above the waist. Rural folk carry a large kerchief, shawl, or towel over one shoulder. Women wear bright-colored saris draped over the left shoulder, with a blouse underneath. Jewelry for hair, ears, neck, wrists, and sometimes ankles is much favored. Cricket, Rugby football, soccer, tennis, horse racing, and hockey are all popular, and national games are enjoyed in the rural areas.

CULTURAL LIFE AND ACHIEVEMENT

The civilization of Ceylon is more than 2,000 years old. Noteworthy among its achievements are those in architecture, painting, and engineering.

ART, MUSIC, AND LITERATURE . . . There are several ruined cities in Ceylon—notably Anuradhapura, the rock fortress of Sigiriya, Polonnaruva, and Yāpahuva, capitals at various periods from the sixth century B.C. to the thirteenth century A.D. They were well planned, ramparted, and moated. They had regular streets and surprisingly modern sanitation. Brick mounds, called dagobas (Sinhalese *dāgabas*), containing relics, were built in massive proportions. The largest, the fourth-century Jetavana Dāgaba, at Anuradhapura, is over 250 feet high and has a diameter of 327 feet. Each dagoba is built on a platform, in a round or oval shape, with three rings and a square on the summit, which is surmounted by a conical spire, capped by a gilded finial. About them are littered sculptured steps, balustrades, and door jambs. Some specimens of the stone sculpture and carvings rank among the finest in the world. There are also baths, rivaling Roman and Pompeian types, and what would today be called swimming pools. In addition, there are the remains of royal palaces, pavilions, and other buildings. All are in the dry zone, where the ancient kingdom flourished. The last of the Sinhalese capitals was Kandy, in the heart of the central mountain range. Architecture reached a very high standard, but gradually, during the period of decadence which culminated in the loss of independence in 1815, developed on folk lines now represented by the term Kandyan.

Under the stimulus of Buddhism the fine arts flourished. The classical period of Sinhalese art was between the fourth and sixth centuries A.D., and there were great revivals under royal patronage in the eleventh, thirteenth, and eighteenth centuries.

The finest paintings are those of the fifth century, represented by the celebrated frescoes of Sigiriya, still amazingly fresh. The next best known are the twelfth-century murals from the Tivanka image house at Polonnaruva. Oils were used in very early times. Folk art is practiced in the Kandyan area, and well-preserved examples exist from the eighteenth century on. The tradition of architecture, painting, sculpture, music, handicrafts, and dancing has been continued by folk artists, with patronage from the Buddhist temples. The painting is flat and restful, resembling ancient Egyptian work. The treatment is narrative, and the object is repeated panel by panel. There is no true perspective. In handicrafts there is a tradition of fineness, fluency, and grace; the commonest objects—even kitchen utensils—are treated artistically. The Sinhalese have reached a high level of achievement in working with ivory, gold, silver, copper, brass, and wood. Most of the designs are traditional. The arts of mat weaving and lacquer and filigree work are widespread in the villages.

Music, played by drums and flutes, is heard at village festivals, and at the annual festival held in connection with the Buddha's sacred tooth at the Daḷadā Mālagāwa in Kandy in August. At this time the best music and dancing native to the island is presented. There are many folk songs, and folk tales, replete with wisdom and a quaint sense of humor, are still told at village gatherings. While the theater is not highly developed, rural dramas, called *nadagam,* are played occasionally, and a movement to revive the drama on modern lines has been started. Western motion pictures are popular, and Indian films attract large audiences. Sinhalese films made in India have revealed considerable talent.

Sinhalese, an Indo-Aryan language with many Dravidian words, dates from the beginning of the island's civilization and continues to be a medium suitable for expressing modern thought. It is written in a script ultimately derived from the

Brāhmī script of North India. Its literature, mainly religious, includes prose and poetry, philosophy, theology, and grammar of a high order.

SCIENCE AND TECHNOLOGY . . . The ancient Sinhalese excelled in engineering and irrigation. Vast artificial lakes, called tanks, dot the old kingdom. Most of them are being restored, and old water channels made to serve modern needs. The tanks were often built in chains, serving a series of villages before they reached their objective, the capital. The fifth-century Jaya Ganga, the principal channel of the Kalaveva, is the best example of these old waterways. It takes water to Anuradhapura, fifty-four miles away; in its first lap of seventeen miles the gradient is six inches to the mile. It is being used with levels intact. Minneri Tank, which covers about 4,500 acres, was built in the fourth century by King Mahasen. Modern counterparts are the Gal Oya project (see p. 208) and the Laxapana hydroelectric project. The island has made great progress in scientific research. There is a medical research institute which has given Ceylon a leading position in the control of malaria and filaria. There are also research institutes for rubber, tea, and coconuts. The Department of Archaeological Survey carries on programs of excavation and conservation. Many valuable monuments have been preserved, and numerous important stone inscriptions discovered and published.

EDUCATION . . . Primary and secondary education is controlled by the minister of education, and administered by the Department of Education. Primary education up to eleven years of age is in the mother tongue. Attendance is compulsory for children from six to fourteen years of age. The schools are either run by the government, or, if conducted by organized religious denominations, aided by government grants. They are supervised by government inspectors acting under provincial education officers. Free education is the accepted policy, although a few older schools have been permitted temporarily to continue to charge fees. In 1948 there were 3,091 government schools, 3,146 assisted schools, and 623 English, central, and bilingual schools. The University of Ceylon, established on July 1, 1942, by the amalgamation of two colleges, has faculties of Oriental studies, arts, science, medicine, law, agriculture, and veterinary science; doctorates are given in letters, law, and medicine. Tuition is free. Courses are given in English. There are also industrial schools, polytechnic academies, and schools for the deaf and blind. Ceylon Technical College prepares students to the level of engineering degrees of the University of London. Adult education has made progress under a special education officer. There are a few public libraries maintained by local government bodies. The Department of National Museums administers Colombo Museum and other museums in the provinces. The attainment of dominion status stimulated the revival of indigenous arts and crafts, with full participation by the government. The Ceylon Society of Arts maintains an art gallery in Colombo, and in 1949 it organized the first of a series of art festivals. There is also an active body, called the '43 Group, of modernist artists.

HISTORY

The story of Ceylon begins traditionally in 543 B.C. (by an alternative system of chronology, 483 B.C.), with its colonization by the legendary Prince Vijaya. The most influential event in Ceylon's history, and the one which scholars generally make the starting point, was the Buddhist mission sent by Emperor Aśoka (r. c. 274–237 B.C.) of India to King Tissa at Anuradhapura.

ANURADHAPURA . . . The Anuradhapura period of Ceylonese history lasted until the end of the tenth century A.D. In the fourth century a chronicle compiled from monastic records and known as the *Dīpavaṃsa* related the history of Ceylon to the end of King Mahasen's reign (A.D. 304). A century later the better-known *Mahāvaṃsa* was compiled. It was continued from time to time, relating the story in 100 chapters to 1815. These two books constitute the chief source of the history of the island; they are often verified by inscriptions. They are written in Buddhist scriptural Pali verse (see Chapter IV). The greatest achievements of the Sinhalese were accomplished during the Anuradhapura period. The kings, though despots, were benevolent, and their rule was democratic to a considerable degree. Villages enjoyed a good deal of autonomy. The economy was agrarian, and cultural connections were largely with north India. The greatest ruler was Dutugemunu (Dutthagamani, r. second or first century B.C.), who is considered the savior of the island and its religion from Elala, a south Indian conqueror. In the second century A.D., King Gajabahu invaded south India and brought back many prisoners. Two centuries later there was a period of great vitality under the dynamic King Mahasen, builder of tanks, monasteries, dagobas, and other monumental structures. Under Kassapa (Kasyapa), of the fifth century, art flourished in its classic period. The island was known to Greeks, Romans, Egyptians, Arabs, and Chinese.

POLONNARUVA . . . At the close of the tenth century the Chola dynasty of southern India conquered the island, destroyed Anuradhapura, and made Polonnaruva its capital. When the Cholas were expelled by Vijayabahu I, in the mid-eleventh century, he continued their policy, and the city remained the capital for two centuries. The Polonnaruva kings, through political considerations, had more dealings with south India, and to this fact can be traced the distinct Dravidian-Hindu influences on the island's culture. Parakramabahu I the Great (r. 1153–1186), is the chief figure of this period. He unified the island, centralized its administration, and knit it together strongly as few of his predecessors had done. He showed great capacity for building and for making the island self-sufficient in food. He sent successful military expeditions to south India and Burma. Another energetic king was Nissaṅka Malla (r. 1187–1196). During the Polonnaruva period Ceylon was in touch with lands as far distant as Cambodia and China. Many Chinese coins and specimens of Sung pottery have been found in various places.

THIRTEENTH TO FIFTEENTH CENTURIES . . . The fall of Polonnaruva in the thirteenth century was followed by a period of instability during which there were sporadic invasions from India, Malaya, and even China; capitals were moved from time to time; and there was a marked trend toward the west coast. Parakramabahu II is the only powerful king of this period. His successors could barely keep the northern part of the island from breaking away into a separate kingdom under descendants of Tamil invaders, and they in fact ultimately established a kingdom of their own. Their power was checked in the fifteenth century by Parakramabahu VI. His capital was Kotte (near Colombo), the last capital of the traditional kingdom.

PORTUGUESE AND DUTCH RULE; THE KINGDOM OF KANDY . . . In 1505 the Portuguese visited Ceylon, and in a few years, profiting by the weakness of the Kotte kings and the internecine warfare, were able to establish a hold on the maritime provinces which, confirmed by the Donation of Dharmapala in 1580, continued for 140 years. During this period the island had its first contact with European ways, with lasting effects. Roman Catholicism was introduced, and gunpowder was made known to the people, who also learned something of Portuguese language, dress, and music. Christianity was the chief contribution of the Portuguese. In 1638–1658, the Dutch drove the Portuguese from Ceylon. The Dutch United East India Company, with trade as its object, then took the place of Portuguese imperial rule in the maritime provinces. Meanwhile, the nationalist Sinhalese, resenting foreign influence in Kotte, left its King Dharmapala and the Portuguese to one side and established for a brief period the Kingdom of Sitawaka in the mid-country; it flourished under kings Mayadunne (r. 1521–1581) and Rājasinha I (r. 1581–1593). Upon the fall of Sitawaka in 1593, Sinhalese aspirations led to the formation of the independent highland Kingdom of Kandy, which in time came to control a large part of the island. (The Tamil kingdom in the north had already been destroyed by the Portuguese.) On several occasions Portuguese attacking Kandy were severely repulsed. Relations with the Dutch were better; they invaded chiefly to preserve their trade. In 1766, by the Treaty of Hanguranketa, King Kīrti Sri (r. 1747–1782) of the Malabar dynasty (founded at Kandy in 1739) was forced to cede the entire seaboard to a depth of four miles to the Dutch. It was under this king that a great national and cultural revival took place. Meanwhile, the Dutch continued in control of the coast until 1796, when they were ousted by the British. The greatest contribution of the Dutch to the island was Roman Dutch law.

BRITISH RULE; THE DOMINION OF CEYLON . . . The British in their turn clashed with the Kandyan king, Sri Wickrema (Vikrama, r. 1798–1815), and his own people rose against him. In 1815 he was forced to abdicate and was deported to India, and the island went under British rule by the terms of a convention between the Sinhalese chieftains and the British governor. Three years later a serious rebellion almost drove the British out; there were other rebellions, in 1843 and 1848, but these were minor. The British introduced a colonial system of administration, and as the island became unified were able to bring about many useful changes. The country was opened up; coffee, tea, and rubber were introduced; coconuts were planted more extensively; and remote places were connected by road and rail. The opening of schools led to the gradual acceptance of English as the language of administration. The island was now brought into line with European developments. Its special place in British strategy, as well as its importance to trade, was quickly realized. The people began to demand political advancement. Political reforms were introduced, culminating, on February 4, 1948, in the end of British rule and the acquisition of dominion status. British occupation had resulted in steady progress. The lasting contribution of the British to the life of the island was parliamentary government.

BIBLIOGRAPHY

Tennent, Sir James Emerson, *Ceylon,* 3d ed., 2 vols. (London, 1859).

Sion, Jules, *Asie des Moussons,* vol. 2 (Paris, 1929).

Cook, E. K., *A Geography of Ceylon* (London, 1931).

Paranavitana, S., *The Stupa in Ceylon,* Archaeological Survey of Ceylon, Memoirs, No. 5 (London, 1943).

Silva, S. F. de, *The New Geography of Ceylon* (Colombo, 1943).

Ladejinsky, W. I., "Agriculture in Ceylon," *Foreign Agriculture,* January 1944.

Codrington, H. W., *A Short History of Ceylon* (New York, 1947).

Ceylon Independence Souvenir (Colombo, 1948).

Wickremasinghe, Martin, *Sinhalese Literature,* tr. by E. R. Sarathchandra (Colombo, 1949).

Census of Ceylon, 1946, vol. 1, pt. 1, General Report (Colombo, 1950).

Ludowyk, E. F. C., ed., *Robert Knox in the Kandyan Kingdom* (Toronto, 1950).

Sarathchandra, E. R., *Sinhalese Novel* (Colombo, 1950).

Guide books to Anuradhapura, Sigiriya, Mihintale, Polonnaruva (Colombo, 1950).

Ferguson's Ceylon Directory (Colombo, annually).

Ceylon Department of Agriculture, *The Tropical Agriculturist* (Colombo, monthly).

The Ceylon Year Book: The Official Government Statistical Annual (Colombo, annually).

Index of Persons and Places

INDEX OF PERSONS AND PLACES

Aurangzeb (Aurangzīb), 80, 145, 147, 149

Australia, viii, 35, 182, 183, 212, 215

Baber (Babur), 146

Bactria, 131, 132, 133, 135-136, 139, 140

Badami, 143

Bādarāyaṇa, 101

Bagh, 86

Bahawalpur, 193, 196

Bala, Friar, 84

Balan gate, 2

Baluchistan, 2, 9, 37, 50, 90, 129, 131, 175, 192, 193, 194

Bāṇa, 60, 61, 72

Banaras (Benares), 5, 6, 91, 105, 108, 178

Bangalore, 27

Barabar Hills, 76

Belur, 78

Bengal, Bay of, vii, 1, 3, 8, 26

Bengal Province, 7, 10, 11, 12, 18, 20, 23, 36, 41, 59, 73, 79, 86, 87, 105, 114, 130, 152, 153, 155, 156, 159, 164, 166, 175

Bengal (East), 3, 8, 37, 90, 175, 193, 194, 199

Bengal (West), 178, 179

Bentinck, Lord William Cavendish, 158

Berar, *see* Madhya Pradesh

Berlin, 160

Bhaja, 83

Bhāravi, 58

Bharhut, 77, 83

Bhartrihari (Bhartṛhari), 60

Bhāsa, 62, 72

Bhaṭṭa Nārāyana, 73

Bhaṭṭi, 58

Bhavabhūti, 62, 72

Bhopal, 178, 182

Bhubaneshwar (Bhuvaneshwar), 77, 86

Bhutan, vii

Bihar, 12, 13, 23, 75, 76, 79, 86, 87, 130, 131, 132, 171, 178

Bijapur, 79, 80, 145, 147

Bilaspur, 178

Bindusāra, 136

Bombay, 18, 20, 26, 27, 29, 114, 153, 156, 159, 165, 171, 177, 178, 189

Borneo, 142, 206

Brahmaputra River, 10, 11

Brahmaputra Valley, 47, 48

British Commonwealth of Nations, v, 182, 196-197, 198, 199, 200; *see also* Great Britain *and* United Kingdom

British East India Company, 17, 149-176, 192

British Indian Empire, 149-176, 192

Brown, W. Norman, 67, 75, 82, 90, 128

Brydon, Dr. William, 158

Buddh (Bodh), 84

Buddha, 83-85, 107-109, 133

Budhasvāmin, 61

Burke, Edmund, 155

Burma, vii, 1, 2, 11, 33, 34, 107, 142, 191, 212, 214, 215

Burma Road, 2

Calcutta, 10, 26, 152, 165, 177

Cambay, 79

Cambodia, 107, 142, 223

Canada, 182, 183

Canning, Earl of, 159

Cardamon Hills, 5, 8

Carnatic, the, 151

Cauvery (Kaveri) River, 93

Cawnpore, *see* Kanpur

Central Provinces, *see* Madhya Pradesh

Ceylon, v-viii, 182, 200-225; *see also* Lanka

Chaitanya, 105

Chanakya (Cāṇakya), 60, 133, 137

Chandernagor, 152, 191

Chandragupta Maurya, 133, 134, 136-137

INDEX OF PERSONS AND PLACES